Praise for

UTOPIA FOR REALISTS

"If you're bored with hackneyed debates, decades-old right-wing and left-wing clichés, you may enjoy the bold thinking, fresh ideas, lively prose, and evidence-based arguments in *Utopia for Realists*."
— Steven Pinker, author of *The Blank Slate* and *The Better Angels of Our Nature*

"Obligatory reading for everyone worried about the wrongs of present-day society and wishing to contribute to their cure."
— Zygmunt Bauman, author of *Consuming Life* and *Liquid Modernity*

"This book is brilliant. Everyone should read it. Bregman shows us we've been looking at the world inside out. Turned right-way out we suddenly see fundamentally new ways forward. If we can get enough people to read this book, the world will start to become a better place."
— Richard Wilkinson, coauthor of *The Spirit Level: Why More Equal Societies Almost Always Do Better*

"An excellent read and full of well-told stories and details I didn't know."
— Tim Harford, senior columnist at the *Financial Times* and author of *The Undercover Economist*

"Learning from history and from up-to-date social science can shatter crippling illusions. It can turn allegedly utopian proposals into plain common sense. It can enable us to face the future with unprecedented enthusiasm. To see how, read this superbly written, upbeat, insightful book."

— Philippe Van Parijs, cofounder of the Basic Income Earth Network and author of *Real Freedom for All*

"A wonderful call to utopian thinking around incomes and the workweek, and a welcome antidote to the pessimism surrounding robots taking our jobs."

— Charles Kenny, senior fellow at the Center for Global Development and author of *The Upside of Down: Why the Rise of the Rest Is Great for the West*

"A bold call for utopian thinking and a world without work — something needed more than ever in an era of defeatism and lack of ambition. Highly recommended!"

— Nick Srnicek, coauthor of *Inventing the Future: Postcapitalism and a World Without Work*

"The impact of this book in the Netherlands has been huge. Not only did Rutger Bregman launch a highly successful and long-running debate in the media, he also inspired a movement across the country that is putting his ideas into practice. Now it's time for the rest of the world."

— Joris Luyendijk, bestselling author of *Swimming with Sharks: My Journey into the World of the Bankers*

"*Utopia for Realists* is an important book, a wonderfully readable breath of fresh air, a window thrown open to a better future. As politicians and economists are asking how to increase productivity, ensure full employment, and downsize government, Bregman asks: What actually makes life worth living and how can we get there? The answers, it turns out, are already there, and Bregman combines deep research with wit, challenging us to think anew about how we want to live and who we want to be. Required reading."

— Philipp Blom, historian and author of *The Vertigo Years: Europe, 1900–1914* and *A Wicked Company: The Forgotten Radicalism of the European Enlightenment*

"If energy, enthusiasm, and aphorism could make the world better, then Rutger Bregman's book would do it. Even in translation from the Dutch, the writing is powerful and fluent. . . . A boisterously good read."

— John Rentoul, *The Independent* (UK)

ALSO BY RUTGER BREGMAN

History of Progress

UTOPIA FOR REALISTS

HOW WE CAN BUILD
THE IDEAL WORLD

RUTGER BREGMAN

Translated from the Dutch by

ELIZABETH MANTON

Little, Brown and Company

NEW YORK • BOSTON • LONDON

Little, Brown and Company
Hachette Book Group
1290 Avenue of the Americas, New York, NY 10104
littlebrown.com

First North American Edition: March 2017
Published simultaneously in English in Great Britain by Bloomsbury Publishing,
March 2017
Originally published in September 2014 in the Netherlands as *Gratis geld voor iedereen:
en nog vijf grote ideeën die de wereld kunnen veranderen* by *The Correspondent*
(thecorrespondent.com), a member-funded journalism
platform for independent voices.

Little, Brown and Company is a division of Hachette Book Group, Inc.
The Little, Brown name and logo are trademarks of Hachette Book Group, Inc.

The publisher is not responsible for websites (or their content)
that are not owned by the publisher.

The Hachette Speakers Bureau provides a wide range of authors for speaking events.
To find out more, go to hachettespeakersbureau.com or call (866) 376-6591.

ISBN 978-0-316-47189-3
Library of Congress Control Number 2016962005

10 9 8 7 6 5 4 3 2 1

LSC-C

Printed in the United States of America

To Maartje

CONTENTS

A map of the world that does not include Utopia is not worth even glancing at, for it leaves out the one country at which Humanity is always landing. And when Humanity lands there, it looks out, and, seeing a better country, sets sail. Progress is the realization of Utopias.

Oscar Wilde (1854–1900)

UTOPIA
FOR
REALISTS

The Return of Utopia

L et's start with a little history lesson:
In the past, everything was worse.

For roughly 99% of the world's history, 99% of humanity was poor, hungry, dirty, afraid, stupid, sick, and ugly. As recently as the seventeenth century, the French philosopher Blaise Pascal (1623–62) described life as one giant vale of tears. "Humanity is great," he wrote, "because it knows itself to be wretched." In Britain, fellow philosopher Thomas Hobbes (1588–1679) concurred that human life was basically "solitary, poor, nasty, brutish, and short."

But in the last 200 years, all of that has changed. In just a fraction of the time that our species has clocked on this planet, billions of us are suddenly rich, well nourished, clean, safe, smart, healthy, and occasionally even beautiful. Where 84% of the world's population still lived in extreme poverty in 1820, by 1981 that percentage had dropped to 44%, and now, just a few decades later, it is under 10%.[1]

If this trend holds, the extreme poverty that has been an abiding feature of life will soon be eradicated for good. Even those we still call poor will enjoy an abundance unprecedented in world history. In the country where I live, the Netherlands, a homeless person receiving public assistance today has more to spend than the average Dutch person in 1950, and four times more than people in Holland's glorious Golden Age, when the country still ruled the seven seas.[2]

For centuries, time all but stood still. Obviously, there was plenty to fill the history books, but life wasn't exactly getting better. If you were to put an Italian peasant from 1300 in a time machine and drop him in 1870s Tuscany he wouldn't notice much of a difference.

Historians estimate that the average annual income in Italy around the year 1300 was roughly $1,600. Some 600 years later – after Columbus, Galileo, Newton, the Scientific Revolution, the Reformation and the Enlightenment, the invention of gunpowder, printing, and the steam engine – it was . . . still $1,600.[3] Six hundred years of civilization, and the average Italian was pretty much where he'd always been.

It was not until about 1880, right around the time Alexander Graham Bell invented the telephone, Thomas Edison patented his lightbulb, Carl Benz was tinkering with his first car, and Josephine Cochrane was ruminating on what may just be the most brilliant idea ever – the dish-washer – that our Italian peasant got swept up in the march of progress. And what a wild ride it has been. The past two centuries have seen explosive growth in both population and prosperity worldwide. Per capita income is now ten

FIGURE I   Two Centuries of Stupendous Progress

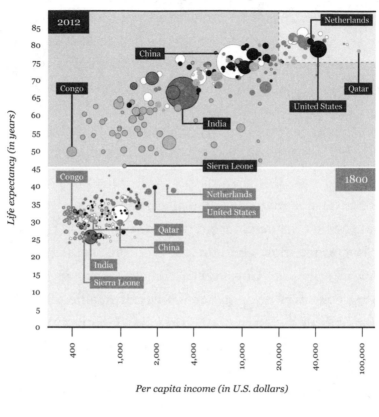

Per capita income (in U.S. dollars)

● North and South America   ● Sub-Saharan Africa

● Europe and Central Asia   ● South Asia

● Middle East and North Africa   ○ East Asia and Pacific

⬚ Land of Plenty

This is a diagram that takes a moment to absorb. Each circle represents a country. The bigger the circle, the bigger the population. The bottom section shows countries in the year 1800; the top shows them in 2012. In 1800, life expectancy in even the richest countries (e.g. the Netherlands, the United States) still fell short of that in the country with the lowest health rating (Sierra Leone) in 2012. In other words: in 1800, all countries were poor in both wealth and health, whereas today, even sub-Saharan Africa outperforms the most affluent countries of 1800 (despite the fact that incomes in the Congo have hardly changed in the last 200 years). Indeed, ever more countries are arriving in the "Land of Plenty," at the top right of the diagram, where the average income now tops $20,000 and life expectancy is over 75.

Source: Gapminder.org

times what it was in 1850. The average Italian is fifteen times as wealthy as in 1880. And the global economy? It is now 250 times what it was before the Industrial Revolution – when nearly everyone, everywhere was still poor, hungry, dirty, afraid, stupid, sick, and ugly.

The Medieval Utopia

The past was certainly a harsh place, and so it's only logical that people dreamed of a day when things would be better.

One of the most vivid dreams was the land of milk and honey known as "Cockaigne." To get there you first had to eat your way through three miles of rice pudding. But it was worth the effort, because on arriving in Cockaigne you found yourself in a land where the rivers ran with wine, roast geese flew overhead, pancakes grew on trees, and hot pies and pastries rained from the skies. Farmer, craftsman, cleric – all were equal and kicked back together in the sun.

In Cockaigne, the Land of Plenty, people never argued. Instead, they partied, they danced, they drank, and they slept around.

"To the medieval mind," the Dutch historian Herman Pleij writes, "modern-day western Europe comes pretty close to a bona fide Cockaigne. You have fast food available 24/7, climate control, free love, workless income, and plastic surgery to prolong youth."[4] These days, there are more people suffering from obesity worldwide than from hunger.[5] In Western Europe, the murder rate is forty times lower, on average, than in the Middle Ages, and if you have the right passport, you're assured an impressive social safety net.[6]

Maybe that's also our biggest problem: Today, the old medieval dream of the utopia is running on empty. Sure, we could manage a little more consumption, a little more security – but the adverse effects in the form of pollution, obesity, and Big Brother are looming ever larger. For the medieval dreamer, the Land of Plenty was a fantasy paradise – "An escape from earthly suffering," in the words of Herman Pleij. But if we were to ask that Italian farmer back in 1300 to describe our modern world, his first thought would doubtless be of Cockaigne.

In fact, we are living in an age of biblical prophecies come true. What would have seemed miraculous in the Middle Ages is now commonplace: the blind restored to sight, cripples who can walk, and the dead returned to life. Take the Argus II, a brain implant that restores a measure of sight to people with genetic eye conditions. Or the Rewalk, a set of robotic legs that enables paraplegics to walk again. Or the Rheobatrachus, a species of frog that became extinct in 1983 but, thanks to Australian scientists, has quite literally been brought back to life using old DNA. The Tasmanian tiger is next on this research team's wish list, whose work is part of the larger "Lazarus Project" (named for the New Testament story of a death deferred).

Meanwhile, science fiction is becoming science fact. The first driverless cars are already taking to the roads. Even now, 3D printers are rolling out entire embryonic cell structures, and people with chips implanted in their brains are operating robotic arms with their minds. Another factoid: Since 1980, the price of one watt of solar energy has plummeted 99% – and that's not a typo. If we're lucky, 3D printers and solar panels may yet turn Karl Marx's ideal (all means of production controlled by the masses) into a reality, all without requiring a bloody revolution.

For a long time, the Land of Plenty was reserved for a small elite in the wealthy West. Those days are over. Since China has opened itself to capitalism, 700 million Chinese have been lifted out of extreme poverty.[7] Africa, too, is fast shedding its reputation for economic devastation; the continent is now home to six of the world's ten fastest-growing economies.[8] By the year 2013, six billion of the globe's seven billion inhabitants owned a cell phone. (By way of comparison, just 4.5 billion had a toilet.)[9] And between 1994 and 2014, the number of people with Internet access worldwide leaped from 0.4% to 40.4%.[10]

Also in terms of health – maybe the greatest promise of the Land of Plenty – modern progress has trumped the wildest imaginings of our ancestors. Whereas wealthy countries have to content themselves with the weekly addition of another weekend to the average lifetime, Africa is gaining four days a week.[11] Worldwide, life expectancy grew from sixty-four years in 1990 to seventy in 2012[12] – more than double what it was in 1900.

Fewer people are going hungry, too. In our Land of Plenty we might not be able to snatch cooked geese from the air, but the number of people suffering from malnutrition has shrunk by more than a third since 1990. The share of the world population that survives on fewer than 2,000 calories a day has dropped from 51% in 1965 to 3% in 2005.[13] More than 2.1 billion people finally got access to clean drinking water between 1990 and 2012. In the same period, the number of children with stunted growth went down by a third, child mortality fell an incredible 41%, and maternal deaths were cut in half.

And what about disease? History's number-one mass murderer, the dreaded smallpox, has been completely wiped out. Polio has all but disappeared, claiming 99% fewer victims in 2013 than in 1988. Meanwhile, more and more children are getting immunized against once common diseases. The worldwide vaccination rate for measles, for example, has jumped from 16% in 1980 to 85% today, while the number of deaths has been cut by more than three-quarters between 2000 and 2014. Since 1990, the TB mortality rate has dropped by nearly half. Since 2000, the number of people dying from malaria has been reduced by a quarter, and so has the number of AIDS deaths since 2005.

Some figures seem almost too good to be true. For example, fifty years ago, one in five children died before reaching their fifth birthday. Today? One in twenty. In 1836, the richest man in the world, one Nathan Meyer Rothschild, died due to a simple lack of antibiotics. In recent decades, dirt-cheap vaccines against measles, tetanus, whooping cough, diphtheria, and polio have saved more lives each year than world peace would have saved in the twentieth century.[14]

Obviously, there are still plenty of diseases to go – cancer, for one – but we're making progress even on that front. In 2013, the prestigious journal *Science* reported on the discovery of a way to harness the immune system to battle tumors, hailing it as the biggest scientific breakthrough of the year. That same year saw the first successful attempt to clone human stem cells, a promising development in the treatment of mitochondrial diseases, including one form of diabetes.

Some scientists even contend that the first person who will live to celebrate their 1,000th birthday has already been born.[15]

FIGURE 2   The Victory of Vaccines

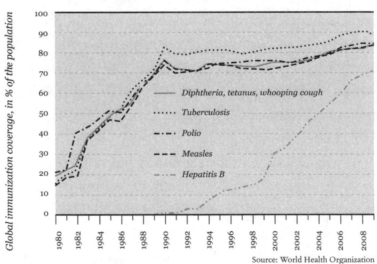

Source: World Health Organization

All the while, we're only getting smarter. In 1962, as many as 41% of kids didn't go to school, as opposed to under 10% today.[16] In most countries, the average IQ has gone up another three to five points every ten years, thanks chiefly to improved nutrition and education. Maybe this also explains how we've become so much more civilized, with the past decade rating as the most peaceful in all of world history. According to the Peace Research Institute in Oslo, the number of war casualties per year has plummeted 90% since 1946. The incidence of murder, robbery, and other forms of criminality is decreasing, too.

"The rich world is seeing less and less crime," the *Economist* reported not long ago. "There are still criminals,

FIGURE 3   War Has Been On the Decline

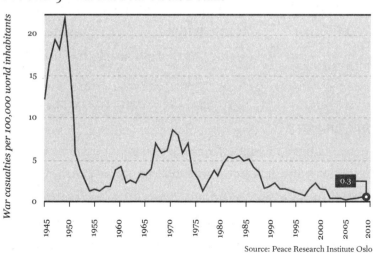

Source: Peace Research Institute Oslo

but there are ever fewer of them and they are getting older."[17]

A Bleak Paradise

Welcome, in other words, to the Land of Plenty.

To the good life, where almost everyone is rich, safe, and healthy. Where there's only one thing we lack: a reason to get out of bed in the morning. Because, after all, you can't really improve on paradise. Back in 1989, the American philosopher Francis Fukuyama already noted that we had arrived in an era where life has been reduced to "economic calculation, the endless solving of technical problems, environmental concerns, and the satisfaction of sophisticated consumer demands."[18]

Notching up our purchasing power another percentage point, or shaving a couple off our carbon emissions; perhaps a new gadget – that's about the extent of our vision. We live in an era of wealth and overabundance, but how bleak it is. There is "neither art nor philosophy," Fukuyama says. All that's left is the "perpetual caretaking of the museum of human history."

According to Oscar Wilde, upon reaching the Land of Plenty, we should once more fix our gaze on the farthest horizon and rehoist the sails. "Progress is the realization of Utopias," he wrote. But the far horizon remains blank. The Land of Plenty is shrouded in fog. Precisely when we should be shouldering the historic task of investing this rich, safe, and healthy existence with meaning, we've buried utopia instead. There's no new dream to replace it because we can't imagine a better world than the one we've got. In fact, most people in wealthy countries believe children will actually be *worse* off than their parents.[19]

But the real crisis of our times, of my generation, is not that we don't have it good, or even that we might be worse off later on.

No, the real crisis is that we can't come up with anything better.

The Blueprint

This book isn't an attempt to predict the future.

It's an attempt to unlock the future. To fling open the windows of our minds. Of course, utopias always say more about the time in which they were imagined than about what's actually in store. The utopian Land of Plenty tells us all about what life was like in the Middle Ages. Grim. Or rather, that the lives of almost everyone almost everywhere have almost always been grim. After all, every culture has its own variation on the Land of Plenty.[20]

Simple desires beget simple utopias. If you're hungry, you dream of a lavish banquet. If you're cold, you dream of a toasty fire. Faced with mounting infirmities, you dream of eternal youth. All of these desires are reflected in the old utopias, conceived when life was still nasty, brutish, and short. "The earth produced nothing fearful, no diseases," fantasized the Greek poet Telecides in the fifth century B.C., and if anything was needed, it would simply appear. "Every creek bed flowed with wine . . . Fish would come into your house, grill themselves, and then lie down on your table."[21]

But before we go any farther, let's first distinguish between two forms of utopian thought.[22] The first is the most familiar, the utopia of the blueprint. Great thinkers like Karl Popper and Hannah Arendt and even an entire current of philosophy, postmodernism, have sought to upend this type of utopia. They largely succeeded; theirs is still the last word on the blueprinted paradise.

Instead of abstract ideals, blueprints consist of immutable rules that tolerate no dissension. The Italian poet Tommaso Campanella's *The City of the Sun* (1602) offers a good example. In his utopia, or rather dystopia, individual ownership is strictly prohibited, everybody is obliged to love everybody else, and fighting is punishable by death. Private life is controlled by the state, procreation included. For instance, smart people can only go to bed with stupid people, and fat ones with skinny ones. Every effort is focused on forging a favorable median. What's more, every person is monitored by a vast network of informants. If someone commits a transgression, the sinner is verbally browbeaten until they are convinced of their own wickedness and freely submit to being stoned by the rest.

With the benefit of hindsight, anyone reading Campanella's book today will see chilling hints of fascism, Stalinism, and genocide.

The Return of Utopia

There is, however, another avenue of utopian thought, one that is all but forgotten. If the blueprint is a high-resolution photo, then this utopia is just a vague outline. It offers not solutions but guideposts. Instead of forcing us into a straitjacket, it inspires us to change. And it understands that, as Voltaire put it, the perfect is the enemy of the good. As one American philosopher has remarked, "any serious utopian thinker will be made uncomfortable by the very idea of the blueprint."[23]

It was in this spirit that the British philosopher Thomas More literally wrote the book on utopia (and coined the term). Rather than a blueprint to be ruthlessly applied, his utopia was, more than anything, an indictment of a grasping aristocracy that demanded ever more luxury as common people lived in extreme poverty.

More understood that utopia is dangerous when taken *too* seriously. "One needs to be able to believe passionately and also be able to see the absurdity of one's own beliefs and laugh at them," observes philosopher and leading utopia expert Lyman Tower Sargent. Like humor and satire, utopias throw open the windows of the mind. And that's vital. As people and societies get progressively older they become accustomed to the status quo, in which liberty can become a prison, and the truth can become lies. The modern creed – or worse, the belief that there's nothing left to believe in – makes us blind to the shortsightedness and injustice that still surround us every day.

To give a few examples: Why have we been working harder and harder since the 1980s despite being richer than ever? Why are millions of people still living in poverty when we are more than rich enough to put an end to it once and for all? And why is more than 60% of your income dependent on the country where you just happen to have been born?[24]

Utopias offer no ready-made answers, let alone solutions. But they do ask the right questions.

The Destruction of the Grand Narrative

Today, sadly enough, our dreams can't even begin before we are woken up. According to the cliché, dreams have a way of turning into nightmares. Utopias are a breeding ground for discord, violence, even genocide. Utopias ultimately become dystopias; in fact, a utopia *is* a dystopia. "Human progress is a myth," goes another cliché. And yet we ourselves have managed to build the medieval paradise.

True, history is full of horrifying forms of utopianism – fascism, communism, Nazism – just as every religion has also spawned fanatical sects. But if one religious radical incites violence, should we automatically write off the whole religion? So why write off the utopianism? Should we simply stop dreaming of a better world altogether?

No, of course not. But that's precisely what is happening. Optimism and pessimism have become synonymous with consumer confidence or the lack thereof. Radical ideas about a different world have become almost literally unthinkable. The expectations of what we as a society can achieve have been dramatically eroded, leaving us with the cold, hard truth that without utopia, all that remains is a technocracy. Politics has been watered down to problem management. Voters swing back and forth not because the parties are so different, but because it's barely possible to tell them apart, and what now separates right from left is a percentage point or two on the income tax rate.[25]

We see it in journalism, which portrays politics as a game in which the stakes are not ideals, but careers. We see it in academia, where everybody is too busy writing to read, too busy publishing to debate. In fact, the twenty-first-century university resembles nothing so much as a factory, as do our hospitals, schools, and TV networks. What counts is achieving targets. Whether it's the growth of the economy, audience shares, publications – slowly but surely, quality is being replaced by quantity.

And driving it all is a force sometimes called "liberalism," an ideology that has been all but hollowed out. What's important now is to "just be yourself" and "do your thing." Freedom may be our highest ideal, but ours has become an empty freedom. Our fear of moralizing in any form has made morality a taboo in the public debate. The public arena should be "neutral," after all – yet never before has it been so paternalistic. On every street corner we're baited to booze, binge, borrow, buy, toil, stress, and swindle. Whatever we may tell ourselves about freedom of speech, our values are suspiciously close to those touted by precisely the companies that can pay for prime-time advertising.[26] If a political party or a religious sect had even a fraction of the influence that the advertising industry has on us and our children, we'd be up in arms. But because it's the market, we remain "neutral."[27]

The only thing left for government to do is patch up life in the present. If you're not following the blueprint of a docile, content citizen, the powers that be are happy to whip you into shape. Their tools of choice? Control, surveillance, and repression.

Meanwhile, the welfare state has increasingly shifted its focus from the causes of our discontent to the *symptoms*. We go to a doctor when we're sick, a therapist when we're sad, a dietitian when we're overweight, prison when we're convicted, and a job coach when we're out of work. All these services cost vast sums of money, but with little to show for it. In the U.S., where the cost of healthcare is the highest on the planet, the life expectancy for many is actually going *down*.

All the while, the market and commercial interests are enjoying free rein. The food industry supplies us with cheap garbage loaded with salt, sugar, and fat, putting us on the fast track to the doctor and dietitian. Advancing technologies are laying waste to ever more jobs, sending us back again to the job coach. And the ad industry encourages us to spend money we don't have on junk we don't need in order to impress people we can't stand.[28] Then we can go cry on our therapist's shoulder.

That's the dystopia we are living in today.

The Pampered Generation

It is not – I can't emphasize this enough – that we don't have it good. Far from it. If anything, kids today are struggling under the burden of too much pampering. According to Jean Twenge, a psychologist at San Diego State University who has conducted detailed research into the attitudes of young adults now and in the past, there has been a sharp rise in self-esteem since the 1980s. The younger generation considers itself smarter, more responsible, and more attractive than ever.

"It's a generation in which every kid has been told, 'You can be anything you want. You're special,'" explains Twenge.[29] We've been brought up on a steady diet of narcissism, but as soon as we're released into the great big world of unlimited opportunity, more and more of us crash and burn. The world, it turns out, is cold and harsh, rife with competition and unemployment. It's not a Disneyland where you can wish upon a star and see all your dreams come true, but a rat race in which you have no one but yourself to blame if you don't make the grade.

Not surprisingly, that narcissism conceals an ocean of uncertainty. Twenge also discovered that we have all become a lot more fearful over the last decades. Comparing 269 studies conducted between 1952 and 1993, she concluded that the average child living in early 1990s North America was more anxious than psychiatric patients in the early 1950s.[30] According to the World Health Organization, depression has even become the biggest health problem among teens and will be the number-one cause of illness worldwide by 2030.[31]

It's a vicious circle. Never before have so many young adults been seeing a psychiatrist. Never before have there been so many early career burnouts. And we're popping antidepressants like never before. Time and again, we blame collective problems like unemployment, dissatisfaction, and depression on the individual. If success is a choice, then so is failure. Lost your job? You should have worked harder. Sick? You must not be leading a healthy lifestyle. Unhappy? Take a pill.

In the 1950s, only 12% of young adults agreed with the statement "I'm a very special person." Today 80% do,[32] when the fact is, we're all becoming more and more alike. We all read the same bestsellers, watch the same blockbusters, and sport the same sneakers. Where our grandparents still toed the lines imposed by family, church, and country, we're hemmed in by the media, marketing, and a paternalistic state. Yet even as we become more and more alike, we're well past the era of the big collectives. Membership of churches and labor unions has taken a tumble, and the traditional dividing line between right and left holds little meaning any more. All we care about is "resolving problems," as though politics could be outsourced to management consultants.

Sure, there are some who try to revive the old faith in progress. Is it any wonder that the cultural archetype of my generation is the Nerd, whose apps and gadgets symbolize the hope of economic growth? "The best minds of my generation are thinking about how to make people click ads," a former math whiz at Facebook recently lamented.[33]

Lest there be any misunderstanding: It is capitalism that opened the gates to the Land of Plenty, but capitalism alone cannot sustain it. Progress has become synonymous with economic prosperity, but the twenty-first century will challenge us to find other ways of boosting our quality of life. And while young people in the West have largely come of age in an era of apolitical technocracy, we will have to return to politics again to find a new utopia.

In that sense, I'm heartened by our dissatisfaction, because dissatisfaction is a world away from indifference. The widespread nostalgia, the yearning for a past that never really was, suggests that we still have ideals, even if we have buried them alive.

True progress begins with something no knowledge economy can produce: wisdom about what it means to live well. We have to do what great thinkers like John Stuart Mill, Bertrand Russell, and John Maynard Keynes were already advocating 100 years ago: to "value ends above means and prefer the good to the useful."[34] We have to direct our minds to the future. To stop consuming our own discontent through polls and the relentlessly bad-news media. To consider alternatives and form new collectives. To transcend this confining zeitgeist and recognize our shared idealism.

Maybe then we'll also be able to again look beyond ourselves and out at the world. There we'll see that good old progress is still marching along on its merry way. We'll see that we live in a marvelous age, a time of diminishing hunger and war and of surging prosperity and life expectancies. But we'll also see just how much there still is left for us – the richest 10%, 5%, or 1% – to do.

The Blueprint

It's time to return to utopian thinking.

We need a new lodestar, a new map of the world that once again includes a distant, uncharted continent – "Utopia." By this I don't mean the rigid blueprints that utopian fanatics try to shove down our throats with their theocracies or their five-year plans – they only subordinate real people to fervent dreams. Consider this: The word *utopia* means both "good place" and "no place." What we need are alternative horizons that spark the imagination.

And I do mean horizons in the plural; conflicting utopias are the lifeblood of democracy, after all.

As always, our utopia will start small. The foundations of what we today call civilization were laid long ago by dreamers who marched to the beat of their own drummers. The Spanish monk Bartolomé de Las Casas (1484–1566) advocated equality between colonists and the native inhabitants of Latin America, and attempted to found a colony in which everyone received a comfortable living. The factory owner Robert Owen (1771–1858) championed the emancipation of English workers and ran a successful cotton mill where employees were paid a fair wage and corporal punishment was prohibited. And the philosopher John Stuart Mill (1806–73) even believed that women and men were equals. (This might also have had something to do with the fact that his wife composed half his oeuvre.)

One thing is certain, however: Without all those wide-eyed dreamers down through the ages, we would all still be poor, hungry, dirty, afraid, stupid, sick, and ugly. Without utopia, we are lost. Not that the present is bad; on the contrary. However, it is bleak, if we have no hope of anything better. "Man needs, for his happiness, not only the enjoyment of this or that, but hope and enterprise and change,"[35] the British philosopher Bertrand Russell once wrote. Elsewhere he continued, "It is not a finished Utopia that we ought to desire, but a world where imagination and hope are alive and active."[36]

Money is better than poverty,
if only for financial reasons.

Woody Allen (b. 1935)

Why We Should Give Free Money to Everyone

L ondon, May 2009 – An experiment is under way. Its subjects: thirteen homeless men. They are veterans of the street. Some have been sleeping on the cold pavement of the Square Mile, Europe's financial center, for going on forty years. Between the police expenses, court costs, and social services, these thirteen troublemakers have racked up a bill estimated at £400,000 ($650,000) or more.[1] Per year.

The strain on city services and local charities is too great for things to go on this way. So Broadway, a London-based aid organization, makes a radical decision: From now on, the city's thirteen consummate drifters will be getting VIP treatment. It's *adiós* to the daily helpings of food stamps, soup kitchens, and shelters. They're getting a drastic and instantaneous bailout.

From now on, these rough sleepers will receive free money.

To be exact, they're getting £3,000 in spending money, and they don't have to do a thing in return.[2] How they spend it is up to them. They can opt to make use of an advisor if they'd like — or not. There are no strings attached, no questions to trip them up.[3]

The only thing they're asked is: What do *you* think you need?

Gardening Classes

"I didn't have enormous expectations," one social worker later recalled.[4] But the drifters' desires proved eminently modest. A telephone, a dictionary, a hearing aid — each had his own ideas about what he needed. In fact, most were downright thrifty. After one year, they had spent an average of just £800.

Take Simon, who had been strung out on heroin for twenty years. The money turned his life around. Simon got clean and started taking gardening classes. "For some reason, for the first time in my life, everything just clicked," he said later. "I'm starting to look after myself, wash and shave. Now I'm thinking of going back home. I've got two kids."

A year and a half after the experiment began, seven of the thirteen rough sleepers had a roof over their heads. Two more were about to move into their own apartments. All thirteen had taken critical steps toward solvency and personal growth. They were enrolled in classes, learning to cook, going through rehab, visiting their families, and making plans for the future.

"It empowers people," one of the social workers said about the personalized budget. "It gives choices. I think it can make a difference." After decades of fruitless pushing, pulling, pampering, penalizing, prosecuting, and protecting, nine notorious vagrants had finally been brought in from the streets. The cost? Some £50,000 a year, including the social workers' wages. In other words, not only did the project help thirteen people, it also cut costs considerably.[5] Even the *Economist* had to conclude that the "most efficient way to spend money on the homeless might be to give it to them."[6]

Hard Data

Poor people can't handle money. This seems to be the prevailing sentiment, almost a truism. After all, if they knew how to manage money, how could they be poor in the first place? We assume that they must spend it on fast food and soda instead of on fresh fruit and books. So to "help," we've rigged up a myriad of ingenious assistance programs, with reams of paperwork, registration systems, and an army of inspectors, all revolving around the biblical principle that "those unwilling to work will not get to eat" (2 Thessalonians 3:10). In recent years, government assistance has become increasingly anchored in employment, with recipients required to apply for jobs, enroll in return-to-work programs, and do mandatory "volunteer" work. Touted as a shift "from welfare to work-fare," the underlying message is clear: Free money makes people lazy.

Except that, according to the evidence, it doesn't.

Meet Bernard Omondi. For years he earned $2 a day working in a stone quarry in an impoverished part of western Kenya. Then, one morning, he received a rather peculiar text message. "When I saw the message, I jumped up," Bernard later recalled. A sum of $500 had just been deposited in his bank account. For Bernard, this was almost a year's wages.

Several months later a journalist from the *New York Times* visited Bernard's village. It was as though the entire population had won the lottery: The village was flush with cash. Yet no one was drinking their money away. Instead, homes had been repaired and small businesses started. Bernard invested his money in a brand-new Bajaj Boxer motorcycle from India and was making $6–$9 a day ferrying people around as a taxi driver. His income had more than tripled.

"This puts the choice in the hands of the poor," says Michael Faye, founder of GiveDirectly, the organization behind Bernard's windfall. "And the truth is, I don't think I have a very good sense of what the poor need."[7] Faye doesn't give people fish, or even teach them to fish. He gives them cash, in the conviction that the real experts on what poor people need are the poor people themselves. When I asked him why there are so few peppy videos or pictures on GiveDirectly's website, Faye explained that he doesn't want to play on emotions too much. "Our data are hard enough."

He's right: According to a study by the Massachusetts Institute of Technology, GiveDirectly's cash grants spur a lasting rise in incomes (up 38% from before the infusion) and also boost homeownership and possession of livestock (up 58%), while reducing the number of days that children go hungry by 42%. Furthermore, 93% of every donation is placed directly in the hands of recipients.[8] Presented with GiveDirectly's figures, Google soon handed over a $2.5 million donation.[9]

But Bernard and his fellow villagers haven't been the only ones to luck out. In 2008, the government of Uganda decided to distribute almost $400 to some 12,000 sixteen-to-thirty-five-year-olds. The money was all but free; the only thing they had to do in return was submit a business plan. Five years later, the effects were staggering. Having invested in their own education and business ventures, the beneficiaries' incomes had gone up nearly 50%. And their odds of getting hired had increased more than 60%.[10]

Another Ugandan program distributed $150 to over 1,800 poor women in the country's north, with similar results: Incomes shot up by almost 100%. Women who received support from an aid worker (cost: $350) benefited slightly more, but researchers subsequently calculated that it would have been much more effective to lump the aid worker's salary in with the grants.[11] As the report dryly concluded, the results imply "a huge change in poverty alleviation programs in Africa and worldwide."[12]

A Southerly Revolution

Studies from all over the world offer proof positive: Free money works.

Already, research has correlated unconditional cash disbursements with reductions in crime, child mortality, malnutrition, teenage pregnancy, and truancy, and with improved school performance, economic growth, and gender equality.[13] "The big reason poor people are poor is because they don't have enough money," notes economist Charles Kenny, "and it shouldn't come as a huge surprise that giving them money is a great way to reduce that problem."[14]

In their book *Just Give Money to the Poor* (2010), scholars at the University of Manchester furnish countless examples of cases where cash handouts with few or no strings attached have worked. In Namibia, figures for malnutrition took a nosedive (from 42% to 10%), as did those for truancy (from 40% to virtually nothing) and crime (by 42%). In Malawi, school attendance among girls and women surged 40%, regardless of whether the cash came with or without conditions. Time and again, the ones to profit most are children. They suffer less hunger and disease, grow taller, perform better at school, and are less likely to be forced into child labor.[15]

From Brazil to India, from Mexico to South Africa, cash-transfer programs have become all the rage across the Global South. When the United Nations formulated its Millennium Development Goals in 2000, these programs weren't even on the radar. Yet by 2010, they were already reaching more than 110 million families in forty-five countries.

Back at the University of Manchester, the researchers summed up these programs' benefits: (1) households put the money to good use, (2) poverty declines, (3) there can be diverse long-term benefits for income, health, and tax revenues, and (4) the programs cost less than the alternatives.[16] So why send over expensive white folks in SUVs when we can simply hand over their salaries to the poor? Especially when this also takes sticky civil service fingers out of the equation. Plus, free cash greases the wheels of the whole economy: People buy more, and that boosts employment and incomes.

Countless aid organizations and governments are convinced that they know what poor people need, and invest in schools, solar panels, or cattle. And, granted, better a cow than no cow. But at what cost? A Rwandan study estimated that donating one pregnant cow costs around $3,000 (including a milking workshop). That's five years' wages for a Rwandan.[17] Or take the patchwork of courses offered to the poor: Study after study has shown that they cost a lot but achieve little, whether the objective is learning to fish, read, or run a business.[18] "Poverty is fundamentally about a lack of cash. It's not about stupidity," stresses the economist Joseph Hanlon. "You can't pull yourself up by your bootstraps if you have no boots."[19]

The great thing about money is that people can use it to buy things they need instead of things that self-appointed experts think they need. And, as it happens, there is one category of product which poor people do *not* spend their free money on, and that's alcohol and tobacco. In fact, a major study by the World Bank demonstrated that in 82% of all researched cases in Africa, Latin America, and Asia, alcohol and tobacco consumption actually *declined*.[20]

But it gets even stranger. In Liberia, an experiment was conducted to see what would happen if you give $200 to the shiftiest of the poor. Alcoholics, addicts, and petty criminals were rounded up from the slums. Three years later, what had they spent the money on? Food, clothing, medicine, and small businesses. "If these men didn't throw away free money," one of the researchers wondered, "who would?"[21]

Yet the "lazy poor people" argument is trotted out time and again. The very persistence of this view has compelled scientists to investigate whether it's true. Just a few years ago, the prestigious medical journal the *Lancet* summed up their findings: When the poor receive no-strings cash they actually tend to work harder.[22] In the final report on the Namibian experiment, a bishop offered this neat biblical explanation. "Look in depth at Exodus 16," he wrote, "the people of Israel in the long journey out of slavery, they received manna from heaven. But," he continued, "it did not make them lazy; instead, it enabled them to be on the move . . ."[23]

Utopia

Free money: It's a notion already proposed by some of history's leading thinkers. Thomas More dreamed about it in his book *Utopia* in 1516. Countless economists and philosophers – Nobel Prize winners among them – would follow.[24] Its proponents have spanned the spectrum from left to right, all the way to the founders of neoliberal thought, Friedrich Hayek and Milton Friedman.[25] And Article 25 of the Universal Declaration of Human Rights (1948) promises that, one day, it will come.

A universal basic income.

And not merely for a few years, or in developing countries alone, or only for the poor, but just what it says on the box: free money for everyone. Not as a favor, but as a right. Call it the "capitalist road to communism."[26] A monthly allowance, enough to live on, without having to lift a finger. The only condition, as such, is that you "have a pulse."[27] No inspectors looking over your shoulder to see if you've spent it wisely, nobody questioning if it's really deserved. No more special benefit and assistance programs; at most an additional allowance for seniors, the unemployed, and those unable to work.

Basic income: It's an idea whose time has come.

Mincome, Canada

In a warehouse attic in Winnipeg, Canada, nearly 2,000 boxes lay gathering dust. The boxes are filled with data – graphs, tables, reports, interviews – about one of the most fascinating social experiments in post-war history.

Mincome.

Evelyn Forget, a professor at the University of Manitoba, first heard about the records in 2004. For five long years she tried to find them, until finally, in 2009, she discovered the boxes in the National Archives. "[Archivists] were in the process of wondering whether, in fact, they could throw them out because they took up a lot of space and nobody seemed interested in it," she later recalled.[28]

Stepping into the attic for the first time, Forget could hardly believe her eyes. It was a treasure trove of information on the real-world implementation of Thomas More's dream from five centuries before.

One of the nearly 1,000 interviews packed away in those boxes was with Hugh and Doreen Henderson. Thirty-five years earlier, when the experiment began, he had been a high-school janitor and she a homemaker taking care of their two kids. The Hendersons didn't have it easy. Doreen kept a garden and raised chickens to ensure they'd have enough to eat. Each dollar was stretched "until it snapped."

Until, on one ordinary day, two sharply dressed men appeared on their doorstep. "We filled out forms, they wanted to see our receipts," Doreen recalled.[29] And then, just like that, the Hendersons' money troubles were a thing of the past. Hugh and Doreen were signed up for Mincome – the first large-scale social experiment in Canada and the largest basic income experiment in the world, ever.

In March 1973, the provincial governor earmarked a sum of $83 million in modern U.S. dollars for the project.[30] He chose Dauphin, a small town of 13,000 northwest of Winnipeg, as the location of the experiment. Everybody in Dauphin was guaranteed a basic income, ensuring that no one fell below the poverty line. In practice, this meant 30% of the town's inhabitants – 1,000 families in all – got a check in the mail each month. A family of four received what would now be around $19,000 a year, *no questions asked*.

At the start of the experiment, an army of researchers descended on the town. Economists would monitor whether its inhabitants worked less, sociologists were there to scrutinize the effects on family life, and anthropologists ensconced themselves in the community to see firsthand how residents would respond.

For four years, all went well, but then elections threw a wrench in the works. A conservative government was voted into power. The new Canadian cabinet saw little point to the expensive experiment, for which the national government was footing three-quarters of the bill. When it became clear that the new administration wouldn't even fund an analysis of the experiment's results, the researchers decided to pack their files away in some 2,000 boxes.

In Dauphin, the letdown was huge. On its launch in 1974, Mincome had been seen as a pilot program that would quickly be rolled out nationwide. Now, it seemed destined to be forgotten. "Government officials opposed [to Mincome] didn't want to spend more money to analyze the data and show what they already thought: that it didn't work," one of the researchers recounted. "And the people who were in favour of Mincome were worried because if the analysis was done and the data wasn't favourable then they would have just spent another million dollars on analysis and be even more embarrassed."[31]

When Professor Forget first heard about Mincome, no one knew what, if anything, the experiment had actually demonstrated. But as coincidence would have it, Canada's Medicare program was introduced around this same time, in 1970. The Medicare archives presented Forget with a wealth of data to compare Dauphin with nearby towns and control groups. For three years, she rigorously subjected the data to all manner of statistical analysis. No matter what she tried, the results were the same every time.

Mincome had been a resounding success.

From Experiment to Law

"Politically, there was a concern that if you began a guaranteed annual income, people would stop working and start having large families," says Forget.[32]

What really happened was precisely the opposite. Young adults postponed getting married, and birth rates dropped. Their school performance improved substantially: The "Mincome cohort" studied harder and faster. In the end, total work hours only notched down 1% for men, 3% for married women, and 5% for unmarried women. Men who were family breadwinners hardly worked less at all, while new mothers used the cash assistance to take several months' maternity leave, and students to stay in school longer.[33]

Forget's most remarkable finding, though, was that hospitalizations decreased by as much as 8.5%. Considering the size of public spending on healthcare in the developed world, the financial implications were huge. Several years into the experiment, domestic violence was also down, as were mental-health complaints. Mincome had made the whole town healthier. Forget could even trace the impacts of receiving a basic income through to the next generation, both in earnings and in health.

Dauphin – the town with no poverty – was one of five guaranteed income experiments in North America. The other four were all conducted in the U.S. Few people today are aware that the U.S. was just a hair's breadth from realizing a social safety net at least as extensive as those in most Western European countries. When President Lyndon B. Johnson declared his "War on Poverty" in 1964, Democrats and Republicans alike rallied behind fundamental welfare reforms.

First, however, some trial runs were needed. Tens of millions of dollars were budgeted to provide a basic income for more than 8,500 Americans in New Jersey, Pennsylvania, Iowa, North Carolina, Indiana, Seattle, and Denver in what were also the first-ever large-scale social experiments to distinguish experimental and control groups. The researchers wanted answers to three questions: (1) Would people work significantly less if they receive a guaranteed income? (2) Would the program be too expensive? (3) Would it prove politically unfeasible?

The answers were no, no, and yes.

Declines in working hours were limited across the board. "The 'laziness' contention is just not supported by our findings," the chief data analyst of the Denver experiment said. "There is not anywhere near the mass defection the prophets of doom predicted." The reduction in paid work averaged 9% per family, and in every state it was mostly the twentysomethings and women with young children who worked less.[34]

Later research showed that even 9% was probably exaggerated. In the original study, this was calculated on the basis of self-reported income, but when the data was compared with official government records, it turned out that a significant portion of earnings had gone unreported. After correcting for this discrepancy, the researchers discovered that the number of hours worked had scarcely decreased at all.[35]

"[The] declines in hours of paid work were undoubtedly compensated in part by other useful activities, such as search for better jobs or work in the home," noted the Seattle experiment's concluding report. For example, one mother who had dropped out of high school worked less in order to earn a degree in psychology and get a job as a researcher. Another woman took acting classes; her husband began composing music. "We're now self-sufficient, income-earning artists," she told the researchers.[36] Among youth included in the experiment, almost all the hours not spent on paid work went into more education. Among the New Jersey subjects, the rate of high-school graduations rose 30%.[37]

And thus, in the revolutionary year of 1968, when young demonstrators the world over were taking to the streets, five famous economists – John Kenneth Galbraith, Harold Watts, James Tobin, Paul Samuelson, and Robert Lampman – wrote an open letter to Congress. "The country will not have met its responsibility until everyone in the nation is assured an income no less than the officially recognized definition of poverty," they said in an article published on the front page of the *New York Times*. According to the economists, the costs would be "substantial, but well within the nation's economic and fiscal capacity."[38]

The letter was signed by 1,200 fellow economists.

And their appeal did not fall on deaf ears. The following August, President Nixon presented a bill providing for a modest basic income, calling it "the most significant piece of social legislation in our nation's history." According to Nixon, the baby boomers would do two things deemed impossible by earlier generations. Besides putting a man on the moon (which had happened the month before), their generation would also, finally, eradicate poverty.

A White House poll found 90% of all newspapers enthusiastically receptive to the plan.[39] The *Chicago Sun-Times* called it "A Giant Leap Forward," the *Los Angeles Times* "A bold new blueprint."[40] The National Council of Churches was in favor, and so were the labor unions and even the corporate sector.[41] At the White House, a telegram arrived declaring, "Two upper middle class Republicans who will pay for the program say bravo."[42] Pundits were even going around quoting Victor Hugo – "Nothing is stronger than an idea whose time has come."

It seemed that the time for a basic income had well and truly arrived.

"Welfare Plan Passes House . . . a Battle Won in Crusade for Reform," headlined the *New York Times* on April 16, 1970. With 243 votes for and 155 against, President Nixon's Family Assistance Plan (FAP) was approved by an overwhelming majority. Most pundits expected the plan to pass the Senate, too, with a membership even more progressive than that of the House of Representatives. But in the Senate Finance Committee, doubts reared up. "This bill represents the most extensive, expensive, and expansive welfare legislation ever handled," one Republican senator said.[43] Most vehemently opposed, however, were the Democrats. They felt the FAP didn't go far enough, and pushed for an even higher basic income.[44] After months of being batted back and forth between the Senate and the White House, the bill was finally canned.

In the following year, Nixon presented a slightly tweaked proposal to Congress. Once again, the bill was accepted by the House, now as part of a larger package of reforms. This time, 288 voted in favor, 132 against. In his 1971 State of the Union address, Nixon considered his plan to "place a floor under the income of every family with children in America" the most important item of legislation on his agenda.[45]

But once again, the bill foundered in the Senate.

Not until 1978 was the plan for a basic income shelved once and for all, however, following a fatal discovery upon publication of the final results of the Seattle experiment. One finding in particular grabbed everybody's attention: The number of divorces had jumped more than 50%. Interest in this statistic quickly overshadowed all the other outcomes, such as better school performance and improvements in health. A basic income, evidently, gave women too much independence.

Ten years later, a reanalysis of the data revealed that a statistical error had been made; in reality, there had been no change in the divorce rate at all.[46]

Futile, Dangerous, and Perverse

"*It Can Be Done!* Conquering Poverty in America by 1976," Nobel Prize winner James Tobin confidently wrote in 1967. At that time, almost 80% of Americans supported a guaranteed basic income.[47] Years later, Ronald Reagan would famously sneer, "In the sixties we waged a war on poverty, and poverty won."

The great milestones of civilization always have the whiff of utopia about them at first. According to renowned sociologist Albert Hirschman, utopias are initially attacked on three grounds: futility (it's not possible), danger (the risks are too great), and perversity (it will degenerate into dystopia). But Hirschman also wrote that almost as soon as a utopia becomes a reality, it often comes to be seen as utterly commonplace.

Not so very long ago, democracy still seemed a glorious utopia. Many a great mind, from the philosopher Plato (427–347 B.C.) to the statesman Edmund Burke (1729–97), warned that democracy was futile (the masses were too foolish to handle it), dangerous (majority rule would be akin to playing with fire), and perverse (the "general interest" would soon be corrupted by the interests of some crafty general or other). Compare this with the arguments against basic income. It's supposedly futile because we can't pay for it, dangerous because people would quit working, and perverse because ultimately a minority would end up having to toil harder to support the majority.

But . . . hold on a minute.

Futile? For the first time in history, we are actually rich enough to finance a sizable basic income. We can get rid of the whole bureaucratic rigmarole designed to force assistance recipients into low-productivity jobs at any cost, and we can help finance the new simplified system by chucking the maze of tax credits and deductions, too. Any further necessary funds can be raised by taxing assets, waste, raw materials, and consumption.

Let's look at the numbers. Eradicating poverty in the U.S. would cost only $175 billion, less than 1% of GDP.[48] That's roughly a quarter of U.S. military spending. Winning the war on poverty would be a bargain compared to the wars in Afghanistan and Iraq, which a Harvard study estimated have cost us a staggering $4–$6 trillion.[49] As a matter of fact, all the world's developed countries had it within their means to wipe out poverty years ago.[50]

And yet, a system that helps solely the poor only drives a deeper wedge between them and the rest of society. "A policy for the poor is a poor policy," observed Richard Titmuss, the great theoretician of the British welfare state. It's an ingrained reflex among those on the left to make every plan, every credit, and every benefit income dependent. The problem is, that tendency is counter-productive.

In a now famous article published in the late 1990s, two Swedish sociologists showed that the countries with the most universal government programs have been the most successful at reducing poverty.[51] Basically, people are more open to solidarity if it benefits them personally. The more we, our family, and our friends stand to gain through the welfare state, the more we're willing to contribute.[52] Logically, therefore, a universal, unconditional basic income would also enjoy the broadest base of support. After all, everyone stands to benefit.[53]

Dangerous? Certainly, some people may opt to work less, but then that's precisely the point. A handful of artists and writers ("all those whom society despises while they are alive and honors when they are dead" – Bertrand Russell) might actually stop doing paid work altogether. There is overwhelming evidence to suggest that the vast majority of people actually want to work, whether they need to or not.[54] In fact, not having a job makes us deeply unhappy.[55]

One of the perks of a basic income is that it would free the poor from the welfare trap and spur them to seek a paid job with true opportunities for growth and advancement. Since basic income is unconditional, and will not be taken away or reduced in the event of gainful employment, their circumstances can only improve.

Perverse? On the contrary, it is the welfare system that has devolved into a perverse behemoth of control and humiliation. Officials keep tabs on public assistance recipients via Facebook to check whether they're spending their money wisely – and woe betide anyone who dares to do unapproved volunteer work. An army of social services workers is needed to guide people through the jungle of eligibility, application, approval, and recapture proced- ures. And then the corps of inspectors has to be mobilized to sift through the paperwork.

The welfare state, which should foster people's sense of security and pride, has degenerated into a system of suspicion and shame. It is a grotesque pact between right and left. "The political right is afraid people will stop working," laments Professor Forget in Canada, "and the left doesn't trust them to make their own choices."[56] A basic income system would be a better compromise. In terms of redistribution, it would meet the left's demands for fairness; where the regime of interference and humili- ation are concerned, it would give the right a more limited government than ever.

Talk Different, Think Different

It's been said before.

We're saddled with a welfare state from a bygone era when the breadwinners were still mostly men and people spent their whole lives working at the same company. The pension system and employment protection rules are still keyed to those fortunate enough to have a steady job, public assistance is rooted in the misconception that we can rely on the economy to generate enough jobs, and welfare benefits are often not a trampoline, but a trap.

Never before has the time been so ripe for the introduction of a universal, unconditional basic income. Look around. Greater flexibility in the workplace demands that we also create greater security. Globalization is eroding the wages of the middle class. The growing rift between those with and those without a college degree makes it essential to give the have-nots a leg-up. And the development of ever-smarter robots could cost even the haves their jobs.

In recent decades the middle class has retained its spending power by borrowing itself into ever-deeper debt. But this model isn't viable, as we now know. The old adage of "those unwilling to work will not get to eat" is now abused as a license for inequality.

Don't get me wrong, capitalism is a fantastic engine for prosperity. "It has accomplished wonders far surpassing Egyptian pyramids, Roman aqueducts, and Gothic cathedrals," as Karl Marx and Friedrich Engels wrote in their *Communist Manifesto*. Yet it's precisely because we're richer than ever that it is now within our means to take the next step in the history of progress: to give each and every person the security of a basic income. It's what capitalism ought to have been striving for all along. See it as a dividend on progress, made possible by the blood, sweat, and tears of past generations. In the end, only a fraction of our prosperity is due to our own exertions. We, the inhabitants of the

Land of Plenty, are rich thanks to the institutions, the knowledge, and the social capital amassed for us by our forebears. This wealth belongs to us all. And a basic income allows all of us to share it.

Of course, this is not to say we should implement this dream without forethought. That could be disastrous. Utopias always start out small, with experiments that ever so slowly change the world. It happened just a few years ago on the streets of London, when thirteen street sleepers got £3,000, no questions asked. As one of the aid workers said, "It's quite hard to just change overnight the way you've always approached this problem. These pilots give us the opportunity to talk differently, think differently, describe the problem differently . . ."

And that's how all progress begins.

So we have inspectors of inspectors and people making instruments for inspectors to inspect inspectors. The true business of people should be to go back to school and think about whatever it was they were thinking about before somebody came along and told them they had to earn a living.

Richard Buckminster Fuller (1895–1983)

3

The End of Poverty

On November 13, 1997, a new casino opened its doors just south of North Carolina's Great Smoky Mountains. Despite the dismal weather, a long line had formed at the entrance, and as people continued to arrive by the hundreds, the casino boss began advising folks to stay at home.

The widespread interest was hardly surprising. After all, it wasn't just some shifty mafia-run gambling den opening its doors that day. Harrah's Cherokee was and still is a massive luxury casino owned and operated by the Eastern Band of Cherokee Indians, and its opening marked the end of a ten-year-long political tug of war. One tribal leader had even predicted that "gambling would be the Cherokee's damnation,"[1] and North Carolina's governor had tried to block the project at every turn.

Soon after the opening, it became apparent that the casino's 35,000-square-foot gaming floor, three hotel towers with over 1,000 rooms and 100 suites, countless stores, restaurants, swimming pool, and fitness center would bring the tribe not damnation, but relief. Nor did it pave the way for organized crime. Far from it: The profits – amounting to $150 million in 2004 and growing to nearly $400 million in 2010[2] – enabled the tribe to build a new school, hospital, and fire station. However, the lion's share of the takings went directly into the pockets of the 8,000 men, women, and children of the Eastern Band Cherokee tribe. From $500 a year at the outset, their earnings from the casino quickly mounted to $6,000 in 2001, constituting a quarter to a third of the average family income.[3]

As coincidence would have it, a Duke University professor by the name of Jane Costello had been researching the mental health of youngsters south of the Great Smoky Mountains since 1993. Every year, the 1,420 kids enrolled in her study took a psychiatric test. The cumulative results had already shown that those growing up in poverty were much more prone to behavioral problems than other children. This wasn't exactly news, though. Correlations between poverty and mental illness had been drawn before by another academic, Edward Jarvis, in his famous paper "Report on Insanity," published in 1855.

But the question still remained: Which was the cause, and which the effect? At the time Costello was doing her research, it was becoming increasingly popular to attribute mental problems to individual genetic factors. If nature was the root cause, then handing over a sack of money every year would be treating the symptoms, but ignoring the disease. If, on the other hand, people's psychiatric problems were not the cause but the consequence of poverty, then that $6,000 might genuinely work wonders. The arrival of the casino, Costello realized, presented a unique opportunity to shed new light on this ongoing question since a quarter of the children in her study belonged to the Cherokee tribe, more than half of them living below the poverty line.

Soon after the casino opened, Costello was already noting huge improvements for her subjects. Behavioral problems among children who had been lifted out of poverty went down 40%, putting them in the same range as their peers who had never known privation. Juvenile crime rates among the Cherokee also declined, along with drug and alcohol use, while their school scores improved markedly.[4] At school, the Cherokee kids were now on a par with the study's non-tribal participants.

Ten years after the casino's arrival, Costello's findings showed that the younger the age at which children escaped poverty, the better their teenage mental health. Among her youngest age cohort, Costello observed a "dramatic decrease" in criminal conduct. In fact, the Cherokee children in her study were now better behaved than the control group.

On seeing the data, Costello's first reaction was disbelief. "The expectation is that social interventions have relatively small effects," she later said. "This one had quite large effects."[5] Professor Costello calculated that the extra $4,000 per annum resulted in an additional year of educational attainment by age twenty-one and reduced the chance of a criminal record at age sixteen by 22%.[6]

But the most significant improvement was in how the money helped parents, well, to parent. Before the casino opened its doors, parents worked hard through the summer but were often jobless and stressed over the winter. The new income enabled Cherokee families to put money aside and to pay bills in advance. Parents who were lifted out of poverty now reported having more time for their children.

They weren't working any less though, Costello discovered. Mothers and fathers alike were putting in just as many hours as before the casino opened. More than anything, says tribe member Vickie L. Bradley, the money helped ease the pressure on families, so the energy they'd spent worrying about money was now freed up for their children. And that "helps parents be better parents," Bradley explains.[7]

What, then, is the cause of mental-health problems among the poor? Nature or culture? Both, was Costello's conclusion, because the stress of poverty puts people genetically predisposed to develop an illness or disorder at an elevated risk.[8] But there's a more important takeaway from this study.

Genes can't be undone. Poverty can.

Why Poor People Do Dumb Things

A world without poverty — it might be the oldest utopia around. But anybody who takes this dream seriously must inevitably face a few tough questions. Why are the poor more likely to commit crimes? Why are they more prone to obesity? Why do they use more alcohol and drugs? In short, why do the poor make so many dumb decisions?

Harsh? Perhaps, but take a look at the statistics: The poor borrow more, save less, smoke more, exercise less, drink more, and eat less healthfully. Offer money-management training and the poor are the last to sign up. When responding to job ads, the poor often write the worst applications and show up at interviews in the least professional attire.

British Prime Minister Margaret Thatcher once called poverty a "personality defect."[9] Though not many politicians would go quite so far, this view that the solution resides with the individual is not exceptional. From Australia to England and from Sweden to the United States there is an entrenched notion that poverty is something people have to overcome on their own. Sure, the government can nudge them in the right direction with incentives – with policies promoting awareness, with penalties, and, above all, with education. In fact, if there's a perceived silver bullet in the fight against poverty, it's a high-school diploma (or even better, a college degree).

But is that all there is to it?

What if the poor aren't actually able to help themselves? What if all the incentives, all the information and education are like water off a duck's back? And what if all those well-meant nudges only make the situation worse?

The Power of Context

These are harsh questions, but then, it's not just anybody asking them; it's Eldar Shafir, a psychologist at Princeton University. He and Sendhil Mullainathan, an economist at Harvard, recently published a revolutionary new theory on poverty.[10] The gist? It's the context, stupid.

Shafir isn't modest in his aspirations. He wants nothing less than to establish a whole new field of science: the science of scarcity. But don't we have that already? Economics? "We get that a lot," laughed Shafir when I met with him at a hotel in Amsterdam. "But my interest is in the psychology of scarcity, on which surprisingly little research has been done."

To economists, everything revolves around scarcity – after all, even the biggest spenders can't buy everything. However, the *perception* of scarcity is not ubiquitous. An empty schedule feels different than a jam-packed workday. And that's not some harmless little feeling. Scarcity impinges on your mind. People behave differently when they perceive a thing to be scarce.

What that thing is doesn't much matter; whether it's too little time, money, friendship, food – it all contributes to a "scarcity mentality." And this has benefits. People who experience a sense of scarcity are good at managing their short-term problems. Poor people have an incredible abil-ity – in the short term – to make ends meet, the same way that overworked CEOs can power through to close a deal.

You Can't Take a Break from Poverty

Despite all this, the drawbacks of a "scarcity mentality" are greater than the benefits. Scarcity narrows your focus to your immediate lack, to the meeting that's starting in five minutes or the bills that need to be paid tomorrow. The long-term perspective goes out the window. "Scarcity consumes you," Shafir explains. "You're less able to focus on other things that are also important to you."

Compare it to a new computer that's running ten heavy programs at once. It gets slower and slower, making errors, and eventually it freezes – not because it's a bad computer, but because it has to do too much at once. Poor people have an analogous problem. They're not making dumb decisions because they *are* dumb, but because they're living in a context in which anyone would make dumb decisions.

Questions like *What's for dinner?* and *How will I make it to the end of the week?* tax a crucial capacity. "Mental band-width," Shafir and Mullainathan call it. "If you want to understand the poor, imagine yourself with your mind elsewhere," they write. "Self-control feels like a challenge. You are distracted and easily perturbed. And this happens every day." This is how scarcity – whether of time or of money – leads to unwise decisions.

There's a key distinction though between people with busy lives and those living in poverty: You can't take a break from poverty.

Two Experiments

So in concrete terms, just how much dumber does poverty make you?

"Our effects correspond to between 13 and 14 IQ points," Shafir says. "That's comparable to losing a night's sleep or the effects of alcoholism." What's remarkable is that we could have figured all this out thirty years ago. Shafir and Mullainathan weren't relying on anything so complicated as brain scans. "Economists have been studying poverty for years and psychologists have been studying cognitive limitations for years," Shafir explains. "We just put two and two together."

It all started a few years ago with a series of experiments conducted at a typical American mall. Shoppers were stopped to ask what they would do if they had to pay to get their car fixed. Some were presented with a $150 repair job, others with one costing $1,500. Would they pay it all in one go, get a loan, work overtime, or put off the repairs? While the mall-goers were mulling it over, they were subjected to a series of cognitive tests. In the case of the less expensive repairs, people with a low income scored about the same as those with a high income. But faced with a $1,500 repair job, poor people scored considerably lower. The mere thought of a major financial setback impaired their cognitive ability.

Shafir and his fellow researchers corrected for all possible variables in the mall survey, but there was one factor they couldn't resolve: The rich folks and the poor folks questioned weren't the same people. Ideally, they'd be able to repeat the survey with subjects who were poor at one moment and rich the next.

Shafir found what he was looking for some 8,000 miles away in the districts of Vilupuram and Tiruvannamalai in rural India. The conditions were perfect; as it happened, the area's sugarcane farmers collect 60% of their annual income all at once right after the harvest. This means they are flush one part of the year and poor the other. So how did they do in the experiment? At the time when they were comparatively poor, they scored substantially worse on the cognitive tests, not because they had become dumber people somehow – they were still the same Indian sugarcane farmers, after all – but purely and simply because their mental bandwidth was compromised.

Gross Domestic Mental Bandwidth

"Fighting poverty has huge benefits that we have been blind to until now," Shafir points out. In fact, he suggests, in addition to measuring our gross domestic product, maybe it's time we also started considering our gross domestic mental bandwidth. Greater mental bandwidth equates to better child-rearing, better health, more productive employees – you name it. "Fighting scarcity could even reduce costs," projects Shafir.

And that's precisely what happened south of the Great Smoky Mountains. Randall Akee, an economist at the University of Los Angeles, calculated that the casino cash distributed to Cherokee kids ultimately *cut* expenditures. According to his conservative estimates, eliminating poverty actually generated more money than the total of all casino payments through reductions in crime, use of care facilities, and repetition of school grades.[11]

Now extrapolate these effects to society as a whole. A British study discovered that the costs of poverty among children in England top £29 billion ($44 billion) a year.[12] According to the researchers, a policy to eliminate poverty "could largely pay for itself."[13]

In the U.S., where more than one in five children grow up poor, countless studies have already shown that anti-poverty measures actually work as a cost-cutting instrument.[14] Greg Duncan, a professor at the University of California, calculated that lifting an American family out of poverty takes an average of about $4,500 annually – less than the Cherokee casino payouts. In the end, the return on this investment, per child, would be:

+ 12.5% more hours worked
+ $3,000 annual savings on welfare
+ $50,000–$100,000 additional lifetime earnings
+ $10,000–$20,000 additional state tax revenues

Professor Duncan concluded that combating poverty

"pays for itself by the time the poor children have reached middle age."[15]

Granted, it would take a big program to tackle such a big problem. A 2013 study estimated the costs of child poverty in the U.S. at as much as $500 billion a year. Kids who grow up poor end up with two years' less educational attainment, work 450 fewer hours per year, and run three times the risk of all-round bad health than those raised in families that are well off. Investments in education won't really help these kids, the researchers say.[16] They have to get above the poverty line first.

A recent meta-analysis of 201 studies on the effectiveness of financial education came to a similar conclusion: Such education makes almost no difference at all.[17] This is not to say no one learns anything – poor people can come out wiser, for sure. But it's not enough. "It's like teaching a person to swim and then throwing them in a stormy sea," laments Professor Shafir.

Educating people certainly isn't entirely pointless, but it can only go so far in helping them to manage their mental bandwidth, already taxed, as it is, by demands like the impossible bureaucratic mire of the welfare state. You might imagine that all the rules and paperwork serve to put off those who aren't genuinely needy. But in fact, it works the other way around: The poor – those whose bandwidth is already overtaxed, whose need is greatest – are the least likely to ask Uncle Sam for help.

Consequently, a whole array of programs goes all but unused by the very people they are meant to benefit. "Some scholarships are applied for by only 30% of those who qualify," says Shafir, "despite the fact that study after study has shown that such a scholarship, of thousands of dollars, can make all the difference." An economist looks at these scholarships and thinks: Since applying is the rational thing to do, poor students will apply. But that's not how it works. The fruits of the scholarship fall well outside the tunnel vision of the scarcity mindset.

Free Money

So what can be done?

Shafir and Mullainathan have a few possible solutions up their sleeves: giving needy students a hand with all that financial-aid paperwork, for instance, or providing pill boxes that light up to remind people to take their meds. This type of solution is called a "nudge." Nudges are hugely popular with politicians in our modern Land of Plenty, mostly because they cost next to nothing.

But, honestly, what difference can a nudge really make? The nudge epitomizes an era in which politics is concerned chiefly with combating symptoms. Nudges might serve to make poverty infinitesimally more bearable, but when you zoom out, you see that they solve exactly nothing. Going back to our computer analogy, I ask Shafir: Why keep tinkering around with the software when you could easily solve the problem by installing some extra memory instead?

Shafir responds with a blank look. "Oh! You mean just hand out more money? Sure, that would be great," he laughs. "But given the evident limitations . . . the brand of left-wing politics you've got here in Amsterdam doesn't even exist in the States."

However, money in itself is not enough; it's also about the distribution. "Scarcity is a relative concept," says Shafir. "It can be based on a lack of income, but equally on excessive expectations." It's simple really: If you'd like to have more money, time, friends, or food, you're more likely to experience a sense of scarcity. And the things you want are determined to a large extent by what people around you have. As Shafir says, "The growing inequality in the Western world is a major obstacle in this respect." If lots of people are buying the latest smartphone, then you want one, too. As long as inequality continues to rise, the gross domestic mental bandwidth will continue to contract.

The Curse of Inequality

But money was supposed to be the key to a happy and healthy life, wasn't it?

Yes. However, nationally speaking, only to a certain extent. Up to a per capita GDP of roughly $5,000 a year, life expectancy increases more or less automatically.[18] But once there's enough food on the table, a roof that doesn't leak, and clean running water to drink, economic growth is no longer a guarantor of welfare. From that point on, equality is a much more accurate predictor.

Take the diagram below. The y-axis shows an index of social problems; on the x-axis are the countries' per capita GDP. It turns out that there's no correlation whatsoever between these two variables. What's more, the world's richest superpower (the U.S.) rates alongside a country with less than half the per capita GDP (Portugal) for the highest incidence of social problems.

"Economic growth has done as much as it can to improve material conditions in the developed countries," concludes

FIGURE 4

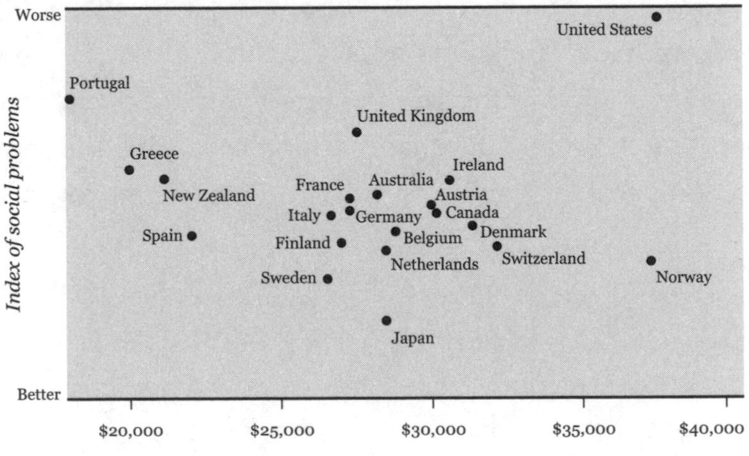

Per capita gross domestic product (corrected for purchasing power)

The index of social problems (here on the y-axis) includes life expectancy, literacy, child mortality, murder rate, inmate population, teenage pregnancy, depression, social trust, obesity, drug and alcohol abuse, and social mobility vs. immobility.

Source: Wilkinson and Pickett

64

the British researcher Richard Wilkinson. "As you get more and more of anything, each addition . . . contributes less and less to your well-being."[19] However, the graph changes dramatically if we replace income on the x-axis with income inequality. Suddenly, the picture crystallizes, with the U.S. and Portugal close together in the top right-hand corner.

Whether you look at the incidence of depression, burnout, drug abuse, high dropout rates, obesity, unhappy childhoods, low election turnout, or social and political distrust, the evidence points to the same culprit every time: inequality.[20]

But hold on. What should it matter if some people are filthy rich, when even those who are the hardest up today are better off than the kings of a few centuries ago?

A lot. Because it's all about *relative* poverty. However

FIGURE 5

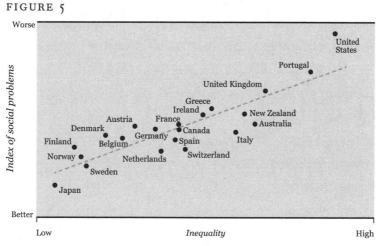

Inequality (here on the x-axis) represents that gap between the richest and the poorest 20% in a given country.

Source: Wilkinson and Pickett

wealthy a country gets, inequality always rains on the parade. Being poor in a rich country is a whole different story to being poor a couple centuries ago, when almost everybody, everywhere was a pauper.

Take bullying. Countries with big disparities in wealth also have more bullying behavior, because there are bigger status differences. Or, in Wilkinson's terms, the "psychosocial consequences" are such that people living in unequal societies spend more time worrying about how others see them. This undercuts the quality of relationships (manifested in a distrust of strangers and status anxiety, for example). The resulting stress, in turn, is a major determinant of illness and chronic health problems.

Okay – but shouldn't we be more concerned with equal opportunities than with equal wealth?

The fact is they both matter, and these two forms of inequality are inextricable. Just look at the global rankings: When inequality goes up, social mobility goes down. Frankly, there's almost no country on Earth where the American Dream is less likely to come true than in the U.S. of A. Anybody eager to work their way up from rags to riches is better off trying their luck in Sweden, where people born into poverty can still hold out hope of a brighter future.[21]

Don't get me wrong – inequality is not the only source of hardship. It's one structural factor that feeds into the evolution of lots of social problems and is intricately linked to a constellation of other factors. And, in point of fact, society can't function *without* some degree of inequality. There still need to be incentives to work, to endeavor, and to excel, and money is a very effective stimulus. Nobody would want to live in a society where cobblers earn as much as doctors. Or rather, nobody living in such a place would want to risk getting sick.

Nonetheless, in almost all developed countries today, inequality far exceeds what could reasonably be deemed desirable. Recently, the International Monetary Fund published a report which revealed that too much inequality even inhibits economic growth.[22] Perhaps the most fascinating finding, however, is that even rich people suffer when inequality becomes too great. They, too, become more prone to depression, suspicion, and myriad other social difficulties.[23]

"Income inequality," say two leading scientists who have studied twenty-four developed countries, "makes us all less happy with our lives, even if we're relatively well-off."[24]

When Poverty Was Still Normal

This is not inevitable.

Sure, 2,000 years ago Jesus of Nazareth said the poor would always be with us.[25] But back then practically all the jobs were in agriculture. The economy simply wasn't productive enough to allow everybody a comfortable existence. And so, well into the eighteenth century, poverty was just another fact of life. "The poor are like the shadows in a painting: they provide the necessary contrast," wrote the French physician Philippe Hecquet (1661–1737). According to the English writer Arthur Young (1741–1820), "Everyone but an idiot knows that the lower classes must be kept poor, or they will never be industrious."[26]

Historians refer to this rationale as "mercantilism" – the notion that one man's loss is another man's gain. Early modern economists believed that countries could prosper only at other countries' expense; it was all a matter of keeping exports high. During the Napoleonic Wars, this line of thinking led to some absurd situations. England was perfectly happy to ship food to France, for example, but banned exports of gold because British politicians had gotten it into their heads that a lack of bullion would crush the enemy faster than famine.

If you were to ask a mercantilist for his top tip, it would be lower wages – the lower the better. Cheap labor hones your competitive edge and therefore boosts exports. In the words of the famous economist Bernard de Mandeville (1670–1733), "It is manifest, that in a free Nation where Slaves are not allow'd of, the surest Wealth consists in a Multitude of laborious Poor."[27]

Mandeville couldn't have been wider of the mark. By now we've learned that wealth begets more wealth, whether you're talking about people or about nations. Henry Ford knew it and that's why he gave his employees a hefty raise in 1914; how else would they ever be able to afford his cars? "Poverty is a great enemy to human happiness; it certainly destroys liberty, and it makes some virtues impracticable, and others extremely difficult," said the British essayist Samuel Johnson in 1782.[28] Unlike many of his contemporaries, he understood that poverty is not a lack of character. It's a lack of cash.

A Roof Over Our Heads

Lloyd Pendleton, the director of Utah's Homeless Task Force, had his lightbulb moment in the early 2000s. Homelessness in the state was out of control, with thousands of people sleeping under bridges, in parks, and on the streets of Utah's cities. Police and social services had their hands full, and Pendleton was fed up. He also had a plan.

In 2005, Utah launched its war on homelessness not, as so often, with Tasers and pepper spray, but by attacking the problem at the root. The goal? To get all the state's homeless off the streets. The strategy? Free apartments. Pendleton started with the seventeen most abject street sleepers he could find. Two years later, after they all had a place to live, he progressively expanded the program. Criminal records, hopeless addictions, towering debts — none of it mattered. In Utah, having a roof over your head became a right.

The program has been a resounding success. While in neighboring Wyoming the number of people living on the streets soared by 213%, Utah saw a 74% decline in chronic homelessness. And all this in an ultraconservative state. The Tea Party has had a big following in Utah for years and Lloyd Pendleton isn't exactly a lefty. "I grew up on a ranch, where you learn to work hard," he remembers. "I used to tell the homeless to get a job, because that's all I thought they needed."[29]

The former executive changed his tune when he heard the full financial story at a conference. Giving away free housing, it turned out, was actually a windfall for the state budget. State economists calculated that a drifter living on the street cost the government $16,670 a year (for social services, police, courts, etc.). An apartment plus professional counseling, by contrast, cost a modest $11,000.[30]

The numbers are clear. Today, Utah is on course to eliminate chronic homelessness entirely, making it the first state in the U.S. to successfully address this problem. All while saving a fortune.

How a Worthy Cause was Lost

Like poverty, solving the homelessness problem is preferable to merely managing it.[31] The principle of "housing first," as this strategy is called, has already circled the globe. Back in 2005, you couldn't walk around downtown

Amsterdam or Rotterdam without seeing people living out on the street. Homeless people were a particular problem around train stations, and a very expensive one at that. Consequently, as Lloyd Pendleton rolled out his plan in Utah, social workers, public officials, and politicians from major Dutch cities convened to figure out how to tackle this problem in the Netherlands. They drew up an action plan.

The budget: $217 million.

The aim: get all homeless people off the street.

The site: Amsterdam, Rotterdam, The Hague, and Utrecht first, then nationwide.

The strategy: counseling and – sure enough – free housing for everyone.

The timeline: February 2006 to February 2014.

It was an unmitigated success. After just a couple of years, the problem of vagrancy in the big cities had been reduced by 65%. Drug use was down by half. The beneficiaries' mental and physical health improved significantly, and park benches were finally vacant. By October 1, 2008, the program had brought nearly 6,500 homeless people in off the streets.[32] And to top it off, the financial returns for society proved double the original investments.[33]

Then came the financial crisis. Before long, budgets were being trimmed and the number of evictions rose. In December 2013, three months before the action plan was slated to conclude, Statistics Netherlands released a bleak press release. Nationwide, homelessness was at a record high. The nation's big cities now counted more street sleepers than when the program launched.[34] And this problem was costing fistfuls of money.

How much exactly? In 2011, the Dutch Ministry of Health commissioned a study to work it out. The resulting report tallied the costs against the benefits of relief for the homeless (including free shelter, assistance programs, free heroin, and prevention services) and concluded that investing in a street sleeper offers the highest return on investment around. Every euro invested in fighting and preventing homelessness in the Netherlands enjoys *double or triple* returns in savings on social services, police, and court costs.[35]

"Relief is preferable and less expensive than living on the street," the researchers concluded. Moreover, their calculations only looked at the savings for government, but of course eliminating the problem of homelessness would have payoffs for a city's businesses and residents, too.

Relief for the homeless, in short, is a win-win-win-win policy.

A Good Lesson

There are lots of problems on which politicians can fiercely disagree, but homelessness should not be one of them. It's a problem that *can* be solved. What's more, solving it will actually free up funds. If you're poor, your main problem is no money. If you're homeless, your main problem is no roof over your head. Speaking of which, in Europe, the number of vacant houses is double the number of homeless.[36] In the U.S., there are five empty homes for each person without one.[37]

Sadly, instead of trying to cure the ailment, we continually opt to fight the symptoms, with police chasing vagrants around, doctors treating rough sleepers only to turn them back out onto the streets, and social workers applying Band-Aid solutions to festering wounds. In Utah, a former executive proved there's another way. Lloyd Pendleton has already turned his efforts to persuading Wyoming to start housing its homeless as well. "These are my brothers and sisters," he said at a meeting in Casper, Wyoming. "When they're hurting, we're hurting as a community. We're all connected."[38]

If this message isn't enough to prick your moral sense, consider the monetary sense it makes. Because whether you're talking about Dutch drifters, Indian sugarcane farmers, or Cherokee children, fighting poverty is good not only for our conscience, but for our wallets, too. As Professor Costello dryly notes, "That's a very valuable lesson for society to learn."[39]

Those who cannot remember the past
are condemned to repeat it.

George Santayana (1863–1952)

4

The Bizarre Tale of President Nixon and His Basic Income Bill

History is not a science that serves up handy, bite-size lessons for daily life. Sure, reflecting on the past can help to put our trials and tribulations into perspective, from leaky faucets to national debts. After all, in the past, pretty much everything was worse. But with the world now changing faster than ever, the past seems more remote from us, too. There's a growing gulf between us and that alien world – a world we can barely comprehend. "The past is a foreign country," a novelist once wrote: "they do things differently there."[1]

Even so, I think historians have more to offer than perspective on our present woes. The foreign country we call the past also lets us look beyond the horizons of what is, to see what could be. Why spin theories about an unconditional basic income when you can trace its actual rise and fall in the 1970s?

Whether we're searching for new dreams or rediscovering old ones, we can't move forward without looking to the past. It's the only place where the abstract becomes concrete, where we can see that we're already living in the Land of Plenty. The past teaches us a simple but crucial lesson: *Things could be different.* The way our world is organized is not the result of some axiomatic evolution. Our current status quo could just as easily be the result of the trivial yet critical twists and turns of history.

Historians don't believe in hard and fast laws of progress or economics; the world is governed not by abstract forces, but by people who plot their own course. Consequently, the past not only puts things into perspective; it can also galvanize our imaginations.

The Shadow of Speenhamland

If there were ever a story to prove that things could be different and that poverty is not a necessary evil, it's the story of Speenhamland, England.

It was the summer of '69, the end of the decade that brought us flower power and Woodstock, rock 'n' roll and Vietnam, Martin Luther King and feminism. It was a time when everything seemed possible, even a conservative president strengthening the welfare state.

Richard Nixon was not the most likely candidate to pursue Thomas More's old utopian dream, but then history sometimes has a strange sense of humor. The same man who was forced to resign after the Watergate scandal in 1974 had been on the verge, in 1969, of enacting an unconditional income for all poor families. It would have been a massive step forward in the War on Poverty, guaranteeing a family of four $1,600 a year, equivalent to roughly $10,000 in 2016.

One man began to realize where all this was heading – to a future where money was considered a basic right. Martin Anderson was an advisor to the president and vehemently opposed to the plan. Anderson greatly admired the writer Ayn Rand, whose utopia revolved around the free market, and the concept of a basic income ran counter to the ideals of small government and individual responsibility that he held dear.

So he launched an offensive.

On the same day that Nixon intended to go public with his plan, Anderson handed him a briefing. Over the weeks that followed, this six-page document, a case report about something that had happened in England 150 years before, did the unthinkable: It completely changed Nixon's mind, and, in the process, changed the course of history.

The report was titled "A Short History of a 'Family Security System'" and consisted almost entirely of excerpts from sociologist Karl Polanyi's classic book *The Great Transformation* (1944). In the seventh chapter, Polanyi describes one of the world's first welfare systems, known as the Speenhamland system, in early nineteenth-century England. This system bore a suspiciously close resemblance to a basic income.

Polanyi's judgment of the system was devastating. Not only did it incite the poor to even greater idleness, damping their productivity and wages; it threatened the very foundations of capitalism. "It introduced no less a social and economic innovation than the 'right to live,'" Polanyi wrote, "and until abolished in 1834, it effectively prevented the establishment of a competitive labor market." In the end, Speenhamland resulted in "the pauperization of the masses," who, according to Polanyi, "almost lost their human shape." A basic income introduced not a floor, he contended, but a ceiling.

At the top of the briefing presented to Nixon was a quotation by the Spanish-American writer George Santayana: "Those who cannot remember the past are condemned to repeat it."[2]

The president was stunned. He called on his key advisors and ordered them to get to the bottom of what had transpired in England a century and a half earlier. They showed him the initial findings of the pilot programs in Seattle and Denver, where people clearly had not started working less. Furthermore, they pointed out, Speenhamland more resembled the social spending mess that Nixon had inherited, which actually kept people trapped in a vicious poverty cycle.

Two of Nixon's leading advisors, the sociologist and later Senator Daniel Moynihan and the economist Milton Friedman, argued that the right to an income already existed, even if it was "a legal entitlement that society has nevertheless managed to stigmatize."[3] According to Friedman, poverty simply meant you were strapped for cash. Nothing more, nothing less.

Yet Speenhamland cast a shadow that extended far beyond the summer of 1969. The president changed tack and settled on a new rhetoric. Where his basic income plan had initially made almost no provision to compel people to work, he now began stressing the importance of gainful employment. And whereas the basic income debate under President Johnson had begun when experts signaled unemployment as becoming endemic, Nixon now spoke of joblessness as a "choice." He deplored the rise of big government, even though his plan would distribute cash assistance to some thirteen million more Americans (90% of them working poor).

"Nixon was proposing a new kind of social provision to the American public," writes the historian Brian Steensland, "but he did not offer them a new conceptual framework through which to understand it."[4] Indeed, Nixon steeped his progressive ideas in conservative rhetoric.

What, we may well ask, was the president doing?

There is a brief anecdote that explains it. On August 7 of that same year, Nixon told Moynihan that he'd been reading biographies of the British prime minister Benjamin Disraeli and the statesman Lord Randolph Churchill (the father of Winston). "Tory men and liberal policies," Nixon remarked, "are what have changed the world."[5] The president wanted to make history. He saw himself presented with the rare, historic chance to cast out the old system, raise up millions of working poor, and win a decisive victory in the War on Poverty. In short, Nixon saw basic income as the ultimate marriage of conservative and progressive politics.

All he had to do was convince the House and Senate. To put his fellow Republicans at ease and manage concerns over the Speenhamland precedent, Nixon decided to attach an additional proviso to his bill. Basic income beneficiaries without a job would have to register with the Department of Labor. Nobody in the White House expected this stipulation would have much effect. "I don't care a damn about the work requirement," Nixon said behind closed doors. "This is the price of getting $1,600."[6]

The next day, the president presented his bill in a televised speech. If "welfare" had to be packaged as "workfare" to get basic income through Congress, then so be it. What Nixon failed to foresee was that his rhetoric of fighting laziness among the poor and unemployed would ultimately turn the country against basic income and the welfare state as a whole.[7] The conservative president who dreamed of going down in history as a progressive leader forfeited a unique opportunity to overthrow a stereotype rooted back in nineteenth-century England: the myth of the lazy poor.

To dispel this stereotype, we have to ask a simple historical question: What was the real deal with Speenhamland?

The Irony of History

Rewind to the year 1795.

The French Revolution had been sending shock waves across the European continent for six years. In England, too, social discontent had reached boiling point. Only two years earlier a young general by the name of Napoleon Bonaparte had crushed the English at the Siege of Toulon in southern France. If that weren't bad enough, the country was suffering another year of bad harvests with no hope of importing grain from the continent. As grain prices continued to rise, the threat of revolution loomed ever closer to British shores.

In one district in southern England, people realized that repression and propaganda would no longer suffice to stem the tide of discontent. On May 6, 1795, the magistrates of Speenhamland gathered at the village inn in Speen and agreed to radically reform assistance for the poor. Specifically, the earnings of "all poor and industrious men and their families" would be supplemented up to the subsistence level, at a rate fixed to the price of bread and paid out per family member.[8] The larger the family, the greater the payments.

This was not the first ever program of public relief, or even the first in England. During the reign of Queen Elizabeth I (1558–1603), the Poor Law had introduced two forms of assistance – one for the deserving poor (the elderly, children, and disabled) and another for those who had to be forced to work. Those in the first category were placed in almshouses. Those in the second were auctioned off to landowners, with the local government supplementing their wages up to an agreed minimum. The Speenhamland system put an end to this distinction, just as Nixon would aspire to do 150 years later. From then on, needy was just plain needy, and everybody in need had a right to relief.

The system quickly caught on across the south of England. Prime Minister William Pitt the Younger even attempted to pass it into national law. To all appearances, it was a great success: Hunger and hardship decreased and, more importantly, revolt was nipped in the bud. In the same period, however, some were raising doubts about the wisdom of aiding the poor. In his 1786 *Dissertation on the Poor Laws*, the vicar Joseph Townsend had already, almost a decade before Speenhamland, warned that "it is only hunger which can spur and goad them on to labour; yet our laws have said, they shall never hunger." Another clergyman, Thomas Malthus, elaborated on Townsend's ideas. In the summer of 1798, on the eve of the Industrial Revolution, he described "the great difficulty" on the road to progress, "that to me appears insurmountable." His premise was twofold: (1) Humans need food to survive, and (2) The passion between the sexes is ineradicable.

His conclusion? Population growth will always exceed food production. According to the pious Malthus, sexual abstinence was the only thing that could prevent the Four Horsemen of the Apocalypse from descending to spread war, famine, disease, and death. Indeed, Malthus was convinced that England was teetering on the brink of a disaster as terrible as the Black Death (the plague) that wiped out half its population in 1349–53.[9]

In any case, the consequences of assistance for the poor were sure to be dire. The Speenhamland system would only encourage people to marry and procreate as fast and as prolifically as possible. One of Malthus' close friends, the economist David Ricardo, believed a basic income would also tempt them to work less, causing food production to fall even further and fan the flames of a French-style revolution on English soil.[10]

In the late summer of 1830, the predicted uprising broke out. Shouting "Bread or Blood!" thousands of agricultural laborers up and down the country wrecked landowners' harvesting machines and demanded a living wage. The authorities cracked down hard, arresting, incarcerating, and deporting 2,000 rioters and sentencing others to death.

In London, government officials realized something had to be done. A national inquiry was launched into agricultural working conditions, rural poverty, and the Speenhamland system itself. The largest government survey to date was undertaken in the spring of 1832, with investigators conducting hundreds of interviews and collecting reams of data that were ultimately compiled in a 13,000-page report. But the bottom line could be summed up in a single sentence: Speenhamland had been a disaster.

The investigators behind this Royal Commission survey blamed the basic income for a population explosion, wage reductions, increased immoral conduct . . . effectively, for the utter deterioration of the English working class. Fortunately, though, no sooner had the basic income been repealed, they wrote, than:

1   The poor once more became industrious.
2   They developed "frugal habits."
3   "Demand for their labour" increased.
4   Their wages "in general advanced."
5   They entered into fewer "improvident and wretched marriages."
6   Their "moral and social condition in every way improved."[11]

Widely circulated and endorsed, the Royal Commission Report was long considered an authoritative source in the emerging social sciences, marking the first time a government had systematically gathered data as input for a complicated decision.

Even Karl Marx used it as the basis for his condemnation of the Speenhamland system in his magnum opus *Das Kapital* (1867) thirty years later. Poor relief, he said, was a tactic employers used to keep wages as low as possible by putting the onus on local government. Like his friend Friedrich Engels, Marx saw the old poor laws as a relic of a feudal past. Releasing the proletariat from the shackles of poverty required a revolution, not a basic income.

Critics of Speenhamland had acquired towering authority, with everyone from left to right relegating it to history's failures. Far into the twentieth century, eminent thinkers such as Jeremy Bentham, Alexis de Tocqueville, John Stuart Mill, Friedrich Hayek, and, above all, Karl Polanyi would denounce it.[12] Speenhamland was the textbook example of a government program that had, with the best of intentions, paved the road to hell.

150 Years Later

But this wasn't quite the whole story.

In the 1960s and 1970s, historians took another look at the Royal Commission Report on Speenhamland and discovered that much of the text had been written before any data was even collected. Of the questionnaires distributed, only 10% were ever filled out. Furthermore, the questions were leading, with the answer choices all fixed in advance. And almost none of the people interviewed were actual beneficiaries. The evidence, such as it was, came mostly from the local elite, and especially the clergy, whose general view was that the poor were only growing more wicked and lazy.

The Royal Commission Report, largely fabricated, supplied the underpinnings of a new, draconian Poor Law. It was even said that the Commission's secretary, Edwin Chadwick, had "the Bill in his head" before the investigation even started, but he was shrewd enough to obtain some substantiating evidence first. Chadwick was furthermore blessed with the "admirable faculty" of getting eyewitnesses to say what he wanted, just like "a French cook who can make an excellent ragout out of a pair of shoes," according to a fellow Commission member.[13]

The investigators barely concerned themselves with analyzing the data, though they did employ "an elaborate structure of appendixes to lend more weight to their 'findings,'" two modern-day researchers note.[14] Their approach could not have been more different than that of the rigorous experiments conducted in Canada and the U.S. in the 1960s and 1970s (see Chapter 2). Those experiments had been groundbreaking and meticulous but had almost no influence at all, whereas the Royal Commission Report was based on bogus science yet still managed to redirect President Nixon's course of action 150 years later.

More recent research has revealed that the Speenhamland system was actually a success. Malthus was wrong about the population explosion, which was attributable chiefly to growing demand for child labor. At the time, children were like walking piggy banks, their earnings a kind of pension plan for parents. Even now, as soon as populations escape poverty, birth rates drop and people find other ways to invest in their future.[15]

Ricardo's analysis was equally faulty. There was no poverty trap in the Speenhamland system and wage earners were permitted to keep their allowance – at least in part – even if their earnings increased.[16] As such, basic income didn't cause poverty, but was adopted in precisely those districts where suffering was already the most acute.[17] And the rural unrest had actually been triggered by the 1819 decision to return to the pre-war gold standard on the advice, incidentally, of David Ricardo.[18]

Marx and Engels were also misguided. With all the competition among landowners to attract decent labor, wages couldn't simply be lowered. On top of this, modern historical research has revealed that the Speenhamland system was more limited than had been assumed. Villages where the system had not been implemented suffered the same hardships attending the gold standard, the advent of northern industry, and the invention of the threshing machine. Threshers, which literally helped separate the wheat from the chaff, destroyed thousands of jobs in one fell swoop, thereby depressing wages and inflating the cost of poor relief.

All the while, the steady upward trend of agricultural production never faltered, increasing by a third between 1790 and 1830.[19] Food was more plentiful than ever, yet a decreasing share of the English population could afford it. Not because they were lazy, but because they were losing the race against the machine.

A Heinous System

In 1834, the Speenhamland system was permanently dismantled. The 1830 uprising, which probably would have happened earlier if not for the basic income, sealed the fate of the first cash transfer trial, with the poor blamed for their own poverty. Where England had previously spent 2% of its national income on poor relief, after 1834 this figure dropped to just 1%.[20]

The new Poor Law introduced perhaps the most heinous form of "public assistance" that the world has ever witnessed. Believing workhouses to be the only effective remedy against sloth and depravity, the Royal Commission forced the poor into senseless slave labor, from breaking stones to walking on treadmills. And all the while, the poor went hungry. In the town of Andover, inmates even resorted to gnawing on the bones they were supposed to grind up for fertilizer.

On entering the workhouse, spouses were separated and children taken away from their parents, never to be seen again. Women were starved as a precaution against pregnancy. Charles Dickens achieved fame with his portrayal of the plight of the poor at this time. "Please, sir, I want some more," says little Oliver Twist in a poorhouse where the boys get three daily helpings of gruel, two onions a week, and a sliver of bread on Sundays. Far from helping the poor, it was this specter of the workhouse that enabled employers to keep wages so miserably low.

Meanwhile, the myth of Speenhamland played a pivotal role in propagating the idea of a free, self-regulating market. According to two contemporary historians, it helped to "cover up the first major policy failure of the new science of political economy."[21] Not until after the Great Depression did it become clear just how shortsighted Ricardo's obsession with the gold standard had been. Ultimately, the perfect, self-regulating market proved an illusion.

The Speenhamland system, by contrast, was an effective means of addressing poverty. In a world that was changing at a breakneck pace, it offered security. "Far from having an inhibitory effect, it probably contributed to economic expansion," concluded a later study.[22] Simon Szreter, a historian at Cambridge University, even argues that anti-poverty legislation was instrumental in England's rise as a world superpower. According to Szreter, by boosting workers' income security and mobility, the old Poor Law and the Speenhamland system made the English agricultural industry the most efficient in the world.[23]

A Pernicious Myth

Now and then politicians are accused of taking too little interest in the past. In this case, however, Nixon was perhaps taking too much. Even a century and a half after the fatal report, the Speenhamland myth was still alive and kicking. When Nixon's bill foundered in the Senate, conservative thinkers began lambasting the welfare state, using the very same misguided arguments applied back in 1834.

These arguments echoed in *Wealth and Poverty*, the 1981 mega-bestseller by George Gilder that would make him Reagan's most cited author and that characterized poverty as a moral problem rooted in laziness and vice. And they appeared again a few years later in *Losing Ground*, an influential book in which the conservative sociologist Charles Murray recycled the Speenhamland myth.[24] Government support, he wrote, would only undermine the sexual morals and work ethic of the poor.

It was like Townsend and Malthus all over again, but as one historian rightly notes, "Anywhere you find poor people, you also find non-poor people theorizing their cultural inferiority and dysfunction."[25] Even former Nixon advisor Daniel Moynihan stopped believing in a basic income when divorce rates were initially thought to have spiked during the Seattle pilot program, a conclusion later debunked as a mathematical error.[26] So did President Carter, though he had once toyed with the idea.

Ayn Rand's faithful follower Martin Anderson smelled victory. "Radical welfare reform is an impossible dream," he crowed in the *New York Times*.[27] The time had come to ax the old welfare state, like the English Poor Law before it in 1834. In 1996 the Democratic president Bill Clinton finally pulled the plug on "the welfare state as we know it." For the first time since the passage of the Social Security Act in 1935, assistance for the poor was again seen as a favor instead of a right. "Personal responsibility" was the new buzzword. The perfectibility of society made way for the perfectibility of the individual, epitomized in the allocation of $250 million to "chastity training" for single mothers.[28] The Reverend Malthus would surely have approved.

Among the few dissident voices was old Daniel Moynihan – not because the system had been so great, but because it was better than nothing.[29] Setting aside his earlier misgivings, Moynihan predicted that child poverty would escalate if the welfare state were further hollowed out. "They should be ashamed," he said of the Clinton government. "History will shame them."[30] Meanwhile, child poverty in the U.S. climbed back to the level of 1964, when the War on Poverty, and Moynihan's career, first began.

The Lessons of History

Yet things could have been different.

At Princeton University, the historian Brian Steensland has meticulously traced the rise and fall of basic income in the U.S., and he emphasizes that, *had* Nixon's plan gone ahead, the ramifications would have been huge. Public assistance programs would no longer be seen as simply pandering to lazy opportunists. No longer would there be such a thing as the "deserving" or "undeserving" poor.

Rooted in the old Elizabethan Poor Law, this historical distinction is, to this day, one of the main obstacles to a world without poverty. Basic income could change that, providing a guaranteed minimum for all.[31] Had the United States, the world's wealthiest nation, gone this route, there's little doubt other countries would have followed suit.

But history took a different turn. Arguments once used in support of basic income (the old system was inefficient, expensive, demeaning) came to be leveled against the welfare state in its entirety. The shadow of Speenhamland and Nixon's misguided rhetoric laid the foundation for Reagan's and Clinton's cutbacks.[32]

These days, the idea of a basic income for all Americans is, in Steensland's words, as "unthinkable" as "women's suffrage and equal rights for racial minorities" were in the past.[33] It's difficult to imagine that we'll ever be able to shake off the dogma that if you want money, you have to work for it. That a president as recent and as conservative as Richard Nixon once sought to implement a basic income seems to have evaporated from the collective memory.

The Surveillance State

According to one of the twentieth century's greatest authors, "It is the peculiar lowness of poverty that you discover first." George Orwell would know, having experienced poverty first hand. In his memoir *Down and Out in Paris and London* (1933), he writes, "You thought it would be quite simple; it is extraordinarily complicated. You thought it would be terrible; it is merely squalid and boring."

Orwell recalls spending entire days simply lying in bed because there was nothing worth getting up for. The crux of poverty, he says, is that "it annihilates the future." All that remains is surviving in the here and now. He also marvels at "how people take it for granted that they have a right to preach at you and pray over you as soon as your income falls below a certain level."

His words are every bit as resonant today. In recent decades, our welfare states have come to look increasingly like surveillance states. Using Big Brother tactics, Big Government is forcing us into a Big Society. Lately, developed nations have been doubling down on this sort of "activating" policy for the jobless, which runs the gamut from job-application workshops to stints picking up trash, and from talk therapy to LinkedIn training. No matter if there are ten applicants for every job, the problem is consistently attributed not to demand, but to supply. That is to say, to the unemployed, who haven't developed their "employment skills" or simply haven't given it their best shot.

What's remarkable is that economists have denounced this unemployment industry all along.[34] Some return-to-work programs even *prolong* unemployment,[35] and the caseworkers appointed to help claimants find a job often cost more than unemployment benefits. Taking a long view, the costs of the surveillance state are higher still.

After all, spending a workweek attending pointless work-shops or performing mindless tasks leaves less time for parenting, education, and looking for a real job.[36]

Imagine this: A welfare mother with two kids has her benefits cut because she hasn't sufficiently developed her job skills. The government saves a couple thousand bucks, but the hidden costs of children who will consequently grow up poor, eat poor food, get poor grades at school, and be more likely to have a run-in with the law, are many times greater.

In fact, conservative criticism of the old nanny state hits the nail on the head. The current tangle of red tape keeps people trapped in poverty. It actually *produces* dependence. Whereas employees are expected to demonstrate their strengths, social services expects claimants to demonstrate their shortcomings; to prove over and over that an illness is sufficiently debilitating, that a depression is sufficiently bleak, and that chances of getting hired are sufficiently slim. Otherwise your benefits are cut. Forms, interviews, checks, appeals, assessments, consultations, and then still more forms – every application for assistance has its own debasing, money-guzzling protocol. "It tramples on privacy and self-respect in a way inconceivable to anyone outside the benefit system," says one British social services worker. "It creates a noxious fog of suspicion."[37]

This isn't a war on poverty; it's a war on the poor. There's no surer way to turn those on the bottom rungs of society – including geniuses like Orwell – into a legion of lazy, frustrated, and even aggressive bums and freeloaders. They're being trained for it. If there's one thing that we capitalists have in common with the communists of old, it's a pathological obsession with gainful employment. Just as Soviet-era shops employed "three clerks to sell a piece of meat," we'll force benefit claimants to perform pointless tasks, even if it bankrupts us.[38]

Capitalist or communist, it all boils down to a pointless distinction between two types of poor, and to a major misconception that we almost managed to dispel some forty years ago – the fallacy that a life without poverty is a privilege you have to work for, rather than a right we all deserve.

The gross national product . . . measures
everything . . . except that which makes
life worthwhile.

Robert F. Kennedy (1925–68)

New Figures for a New Era

It started at about a quarter to three in the afternoon –
with tremors some six miles under the Earth's surface
the likes of which hadn't been felt in half a century or more.
Sixty miles away, seismographs started going crazy, scrib-
bling a magnitude of 9 on the Richter scale. Less than half
an hour later, the first waves crashed onto Japan's shore,
towering twenty, forty, even sixty feet high. In the space of
a few hours, 150 square miles of land had been buried
under mud, debris, and water.

Nearly 20,000 people were left dead.

"JAPAN'S ECONOMY HEADS INTO FREEFALL," a head-
line in the *Guardian* proclaimed shortly after the disaster.[1]
A few months later, the World Bank tallied the damage at
$235 billion, on a par with the entire GDP of Greece. The
Sendai seaquake on March 11, 2011, went down in history
as the costliest disaster ever.

But the story doesn't end there. In a TV appearance on
the day of the quake, American economist Larry Summers
said that, ironically, this tragedy would help to lift the
Japanese economy. Sure, in the short run production would

slow, but after a couple of months, recovery efforts would boost demand, employment, and consumption.

And Larry Summers was right.

After a slight dip in 2011, the following year saw the country's economy grow 2%, and figures for 2013 were even better. Japan was experiencing the effects of an enduring economic law which holds that every disaster has a silver lining – at least for the GDP.

It was the same with the Great Depression. The United States only really started to climb out of the crisis when it entered the biggest catastrophe of the last century: World War II. Or take the flood that killed almost 2,000 people in my own country of the Netherlands in 1953. Rebuilding after the disaster provided a terrific impetus for the Dutch economy. With national industry in a slump in the early 1950s, the inundation of large parts of the southwest buoyed annual growth from 2% to 8%. "We pulled ourselves up out of the muck by our bootstraps," was how one historian summed it up.[2]

What You See

So should we welcome climate disasters? Raze entire neighborhoods? Blow up factories? It could be a great antidote to unemployment and work wonders for the economy.

But before we get too excited, not everyone would agree with this line of thinking. In 1850, the philosopher Frédéric

Bastiat penned an essay titled *"Ce qu'on voit et ce qu'on ne voit pas,"* which means roughly "What you see and what you don't."[3] From a certain perspective, he says, breaking a window sounds like a fine idea. "Imagine it costs six francs to repair the damage. And imagine that this creates a commercial gain of six francs – I confess, there's no arguing with this reasoning. The glazier comes along, does his work, and happily pockets six francs . . ." *Ce qu'on voit.*

But, as Bastiat realized, this theory doesn't take account of what we don't see. Imagine (again), that the Attorney General's Office reports a 15% increase in street activity. It's only natural that you'd want to know what kind of activity. Neighborhood barbecues or public nudity? Street musicians or street robberies? Lemonade stands or broken windows? What's the *nature* of the activity?

That is precisely what modern society's sacred measure of progress, the Gross Domestic Product, does not measure. *Ce qu'on ne voit pas.*

What You Don't See

The Gross Domestic Product. So, what is it really?

Well, that's easy, you say: The GDP is the sum of all goods and services that a country produces, corrected for seasonal fluctuations, inflation, and perhaps purchasing power.

To which Bastiat would respond: You've overlooked a huge part of the picture. Community service, clean air, free refills on the house – none of these things make the GDP an iota bigger. If a businesswoman marries her cleaner, the GDP dips when her hubby trades his job for unpaid housework. Or take Wikipedia. Supported by investments of time rather than money, it has left the old *Encyclopedia Britannica* in the dust – and taken the GDP down a few notches in the process.

Some countries do factor in an estimate of their shadow economies. The Greek GDP spiked 25% when statisticians dove into the country's black market in 2006, for instance, thereby enabling the government to take out several hefty loans shortly before the European debt crisis broke out. Italy started including its black market back in 1987, which swelled its economy by 20% overnight. "A wave of euphoria swept over Italians," reported the *New York Times*, "after economists recalibrated their statistics taking into account for the first time the country's formidable underground economy of tax evaders and illegal workers."[4]

And that's to say nothing of all the unpaid labor that doesn't even qualify as part of the black market, from volunteering to childcare to cooking, which together represents more than half of all our work. Of course, we can hire cleaners or nannies to do some of these chores, in which case they count toward the GDP, but we still do most ourselves. Adding all this unpaid work would expand the economy by anywhere from 37% (in Hungary) to 74% (in the UK).[5] However, as the economist Diane Coyle notes, "generally official statistical agencies have never bothered – perhaps because it has been carried out mainly by women."[6]

While we're on the subject, only Denmark has ever attempted to quantify the value of breastfeeding in its GDP. And it's no paltry sum: In the U.S., the potential contribution of breast milk has been estimated at an incredible $110 billion a year[7] – about the size of China's military budget.[8]

The GDP also does a poor job of calculating advances in knowledge. Our computers, cameras, and phones are all smarter, speedier, and snazzier than ever, but also cheaper, and therefore they scarcely figure.[9] Where we still had to shell out $300,000 for a single storage gigabyte thirty years ago, today it costs less than a dime.[10] Such stunning technological advances figure as little more than pocket change in the GDP. Free products can even cause the economy to contract (like the call service Skype, which cost telecom companies a fortune). Today, the average African with a cell phone has access to more information than President Clinton did in the 1990s, yet the information sector's share of the economy hasn't budged from twenty-five years ago, before we had the Internet.[11]

Besides being blind to lots of good things, the GDP also benefits from all manner of human suffering. Gridlock, drug abuse, adultery? Goldmines for gas stations, rehab centers, and divorce attorneys. If you were the GDP, your ideal citizen would be a compulsive gambler with cancer who's going through a drawn-out divorce that he copes with by popping fistfuls of Prozac and going berserk on Black Friday. Environmental pollution even does double duty: One company makes a mint by cutting corners while another is paid to clean up the mess. By contrast, a centuries-old tree doesn't count until you chop it down and sell it as lumber.[12]

Mental illness, obesity, pollution, crime – in terms of the GDP, the more the better. That's also why the country with the planet's highest per capita GDP, the United States, also leads in social problems. "By the standard of the GDP," says the writer Jonathan Rowe, "the worst families in America are those that actually function as families – that cook their own meals, take walks after dinner and talk together instead of just farming the kids out to the commercial culture."[13]

The GDP is equally indifferent to inequality, which is on the rise in most developed countries, and to debts, which make living on credit a tempting option. In the last quarter of 2008, when the global financial system very nearly imploded, British banks were growing faster than ever. As a share of the GDP, they represented 9% of the English economy at the height of the crisis, almost as much as the whole manufacturing industry. And to think that in the 1950s their contribution was still virtually nil.

It was during the 1970s that statisticians decided it would be a good idea to measure banks' "productivity" in terms of their risk-taking behavior. The more risk, the bigger their slice of the GDP.[14] Hardly any wonder, then, that banks have continually upped their lending, egged on by politicians who have been convinced that the financial sector's slice is every bit as valuable as the whole manufacturing industry. "If banking had been subtracted from the GDP, rather than added to it," the *Financial Times* recently reported, "it is plausible to speculate that the financial crisis would never have happened."[15]

The CEO who recklessly hawks mortgages and derivatives to lap up millions in bonuses currently contributes more to the GDP than a school packed with teachers or a factory full of car mechanics. We live in a world where the going rule seems to be that the more vital your occupation (cleaning, nursing, teaching), the lower you rate in the GDP. As the Nobel laureate James Tobin said back in

FIGURE 6   The Growth of the Banking Sector

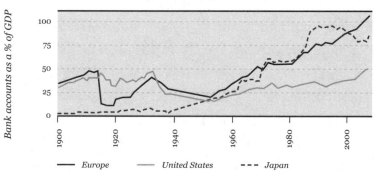

This graph shows lending to households and organizations outside the financial sector. "Europe" is the mean of Denmark, England, France, Germany, Italy, the Netherlands, Spain, and Sweden.

Source: Schularick and Taylor (2012)

1984, "We are throwing more and more of our resources, including the cream of our youth, into financial activities remote from the production of goods and services, into activities that generate high private rewards disproportionate to their social productivity."[16]

To Each Era its Own Figures

Don't get me wrong – in plenty of countries economic growth, welfare, and health still go happily hand in hand. These are places where there are still stomachs to fill and houses to build. It's a privilege of the rich to rank other goals ahead of growth. But for most of the world's population, money takes the cake. "There is only one class in the community that thinks more about money than the rich," said Oscar Wilde, "and that is the poor."[17]

Nevertheless, in the Land of Plenty we have come to the end of a long and historic voyage. For more than thirty years now, growth has hardly made us better off, and in some cases quite the reverse. If we want a higher quality of life, we will have to take the first step in search of other means, and alternative metrics.

The idea that the GDP still serves as an accurate gauge of social welfare is one of the most widespread myths of our times. Even politicians who fight over everything else can always agree that the GDP must grow. Growth is good. It's good for employment, it's good for purchasing power, and it's good for our government, giving it more to spend.

Modern journalism would be all but lost without the GDP, wielding the latest national growth figures as a kind of government report card. A shrinking GDP spells recession and, if it really shrivels, depression. In fact, the GDP offers pretty much everything a journalist could want: hard figures, issued at regular intervals, and the chance to quote experts. Most importantly, the GDP offers a clear benchmark. Is the government doing its job? How do we as a country stack up? Has life gotten a little better? Never fear, we have the latest figures on the GDP, and they'll tell us everything we need to know.

Given our obsession with it, it's hard to believe that just eighty years ago the GDP didn't even exist.

Of course, the desire to measure wealth goes way back, all the way back to the era of powdered wigs. Economists in those days, who were known as "Physiocrats," believed that all wealth came from the land. Consequently, they were preoccupied mainly with harvest yields. In 1665, the Englishman William Petty was the first to present an estimate of what he termed the "national income." His purpose was to discover how much England could raise in tax revenues, and, by extension, how long it could continue to finance war with Holland. Unlike the Physiocrats, Petty believed that true wealth derived not from the land, but from wages. Therefore, he reasoned, wages should be taxed more heavily. (Petty, as it happens, was a rich landowner.)

A different definition of national income was advanced by the British politician Charles Davenant, who gives the game away in the title of his 1695 essay "Upon Ways and Means of Supplying the War." Estimates like his gave England a considerable advantage as it vied with France. The French king, for his part, had to wait until the end of the eighteenth century to get decent economic statistics of his own. In 1781 his finance minister, Jacques Necker, submitted the *Compte rendu au roi*, or "Financial statement for the king," to Louis XVI, who was then already teetering on the brink of bankruptcy. Although this document enabled the king to take out a few more loans, it came too late to stop the Revolution in 1789.

The meaning of the term "national income" has actually never been fixed, fluctuating with the latest intellectual currents and the imperatives of the moment. Every era has its own idiosyncratic ideas about what defines a country's wealth. Take Adam Smith, father of modern economics, who believed that the wealth of nations was founded not only on agriculture, but also on manufacturing. The entire service economy, by contrast – a sector that spans everything from entertainers to lawyers and constitutes roughly two-thirds of the modern economy – Smith argued "adds to the value of nothing."[18]

Nevertheless, as cash flows shifted from farms to factories and then from production lines to office towers, figures for tabulating all this wealth kept pace. The first person to argue that what matters is not the *nature* but the *price* of products was the economist Alfred Marshall (1842–1924). By Marshall's measure, a Paris Hilton movie, an hour of *Jersey Shore*, and a Bud Light Lime can all boost a country's wealth, as long as they carry a price tag.

Yet just eighty years ago it still seemed an impossible mission when U.S. President Herbert Hoover was tasked with beating back the Great Depression with only a mixed bag of numbers, ranging from share values to the price of iron to the volume of road transport. Even his most important metric – the "blast-furnace index" – was little more than an unwieldy construct that attempted to pin down production levels in the steel industry.

If you had asked Hoover how "the economy" was doing, he would have given you a puzzled look. Not only because this wasn't among the numbers in his bag, but because he would have had no notion of our modern understanding of the word "economy." "Economy" isn't really a thing, after all – it's an idea, and that idea had yet to be invented.

In 1931, Congress called together the country's leading statisticians and found them unable to answer even the most basic questions about the state of the nation. That something was fundamentally wrong seemed evident, but their last reliable figures dated from 1929. It was obvious that the homeless population was growing and that companies were going bankrupt left and right, but as to the actual extent of the problem, nobody knew.

A few months earlier, President Hoover had dispatched a number of Commerce Department employees around the country to report on the situation. They returned with mainly anecdotal evidence that aligned with Hoover's own belief that economic recovery was just around the bend. Congress wasn't reassured, however. In 1932, it appointed a brilliant young Russian professor by the name of Simon Kuznets to answer a simple question: How much stuff can we make?

Over the next few years, Kuznets laid the foundations of what would later become the GDP. His initial calculations caused a flurry of excitement and the report he presented to Congress became a national bestseller (itself adding to the GDP, one 20-cent copy at a time). Soon, you couldn't switch on the radio without hearing about "national income" this or "the economy" that.

It's hard to overstate the importance of the GDP. Even the atomic bomb pales in comparison, according to some historians. The GDP, it turned out, was an excellent yardstick for the power of a nation in times of war. "Only those who had a personal share in the economic mobilization for World War I could realize in how many ways and how much estimates of national income covering 20 years and classified in several ways facilitated the World War II effort," U.S. National Bureau of Economic Research Director Wesley C. Mitchell wrote shortly after the war.[19]

Solid figures can even tip the balance between life and death. In his 1940 essay "How to Pay for the War," Keynes complained of spotty British statistics. Hitler likewise lacked the figures needed to get the German economy back up to speed. It wasn't until 1944, as the Russians bore down on the Eastern Front and the Allies landed in the west, that the German economy achieved peak production.[20]

But by that time, the American GDP – the measurement of which would eventually earn Kuznets the Nobel Prize – had already won the day.

The Ultimate Yardstick

From the wreckage of depression and war, the GDP emerged as the ultimate yardstick of progress – the crystal ball of nations, the number to trump all others. And this time, its job was not to bolster the war effort, but to anchor the consumer society. "Much like a satellite in space can survey the weather across an entire continent so can the GDP give an overall picture of the state of the economy," economist Paul Samuelson wrote in his bestselling textbook *Economics*. "Without measures of economic aggregates like GDP, policymakers would be adrift in a sea of unorganized data," he continued. "The GDP and related data are like beacons that help policymakers steer the economy toward the key economic objectives."[21]

At the start of the twentieth century the U.S. government employed a grand total of one economist; more accurately, an "economic ornithologist," whose job was to study birds. Less than forty years later, the National Bureau of Economic Research payrolled some 5,000 economists, in the sense that we use the word. These included Simon Kuznets and Milton Friedman, ultimately two of the century's most important thinkers.[22] All across the world, economists began to play a dominant role in politics. Most were educated in the United States, the cradle of the GDP, where practitioners pursued a new, scientific brand of economics revolving around models, equations, and numbers. Lots and lots of numbers.

This was a completely different form of economics to what John Maynard Keynes and Friedrich Hayek had learned at school. When people around 1900 talked about "the economy," they usually just meant "society." But the 1950s introduced a new generation of technocrats who invented a whole new objective: getting the "economy" to "grow." More important, they thought they knew how to accomplish it.

Before the invention of the GDP, economists were rarely quoted by the press, but in the years after World War II they became a fixture in the papers. They had mastered a trick no one else could do: managing reality and predicting the future. Increasingly, the economy was regarded as a machine with levers that politicians could pull to promote "growth." In 1949, the inventor and economist Bill Phillips even constructed a real machine from plastic containers and pipes to represent the economy, with water pumping around to represent federal revenue flows.

As one historian explains, "The first thing you do in 1950s and '60s if you're a new nation is you open a national

FIGURE 7   The Prevalence of the Terms "GNP" and "GDP" in Books
Published in English, 1930–2008

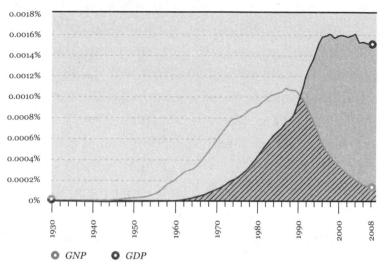

*Initially, the more common measure was the gross national product (GNP), but
in the 1990s this was superseded by the GDP. The GNP adds up all a country's
economic activity (including activities abroad), while the GDP adds up all
activities within its borders (including by foreign enterprises). In most countries,
the gap between GNP and GDP is never more than a few percent.*

Source: Google Ngram

airline, you create a national army, and you start measuring
GDP."[23] But that last item became progressively trickier.
When the United Nations published its first standard
guideline for figuring GDP in 1953, it totaled just under
fifty pages. The most recent edition, issued in 2008, comes
in at 722. Though it's a number bandied about freely in the
media, there are few people who really understand how the
GDP is determined. Even many professional economists
have no clue.[24]

To calculate the GDP, numerous data points have to be linked together and hundreds of wholly subjective choices made regarding what to count and what to ignore. In spite of this methodology, the GDP is never presented as anything less than hard science, whose fractional vacillations can make the difference between reelection and political annihilation. Yet this apparent precision is an illusion. The GDP is not a clearly defined object just waiting around to be "measured." To measure GDP is to seek to measure an idea.

A great idea, admittedly. There's no denying that GDP came in very handy during wartime, when the enemy was at the gates and a country's very existence hinged on production, on churning out as many tanks, planes, bombs, and grenades as possible. During wartime, it's perfectly reasonable to borrow from the future. During wartime, it makes sense to pollute the environment and go into debt. It can even be preferable to neglect your family, put your children to work on a production line, sacrifice your free time, and forget everything that makes life worth living.

Indeed, during wartime, there's no metric quite as useful as the GDP.

Alternatives

The point, of course, is that the war is over. Our standard of progress was conceived for a different era with different problems. Our statistics no longer capture the shape of our economy. And this has consequences. Every era needs its own figures. In the eighteenth century, they concerned the size of the harvest. In the nineteenth century, the radius of the rail network, the number of factories, and the volume of coal mining. And in the twentieth, industrial mass production within the boundaries of the nation-state.

But today it's no longer possible to express our prosperity in simple dollars, pounds, or euros. From healthcare to education, from journalism to finance, we're all still fixated on "efficiency" and "gains," as though society were nothing but one big production line. But it's precisely in a service-based economy that simple quantitative targets fail. "The gross national product . . . measures everything . . . except that which makes life worthwhile," said Robert Kennedy.[25]

It's time for a new set of figures.

As long ago as 1972, the Fourth Dragon King of Bhutan proposed a switch to measuring "gross national happiness," since GDP ignored vital facets of culture and well-being (for starters, knowledge of traditional songs and dances). But happiness seems no less one-dimensional and arbitrary a quality to quantify than GDP; after all, you could be happy just because you're three sheets to the wind – *ce qu'on ne voit pas*. And don't setbacks, sorrow, and sadness have a place in a full life, too? It's like the philosopher John Stuart Mill once said: "Better to be Socrates dissatisfied than a fool satisfied."[26]

Not only that, we *need* a good dose of irritation, frustration, and discontent to propel us forward. If the Land of

Plenty is a place where everybody is happy, then it's also a place steeped in apathy. Had women never protested, they would never have gained the vote; had African Americans never rebelled, Jim Crow might still be the law of the land. If we prefer to salve our grievances with a fixation on gross national happiness, that would spell the end of progress. "Discontent," said Oscar Wilde, "is the first step in the progress of a man or a nation."[27]

So how about some other options? Two candidates are the Genuine Progress Indicator (GPI) and the Index of Sustainable Economic Welfare (ISEW), which also incorporate pollution, crime, inequality, and volunteer work in their equations. In Western Europe, GPI has advanced a good deal slower than GDP, and in the U.S. it has even receded since the 1970s. Or how about the Happy Planet Index, a ranking that factors in ecological footprints, in which most developed countries figure somewhere around the middle and the U.S. dangles near the bottom?

But even these calculations leave me skeptical.

Bhutan rocks the charts in its own index, which conveniently leaves out the Dragon King's dictatorship and the ethnic cleansing of the Lhotshampa. Communist East Germany had a "gross social product" that rose steadily year after year despite the massive social, ecological, and economic harms perpetrated by the regime. Likewise, though GPI and ISEW do correct some of GDP's failings, they totally pass over the huge technological leaps made in recent decades. Both indices testify that all is not well in the world – but that's also precisely what they've been designed to show.

In fact, simple rankings consistently conceal more than they reveal. A high score on the UN's Human Development Index or the OECD's Better Life Index may be something we should applaud, *but not if we don't know what is being measured*. What's certain is that the wealthier countries become, the more difficult it is to measure that wealth. Paradoxically, we're living in an information age where we spend increasing amounts of money on activities about which we have little solid information.

The Secret of the Expanding Government

It all goes back to Mozart.

When the musical mastermind composed his 14th string quartet in G major (K. 387) in 1782, he needed four people to perform it. Now, 250 years later, it still requires exactly four.[28] If you're looking to up your violin's production capacity, the most you can do is play a little faster. Put another way: Some things in life, like music, resist all attempts at greater efficiency. While we can produce coffee machines ever faster and more cheaply, a violinist can't pick up the pace without spoiling the tune.

In our race against the machine, it's only logical that we'll continue to spend less on products that can be easily made more efficiently and more on labor-intensive services and amenities such as art, healthcare, education, and safety. It's no accident that countries that score high on well-being, like Denmark, Sweden, and Finland, have a large public sector. Their governments subsidize the domains where productivity can't be leveraged. Unlike the manufacture of a fridge or a car, history lessons and doctor's checkups can't simply be made "more efficient."[29]

The natural consequence is that the government is gobbling up a growing share of the economic pie. First noted by the economist William Baumol in the 1960s, this phenomenon, now known as "Baumol's cost disease," basically says that prices in labor-intensive sectors such as healthcare and education increase faster than prices in sectors where most of the work can be more extensively automated.

But hold on a minute.

Shouldn't we be calling this a blessing, rather than a disease? After all, the more efficient our factories and our computers, the *less* efficient our healthcare and education need to be; that is, the more time we have left to attend to the old and infirm and to organize education on a more personal scale. Which is great, right? According to Baumol, the main impediment to allocating our resources toward such noble ends is "the illusion that we cannot afford them."

As illusions go, this one is pretty stubborn. When you're obsessed with efficiency and productivity, it's difficult to see the real value of education and care. Which is why so many politicians and taxpayers alike see only costs. They don't realize that the richer a country becomes the more it should be spending on teachers and doctors. Instead of regarding these increases as a blessing, they're viewed as a disease.

Yet unless we prefer to run our schools and hospitals as if they were factories, we can be certain that, in the race against the machine, the costs of healthcare and education will only go up. At the same time, products like refrigerators and cars have become *too cheap*. To look solely at the price of a product is to ignore a large share of the costs. In fact, a British think tank estimated that for every pound earned by advertising executives, they destroy an equivalent of £7 in the form of stress, overconsumption, pollution, and debt; conversely, each pound paid to a trash collector creates an equivalent of £12 in terms of health and sustainability.[30]

Whereas public sector services often bring a plethora of hidden benefits, the private sector is riddled with hidden costs. "We can afford to pay more for the services we need – chiefly healthcare and education," Baumol writes. "What we may not be able to afford are the consequences of falling costs."

You may brush this aside with the argument that such "externalities" can't simply be quantified because they involve too many subjective assumptions, but that's precisely the point. "Value" and "productivity" cannot be expressed in objective figures, even if we pretend the opposite: "We have a high graduation rate, therefore we offer a good education" – "Our doctors are focused and efficient, therefore we provide good care" – "We have a high publication rate, therefore we are an excellent university" – "We have a high audience share, therefore we are producing good television" – "The economy is growing, therefore our country is doing fine . . ."

The targets of our performance-driven society are no less absurd than the five-year plans of the former U.S.S.R. To found our political system on production figures is to turn the good life into a spreadsheet. As the writer Kevin Kelly says, "Productivity is for robots. Humans excel at wasting time, experimenting, playing, creating, and exploring."[31] Governing by numbers is the last resort of a country that no longer knows what it wants, a country with no vision of utopia.

A Dashboard for Progress

"There are three kinds of lies: lies, damned lies, and statistics," the British prime minister Benjamin Disraeli purportedly scoffed. Nevertheless, I firmly believe in the old Enlightenment principle that decisions require a foundation of reliable information and numbers.

The GDP was contrived in a period of deep crisis and provided an answer to the great challenges of the 1930s. As we face our own crises of unemployment, depression, and climate change, we, too, will have to search for a new figure. What we need is a "dashboard" complete with an array of indicators to track the things that make life worthwhile – money and growth, obviously, but also community service, jobs, knowledge, social cohesion. And, of course, the scarcest good of all: time.

"But such a dashboard couldn't possibly be objective," you might counter. True. But there's no such thing as a neutral metric. Behind every statistic is a certain set of assumptions and prejudices. What's more, those figures – and their assumptions – guide our actions. That's true of GDP but equally true of the Human Development and Happy Planet indices. And it's precisely because we need to change our actions that we need new figures to guide us.

Simon Kuznets warned us about this eight years ago. "The welfare of a nation can . . . scarcely be inferred from a measurement of national income," he reported to Congress. "Measurements of national income are subject to this type of illusion and resulting abuse, especially since they deal with matters that are the center of conflict of opposing social groups where the effectiveness of an argument is contingent upon oversimplification."[32]

The inventor of GDP cautioned against including in its calculation expenditure for the military, advertising, and the financial sector,[33] but his advice fell on deaf ears. After World War II, Kuznets grew increasingly concerned about the monster he had created. "Distinctions must be kept in mind between quantity and quality of growth," he wrote in

1962, "between costs and returns, and between the short and long run. Goals for more growth should specify more growth of what and for what."[34]

Now it's up to us to reconsider these old questions. What is growth? What is progress? Or even more fundamentally, what makes life truly worthwhile?

To be able to fill leisure intelligently
is the last product of civilization.

Bertrand Russell (1872–1970)

6

A Fifteen-Hour Workweek

Had you asked the greatest economist of the twentieth century what the biggest challenge of the twenty-first would be, he wouldn't have had to think twice.

Leisure.

In the summer of 1930, just as the Great Depression was gathering momentum, the British economist John Maynard Keynes gave a curious lecture in Madrid. He had already bounced some novel ideas off a few of his students at Cambridge and decided to reveal them publicly in a brief talk titled "Economic Possibilities for our Grandchildren."[1]

In other words, for us.

At the time of his visit, Madrid was a mess. Unemployment was spiraling out of control, fascism was gaining ground, and the Soviet Union was actively recruiting supporters. A few years later, a devastating civil war would break out. How, then, could *leisure* be the biggest challenge? That summer, Keynes seemed to have landed from a different planet. "We are suffering just now from a bad attack of economic pessimism," he wrote. "It is common to hear people say that the epoch of enormous economic progress

which characterized the nineteenth century is over ..."
And not without cause. Poverty was rampant, international tensions were running high, and it would take the death machine of World War II to breathe life back into global industry.

Speaking in a city on the precipice of disaster, the British economist hazarded a counterintuitive prediction. By 2030, Keynes said, mankind would be confronted with the greatest challenge it had ever faced: what to do with a sea of spare time. Unless politicians make "disastrous mistakes" (austerity during an economic crisis, for instance), he anticipated that within a century the Western standard of living would have multiplied to at least four times that of 1930.

The conclusion? In 2030, we'll be working just fifteen hours a week.

A Future Filled with Leisure

Keynes was neither the first nor the last to foresee a future awash in leisure. A century and a half earlier, American Founding Father Benjamin Franklin had already predicted that four hours of work a day would eventually suffice. Beyond that, life would be all "leisure and pleasure." And Karl Marx similarly looked forward to a day when everyone would have the time "to hunt in the morning, fish in the afternoon, raise cattle in the evening, criticize after dinner ... without ever becoming hunter, fisherman, herdsman or critic."

At around the same time, the father of classical liberalism, British philosopher John Stuart Mill, was arguing that the best use of more wealth was more leisure. Mill opposed the "gospel of work" proclaimed by his great adversary Thomas Carlyle (a great proponent of slavery, too, as it happens), juxtaposing it with his own "gospel of leisure." According to Mill, technology should be used to curb the workweek as far as possible. "There would be as much scope as ever for all kinds of mental culture, and moral and social progress," he wrote, "as much room for improving the Art of Living."[2]

Yet the Industrial Revolution, which propelled the nineteenth century's explosive economic growth, had brought about the exact opposite of leisure. Where an English farmer in the year 1300 had to work some 1,500 hours a year to make a living, a factory worker in Mill's era had to put in twice the time simply to survive. In cities like Manchester, a seventy-hour workweek – no vacations, no weekends – was the norm, even for children. "What do the poor want with holidays?" an English duchess wondered toward the end of the nineteenth century. "They ought to work!"[3] Too much free time was simply an invitation to wickedness.

Nevertheless, starting around 1850 some of the prosperity created by the Industrial Revolution began to trickle down to the lower classes. And money is time. In 1855, the stonemasons of Melbourne, Australia, were the first to secure an eight-hour workday. By century's end, work-weeks in some countries had already dipped south of sixty hours. Nobel Prize-winning playwright George Bernard Shaw predicted in 1900 that, at this rate, workers in the year 2000 would be clocking just two hours a day.

Employers resisted, naturally. When in 1926 a group of thirty-two prominent American businessmen were asked how they felt about a shorter workweek, a grand total of two thought the idea had merit. According to the other thirty, more free time would only result in higher crime rates, debts, and degeneration.[4] Yet it was none other than Henry Ford – titan of industry, founder of Ford Motor Company, and creator of the Model-T – who, in that same year, became the first to implement a five-day workweek.

People called him crazy. Then they followed in his footsteps.

A dyed-in-the-wool capitalist and the mastermind behind the production line, Henry Ford had discovered that a shorter workweek actually increased productivity among his employees. Leisure time, he observed, was a "cold business fact."[5] A well-rested worker was a more effective worker. And besides, an employee toiling at a factory from dawn till dusk, with no free time for road trips or joy rides, would never buy one of his cars. As Ford told a journalist, "It is high time to rid ourselves of the notion that leisure for workmen is either 'lost time' or a class privilege."[6]

Within a decade, the skeptics had been won over. The National Association of Manufacturers, which twenty years earlier had been warning that a shorter workweek would ruin the economy, now proudly advertised that the U.S. had the shortest workweek in the world. In their newfound leisure hours, workers were soon driving their Ford cars past NAM billboards that proclaimed, "There is no way like the American way."[7]

"A Race of Machine Tenders"

All evidence seemed to suggest that the great minds, from Marx to Mill to Keynes to Ford, would be proven right.

In 1933, the U.S. Senate approved legislation introducing a thirty-hour workweek. Although the bill languished in the House of Representatives under industry pressure, a shorter workweek remained the labor unions' top priority. In 1938, legislation protecting the five-day workweek was finally passed. The following year, the folk song "Big Rock Candy Mountain" climbed to the top of the charts, describing a utopia in which "hens lay soft-boiled eggs," cigarettes grow on trees, and "the jerk that invented work" is strung up from the tallest tree.

After World War II, leisure time continued its steady rise. In 1956, Vice President Richard Nixon promised Americans that they would only have to work four days a week "in the not too distant future." The country had reached a "plateau of prosperity," and he believed a shorter workweek was inevitable.[8] Before long, machines would be doing all the work. This would free up "abundant scope for recreation," enthused an English professor, "by immersion in the imaginative life, in art, drama, dance, and a hundred other ways of transcending the constraints of daily life."[9]

Keynes' bold prediction had become a truism. In the mid-1960s, a Senate committee report projected that by 2000 the workweek would be down to just fourteen hours, with at least seven weeks off a year. The RAND Corporation, an influential think tank, foresaw a future in which just 2% of the population would be able to produce everything society needed.[10] Working would soon be reserved for the elite.

In the summer of 1964, the *New York Times* asked the great science-fiction author Isaac Asimov to take a shot at forecasting the future.[11] What would the world be like in fifty years? About some things, Asimov was cautious: The robots of 2014 would "neither be common nor very good." But in other respects, his expectations were high. Cars would be cruising through the air and entire cities would be built underwater.

There was just one thing, ultimately, that worried him: the spread of boredom. Mankind, he wrote, would become "largely a race of machine tenders," and there would be "serious mental, emotional and sociological consequences." Psychiatry would be the largest medical specialty in 2014 due to the millions of people who found themselves adrift in a sea of "enforced leisure." "Work," he said, would become "the most glorious single word in the vocabulary."

As the 1960s progressed, more thinkers began to voice concerns. Pulitzer Prize-winning political scientist Sebastian de Grazia told the Associated Press, "There is reason to fear . . . that free time, forced free time, will bring on the restless tick of boredom, idleness, immorality, and increased personal violence." And in 1974, the U.S. Department of the Interior sounded the alarm, declaring that "Leisure, thought by many to be the epitome of paradise, may well become the most perplexing problem of the future."[12]

Despite these concerns, there was little doubt about the course history would ultimately take. By around 1970, sociologists talked confidently of the imminent "end of work." Mankind was on the brink of a veritable leisure revolution.

George and Jane

Meet George and Jane Jetson. They're an upstanding couple who live with their two kids in a spacious apartment in Orbit City. He's got a job as a "digital index operator" at a large company; she's a traditional American homemaker. George is plagued by nightmares about his job. And who could blame him? He is tasked with pushing a single button at intervals, and his boss Mr. Spacely – short, rotund, and impressively mustachioed – is a tyrant.

"Yesterday, I worked *two full hours*!" George complains after the umpteenth nightmare. His wife Jane is appalled. "Well, what does Spacely think he's running? A sweatshop?!"[13]

The average Orbit City workweek is nine hours. Sadly, it only exists on TV, in "the single most important piece of 20th century futurism," *The Jetsons*.[14] Premiering in 1962, the series was set in 2062; basically, it's *The Flintstones* but in the future. With its endless reruns, several generations have now grown up with *The Jetsons*.

Fifty years later, it turns out that many of the predictions its creators made about the year 2062 have already come true. A housekeeping robot? Check. Tanning beds? Been there. Touchscreens? Done that. Video chat? Natch. But in other respects, we're still a long way off from Orbit City. When will those flying cars get off the ground? No sign of moving city sidewalks either.

But the most disappointing fail? The rise of leisure.

The Forgotten Dream

In the 1980s, workweek reductions came to a grinding halt. Economic growth was translating not into more leisure, but into more stuff. In countries like Australia, Austria, Norway, Spain, and England, the workweek stopped shrinking altogether.[15] In the U.S., it actually grew. Seventy years after the country passed the forty-hour workweek into law, three-quarters of the labor force was putting in more than forty hours a week.[16]

But that's not all. Even in countries that have seen a reduction in the *individual* workweek, families have nevertheless become more pressed for time. Why? It all has to do with the most important development of the last decades: the feminist revolution.

The futurists never saw it coming. After all, the Jane Jetson of 2062 was still an obedient homemaker. In 1967, the *Wall Street Journal* predicted that the availability of robots would enable the twenty-first-century man to spend hours relaxing at home on the sofa with his wife.[17] No one could have suspected that by January 2010, for the first time since men were conscripted to fight in World War II, the bulk of the U.S. labor force would be made up of women.

Where they contributed only 2–6% of the family income in 1970, now this figure has already topped 40%.[18]

The pace at which this revolution has taken place is head-spinning. If you include unpaid labor, women in Europe and North America work more than men.[19] "My grandma didn't have the vote, my mom didn't have the pill, and I don't have any time," as a Dutch comedienne pithily summed it up.[20]

With women storming the labor market, men should have started working less (and cooking, cleaning, and taking care of the family more).

FIGURE 8   Women in the Workplace, 1970–2012

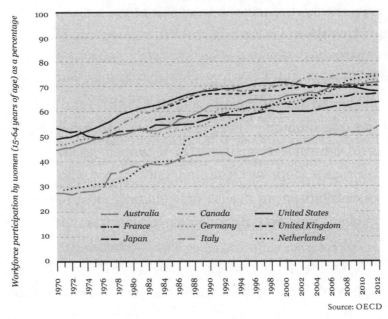

Source: OECD

But that didn't really happen. Whereas couples worked a combined total of five to six days a week in the 1950s, nowadays it's closer to seven or eight. At the same time, parenting has become a much more time-intensive job. Research suggests that across national boundaries, parents are dedicating substantially more time to their children.[21] In the U.S., working mothers actually spend more time with their kids today than stay-at-home moms did in the 1970s.[22]

Even citizens of the Netherlands – the nation with the shortest workweek in the world – have felt the steadily increasing weight of work, overtime, care tasks, and education since the 1980s. In 1985 these activities were taking up 43.6 hours a week; by 2005, 48.6 hours.[23] Three-quarters

FIGURE 9 We Have Been Working Progressively Less (up to 1980)

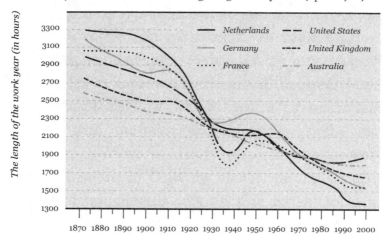

The number of annual work hours per capita has taken a nosedive since the nineteenth century. Yet after 1970, the figures are misleading as an increasing number of women joined the workforce. As a consequence, families have been increasingly pressed for time, even though the numbers of hours worked per employee was still decreasing in some countries.

Source: International Labour Organization

of the Dutch workforce is feeling overburdened by time pressures, a quarter habitually works overtime, and one in eight is suffering the symptoms of burnout.[24]

What's more, work and leisure are becoming increasingly difficult to disentangle. A study conducted at the Harvard Business School has shown that, thanks to modern technology, managers and professionals in Europe, Asia, and North America now spend eighty to ninety hours per week "either working, or 'monitoring' work and remaining accessible."[25] And according to Korean research, the smartphone has the average employee working eleven more hours per week.[26]

It's safe to say the predictions of the great minds didn't exactly come true. Not by a long shot, in fact. Asimov may have been right that by 2014 "work" would be the most glorified word in our vocabulary, but for a completely different reason. We aren't bored to death; we're working ourselves to death. The army of psychologists and psychiatrists are fighting not the advance of ennui, but an epidemic of stress.

We are long past due for the fulfillment of Keynes' prophecy. Around the year 2000, countries like France, the Netherlands, and the United States were already five times as wealthy as in 1930.[27] Yet nowadays our biggest challenges are not leisure and boredom, but stress and uncertainty.

Cornflake Capitalism

It is a place "Where money has been exchanged for the good life," wrote a medieval poet in an enthusiastic description of Cockaigne, the mythical Land of Plenty, "and he who sleeps the longest, earns the most."[28] In Cockaigne, the year is an endless succession of holidays: four days each for Easter, Pentecost, St. John's Day, and Christmas. Anyone who wants to work is locked up in a subterranean cellar. Even uttering the word "work" is a serious offense.

Ironically, medieval people were probably closer to achieving the contented idleness of the Land of Plenty than we are today. Around 1300, the calendar was still packed with holidays and feasts. Harvard historian and economist Juliet Schor has estimated that holidays accounted for no less than one-third of the year. In Spain, the share was an astounding five months, and in France, nearly six. Most peasants didn't work any harder than necessary for their living. "The tempo of life was slow," Schor writes. "Our ancestors may not have been rich, but they had an abundance of leisure."[29]

So where has all that time gone?

It's quite simple, really. Time is money. Economic growth can yield either more leisure or more consumption. From 1850 until 1980, we got both, but since then, it is mostly consumption that has increased. Even where real incomes have stayed the same and inequality has exploded, the consumption craze has continued, but on credit.

And that's precisely the main argument that has been brought to bear against the shorter workweek: We can't afford it. More leisure is a wonderful ideal, but it's simply too expensive. If we were all to work less, our standard of living would collapse and the welfare state would crumble.

But would it?

At the beginning of the twentieth century, Henry Ford conducted a series of experiments which demonstrated that his factory workers were most productive when they worked a forty-hour week. Working an additional twenty hours would pay off for four weeks, but after that, productivity *declined*.

Others took his experiments a step farther. On December 1, 1930, as the Great Depression was raging, the cornflake magnate W. K. Kellogg decided to introduce a six-hour workday at his factory in Battle Creek, Michigan. It was an unmitigated success: Kellogg was able to hire an additional 300 employees and slashed the accident rate by 41%. Moreover, his employees became noticeably more productive. "This isn't just a theory with us," Kellogg proudly told a local newspaper. "The unit cost of production is so lowered that we can afford to pay as much for six hours as we formerly paid for eight."[30]

For Kellogg, like Ford, a shorter workweek was simply a matter of good business.[31] But for the residents of Battle Creek, it was much more than that. For the first time ever, a local paper reported, they had "real leisure."[32] Parents had time to spare for their children. They had more time to read, garden, and play sports. Suddenly, churches and community centers were bursting at the seams with citizens who now had time to spend on civic life.[33]

Nearly half a century later, British Prime Minister Edward Heath also discovered the benefits of cornflake capitalism, albeit inadvertently. It was late 1973 and he was at his wits' end. Inflation was reaching record highs and government expenditures were skyrocketing, and labor unions were dead set against compromise of any kind. As if that weren't enough, the miners decided to go on strike. With energy consequently in short supply, the Brits turned down their thermostats and donned their heaviest sweaters. December came, and even the Christmas tree in Trafalgar Square remained unlit.

Heath decided on a radical course of action. On January 1, 1974, he imposed a three-day workweek. Employers were not permitted to use more than three days' electricity until energy reserves had recovered. Steel magnates predicted that industrial production would plunge 50%. Government ministers feared a catastrophe. When the five-day workweek was reinstated in March 1974, officials set about calculating the total extent of production losses. They had trouble believing their eyes: The grand total was 6%.[34]

What Ford, Kellogg, and Heath had all discovered is that productivity and long work hours do *not* go hand in hand. In the 1980s, Apple employees sported T-shirts that read, "Working 90 hours a week and loving it!" Later, productivity experts calculated that if they had worked half the hours then the world might have enjoyed the groundbreaking Macintosh computer a year earlier.[35]

There are strong indications that in a modern knowledge economy, even forty hours a week is too much. Research suggests that someone who is constantly drawing on their creative abilities can, on average, be productive for no more than six hours a day.[36] It's no coincidence that the world's wealthy countries, those with a large creative class and highly educated populations, have also shaved the most time off their workweeks.

The Solution to (Almost) Everything

Recently, a friend asked me: What does working less actually solve?

I'd rather turn the question around: Is there anything that working less does *not* solve?

Stress? Countless studies have shown that people who work less are more satisfied with their lives.[37] In a recent poll conducted among working women, German researchers even quantified the "perfect day." The largest share of minutes (106) would go toward "intimate relationships." "Socializing" (82), "relaxing" (78), and "eating" (75) also scored high. At the bottom of the list were "parenting" (46), "work" (36), and "commuting" (33). The researchers dryly noted that "in order to maximize well-being it is likely that working and consuming (which increases GDP) might play a smaller role in people's daily activities compared to now."[38]

Climate change? A worldwide shift to a shorter workweek could cut the CO_2 emitted this century by half.[39] Countries with a shorter workweek have a smaller ecological footprint.[40] Consuming less starts with working less – or, better yet, with consuming our prosperity in the form of leisure.

Accidents? Overtime is deadly.[41] Long workdays lead to more errors: Tired surgeons are more prone to slip-ups, and soldiers who get too little shuteye are more prone to miss targets. From Chernobyl to the Space Shuttle *Challenger*, overworked managers often prove to have played a fatal role in disasters. It's no coincidence that the financial sector, which triggered the biggest disaster of the last decade, is absolutely drowning in overtime.

Unemployment? Obviously, you can't simply chop a job up into smaller pieces. The labor market isn't a game of musical chairs in which anyone can fit into any seat and all we need to do is dole out places. Nevertheless, researchers at the International Labour Organization have concluded that work sharing – in which two part-time employees share a workload traditionally assigned to one full-time worker – went a long way toward resolving the last crisis.[42] Particularly in times of recession with spiking unemployment and production exceeding demand, sharing jobs can help to soften the blow.[43]

Emancipation of women? Countries with short workweeks consistently top gender-equality rankings. The central issue is achieving a more equitable distribution of work. Not until men do their fair share of cooking, cleaning, and other domestic labor will women be free to fully participate in the broader economy. In other words, the emancipation of women is a men's issue. These changes, however, are not only dependent on the choices of individual men; legislation has an important role to play. Nowhere is the time gap between men and women smaller than in Sweden, a country with a truly decent system in place for childcare and paternity leave.

And paternity leave, in particular, is crucial: Men who spend a few weeks at home after the birth of a child devote more time to their wives, to their children, and to the kitchen stove than they would have otherwise. Plus, this effect lasts — are you ready for it? — *for the rest of their lives*. Research in Norway has shown that men who take paternity leave are then 50% more likely to share laundry duty with their wives.[44] Canadian research shows that they'll spend more time on domestic chores and child-care.[45] Paternity leave is a Trojan horse with the potential to truly turn the tide in the struggle for gender equality.[46]

Aging population? An increasing share of the older population wants to continue working even after hitting retirement age. But where thirtysomethings are drowning in work, family responsibilities, and mortgages, seniors struggle to get hired, even though working is excellent for their health. So, besides distributing jobs more equally between the sexes, we also have to share them across the generations. Young workers who are just now entering the labor market may well continue working into their eighties. In exchange, they could put in not forty hours, but perhaps thirty or even twenty per week. "In the 20th century we had a redistribution of wealth," one leading demographer has observed. "I believe that in this century, the great redis-tribution will be in terms of working hours."[47]

Inequality? The countries with the biggest disparities in wealth are precisely those with the longest workweeks. While the poor are working longer and longer hours just to get by, the rich are finding it ever more "expensive" to take time off as their hourly rates rise.

In the nineteenth century, it was typical for wealthy people to flatly refuse to roll up their sleeves. Work was for peasants. The more someone worked, the poorer they were. Since then, social mores have flipped. Nowadays, excessive work and pressure are status symbols. Moaning about too much work is often just a veiled attempt to come across as important and interesting. Time to oneself is sooner equated with unemployment and laziness, certainly in countries where the wealth gap has widened.

Growing Pains

Nearly a hundred years ago, our old friend John Maynard Keynes made another outrageous prediction. Keynes understood that the stock-market crash of 1929 hadn't called curtains on the entire world economy. Producers could still supply just as much as they had the year before; only the demand for many products had dried up. "We are suffering, not from the rheumatics of old age," Keynes wrote, "but from the growing-pains of over-rapid changes."

More than eighty years on, we're facing the very same problem. It's not that we are poor. It's that there simply is not enough paid work to go around. And, actually, that is good news.

It means we can begin gearing up for what may be our greatest challenge yet: filling up a veritable sea of leisure time. Obviously, the fifteen-hour workweek is still a distant utopia. By 2030, Keynes predicted, economists would play only a minor role, "on a level with dentists." But this dream now seems farther off than ever. Economists dominate the arenas of media and politics. And the dream of a shorter workweek, too, has been trampled. There is hardly a politician around still willing to endorse it, even with stress and unemployment surging to record levels.

Yet Keynes wasn't crazy. In his own day, workweeks were shrinking fast and he simply extrapolated into the future the trend that had begun around 1850. "Of course, it will all happen gradually," he qualified, "not as a catastrophe." Imagine that the leisure revolution were to gain steam again in this century. Even in conditions of slow economic growth, we inhabitants of the Land of Plenty could work fewer than fifteen hours a week by 2050, and earn the same amount as in 2000.[48]

If we can indeed make that happen, it's high time we start to prepare.

National Strategy

First we must ask ourselves: Is this what we want?

As it happens, pollsters have already asked us this question. Our answer: Yes, very much, please. We're even willing to trade in precious purchasing power for more free time.[49] It is worth noting, however, that the line between work and leisure has blurred in recent times. Work is now often perceived as a kind of hobby, or even as the very crux of our identity. In his classic book *The Theory of the Leisure Class* (1899), the sociologist Thorstein Veblen still described leisure as the badge of the elite. But things that used to be categorized as leisure (art, sports, science, care, philanthropy) are now classed as work.

Clearly, our modern Land of Plenty still features plenty of badly paid, crummy jobs. And the jobs that do pay well are often viewed as not being particularly useful. Yet the objective here is not to plead for an end to the workweek. Quite the reverse. It's time that women, the poor, and seniors got the chance to do more, not less, good work. Stable and meaningful work plays a crucial part in every life well lived.[50] By the same token, forced leisure – getting fired – is a catastrophe. Psychologists have demonstrated that protracted unemployment has a greater impact on well-being than divorce or the loss of a loved one.[51] Time heals all wounds, except unemployment. Because the longer you're sidelined, the deeper you slide.

But no matter how important work is in our lives, folks all over the world, from Japan to the U.S., yearn for a shorter workweek.[52] When American scientists surveyed employees to find out whether they would rather have two weeks' additional salary or two weeks off, twice as many people opted for the extra time. And when British researchers asked employees if they would rather win the lottery or work less, again, twice as many choose the latter.[53]

All the evidence points to the fact that we can't do without a sizable daily dose of unemployment. Working less provides the bandwidth for other things that are also important to us, like family, community involvement, and recreation. Not coincidentally, the countries with the shortest workweeks also have the largest number of volunteers and the most social capital.

So now that we know we want to work less, the second question then is: How can we manage to do so?

We can't all just go ahead and switch to a twenty-hour or thirty-hour workweek. Reduction of work first has to be reinstated as a political ideal. Then, we can curb the workweek step by step, trading in money for time, investing more money in education, and developing a more flexible retirement system and good provisions for paternity leave and childcare.

It all starts with reversing incentives. Currently, it's cheaper for employers to have one person work overtime than to hire two part-time.[54] That's because many labor costs, such as healthcare benefits, are paid per employee instead of per hour.[55] And that's also why we as individuals can't just unilaterally decide to start working less. By doing so we would risk losing status, missing out on career opportunities, and, ultimately, maybe losing our jobs altogether. And employees keep tabs on each other: Who has been at their desk the longest? Who clocks the most hours? At the end of the workday in almost every office you can find exhausted staff sitting at their desks aimlessly browsing the Facebook profiles of people they don't know, waiting until the first of their coworkers has left for the day.

Breaking this vicious circle will require collective action – by companies or, better yet, by countries.

The Good Life

When I told people, in the course of writing this book, that I was addressing the biggest challenge of the century, their interest was immediately piqued. Was I writing on terrorism? Climate change? World War III?

Their disappointment was palpable when I launched into the subject of leisure. "Wouldn't everybody just be glued to the TV all the time?"

I was reminded of the dour priests and salesmen of the nineteenth century who believed that the plebs wouldn't be able to handle getting the vote, or a decent wage, or, least of all, leisure, and who backed the seventy-hour workweek as an efficacious instrument in the fight against liquor. But the irony is that it was precisely in overworked, industrialized cities that more and more people sought refuge in the bottle.

Now we're living in a different era, but the story is the same: In overworked countries like Japan, Turkey, and, of course, the United States, people watch an absurd amount of television. Up to five hours a day in the U.S., which adds up to nine years over a lifetime. American children spend half again as much time in front of the TV as they do at school.[56]

True leisure, however, is neither a luxury nor a vice. It is as vital to our brains as vitamin C is to our bodies. There's not a person on earth who on their deathbed thinks, "Had I only put in a few more hours at the office or sat in front of the tube some more." Sure, swimming in a sea of spare time will not be easy. A twenty-first-century education should prepare people not only for joining the workforce, but also (and more importantly) for life. "Since men will not be tired in their spare time," the philosopher Bertrand Russell wrote in 1932, "they will not demand only such amusements as are passive and vapid."[57]

We can handle the good life, if only we take the time.

Work is the refuge of people who have nothing
better to do.

Oscar Wilde (1854–1900)

7

Why It Doesn't Pay to
Be a Banker

Thick fog envelops City Hall Park at daybreak on February 2, 1968.[1] Seven thousand New York City sanitation workers stand crowded together, their mood rebellious. Union spokesman John DeLury addresses the multitude from the roof of a truck. When he announces that the mayor has refused further concessions, the crowd's anger threatens to boil over. As the first rotten eggs sail overhead, DeLury realizes the time for compromise is over. It's time to take the illegal route, the path prohibited to sanitation workers for the simple reason that the job they do is too important.

It's time to strike.

The next day, trash goes uncollected throughout the Big Apple. Nearly all the city's garbage crews have stayed home. "We've never had prestige, and it never bothered me before," one garbageman is quoted as saying in a local newspaper. "But it does now. People treat us like dirt."

When the mayor goes out to survey the situation two days later, the city is already knee-deep in refuse, with another 10,000 tons added every day. A rank stench begins to percolate through the city's streets, and rats have been sighted in even the swankiest parts of town. In the space of just a few days, one of the world's most iconic cities has started to look like a slum. And for the first time since the polio epidemic of 1931, city authorities declare a state of emergency.

Still the mayor refuses to budge. He has the local press on his side, which portrays the strikers as greedy narcissists. It takes a week before the realization begins to kick in: The garbagemen are actually going to win. "New York is helpless before them," the editors of the *New York Times* declare despairingly. "This greatest of cities must surrender or see itself sink in filth." Nine days into the strike, when the trash has piled up to 100,000 tons, the sanitation workers get their way. "The moral of New York's latest step towards chaos," *Time* magazine later reported, is "that it pays to strike."[2]

Rich Without Lifting a Finger

Perhaps, but not in every profession.

Imagine, for instance, that all of Washington's 100,000 lobbyists were to go on strike tomorrow.[3] Or that every tax accountant in Manhattan decided to stay home. It seems unlikely the mayor would announce a state of emergency. In fact, it's unlikely that either of these scenarios would do much damage. A strike by, say, social media consultants, telemarketers, or high-frequency traders might never even make the news at all.

When it comes to garbage collectors, though, it's different. Any way you look at it, they do a job we can't do without. And the harsh truth is that an increasing number of people do jobs that we can do just fine without. Were they to suddenly stop working the world wouldn't get any poorer, uglier, or in any way worse. Take the slick Wall Street traders who line their pockets at the expense of another retirement fund. Take the shrewd lawyers who can draw a corporate lawsuit out until the end of days. Or take the brilliant ad writer who pens the slogan of the year and puts the competition right out of business.

Instead of *creating* wealth, these jobs mostly just *shift* it around.

Of course, there's no clear line between who creates wealth and who shifts it. Lots of jobs do both. There's no denying that the financial sector can contribute to our wealth and grease the wheels of other sectors in the process. Banks can help to spread risks and back people with bright ideas. And yet, these days, banks have become so big that much of what they do is merely shuffle wealth around, or even destroy it. Instead of growing the pie, the explosive expansion of the banking sector has increased the share it serves itself.[4]

Or take the legal profession. It goes without saying that the rule of law is necessary for a country to prosper.

But now that the U.S. has seventeen times the number of lawyers per capita as Japan, does that make American rule of law seventeen times as effective?[5] Or Americans seventeen times as protected? Far from it. Some law firms even make a practice of buying up patents for products they have no intention of producing, purely to enable them to sue people for patent infringement.

Bizarrely, it's precisely the jobs that shift money around – creating next to nothing of tangible value – that net the best salaries. It's a fascinating, paradoxical state of affairs. How is it possible that all those agents of prosperity – the teachers, the police officers, the nurses – are paid so poorly, while the unimportant, superfluous, and even destructive *shifters* do so well?

When Idleness was Still a Birthright

Maybe history can shed some light on this conundrum.

Up until a few centuries ago, almost everybody worked in agriculture. That left an affluent upper class free to loaf around, live off their private assets, and wage war – all hobbies that don't create wealth but at best shift it about, or at worst destroy it. Any blue-blooded noble was proud of this lifestyle, which gave the happy few the hereditary right to line their pockets at the expense of others. Work? That was for peasants.

In those days, before the Industrial Revolution, a farmers' strike would have paralyzed the entire economy. These days, all the graphs, diagrams, and pie charts suggest that everything has changed. As a portion of the economy, agriculture seems marginal. Indeed, the U.S. financial sector is seven times as large as its agricultural sector.

So, does this mean that if farmers were to stage a strike, it would put us in less of a bind than a boycott by bankers? (No, quite the reverse.) And, besides, hasn't agricultural production actually soared in recent decades? (Certainly.) Well then, aren't farmers earning more than ever? (Sadly, no.)

You see, in a market economy, things work precisely the other way around. The larger the supply, the lower the price. And there's the rub. Over the last few decades, the supply of food has skyrocketed. In 2010, American cows produced twice as much milk as they did in 1970.[6] Over that same period, the productivity of wheat has also doubled, and that of tomatoes has tripled. The better agriculture has become, the less we're willing to pay for it. These days, the food on our plates has become dirt cheap.

This is what economic progress is all about. As our farms and factories grew more efficient, they accounted for a shrinking share of our economy. And the more productive agriculture and manufacturing became, the fewer people they employed. At the same time, this shift generated more work in the service sector. Yet before we could get ourselves a job in this new world of consultants, accountants, programmers, advisors, brokers, and lawyers, we first had to earn the proper credentials.

This development has generated immense wealth.

Ironically, however, it has also created a system in which an increasing number of people can earn money without contributing anything of tangible value to society. Call it the paradox of progress: Here in the Land of Plenty, the richer and the smarter we get, the more expendable we become.

When Bankers Struck

"CLOSURE OF BANKS."

On May 4, 1970, this notice ran in the *Irish Independent*. After lengthy but fruitless negotiations over wages that had failed to keep pace with inflation, Ireland's bank employees decided to go on strike.

Overnight, 85% of the country's reserves were locked down. With all indications suggesting that the strike could last a while, businesses across Ireland began to hoard cash. Two weeks into the strike, the *Irish Times* reported that half of the country's 7,000 bankers had already booked flights to London in search of other work.

At the outset, pundits predicted that life in Ireland would come to a standstill. First, cash supplies would dry up, then trade would stagnate, and finally unemployment would explode. "Imagine all the veins in your body suddenly shrinking and collapsing," was how one economist described the prevailing fear, "and you might begin to see how economists conceive of banking shutdowns."[7] Heading into the summer of 1970, Ireland braced itself for the worst.

And then something odd happened. Or more accurately, nothing much happened at all.

In July, the London *Times* reported that the "figures and trends which are available indicate that the dispute has not had an adverse effect on the economy so far." A few months later, the Central Bank of Ireland drew up the final balance. "The Irish economy continued to function for a reasonably long period of time with its main clearing banks closed for business," it concluded. Not only that, the economy had continued to grow.

In the end, the strike would last a whole six months — twenty times as long as the New York City sanitation workers' strike. But whereas across the pond a state of emergency had been declared after just six days, Ireland was still going strong after six months without bankers. "The main reason I cannot recollect much about the bank strike," an Irish journalist reflected in 2013, "was because it did not have a debilitating impact on daily life."[8]

But without bankers, what did they do for money?

Something quite simple: The Irish started issuing their own cash. After the bank closures, they continued writing checks to one another as usual, the only difference being that they could no longer be cashed at the bank. Instead, that other dealer in liquid assets — the Irish pub — stepped in to fill the void. At a time when the Irish still stopped for a pint at their local pub at least three times a week, everyone – and especially the bartender – had a pretty good idea who could be trusted. "The managers of these retail outlets and public houses had a high degree of information about their customers," explains the economist Antoin Murphy. "One does not after all serve drink to someone for years without discovering something of his liquid resources."9

In no time, people forged a radically decentralized monetary system with the country's 11,000 pubs as its key nodes and basic trust as its underlying mechanism. By the time the banks finally reopened in November, the Irish had printed an incredible £5 billion in homemade currency. Some checks had been issued by companies, others were scribbled on the backs of cigar boxes, or even on toilet paper. According to historians, the reason the Irish were able to manage so well without banks was all down to social cohesion.

So were there no problems at all?

No, of course there were problems. Take the guy who bought a racehorse on credit and then paid the debt with money he won when his horse came in first – basically, gambling with another person's cash.10 It sounds an awful lot like what banks do now, but then on a smaller scale. And, during the strike, Irish companies had a harder time acquiring capital for big investments. Indeed, the very fact that people began do-it-yourself banking makes it patently clear that they couldn't do without some kind of financial sector.

But what they *could* do perfectly well without was all the smoke and mirrors, all the risky speculation, the glittering skyscrapers, and the towering bonuses paid out of taxpayers' pockets. "Maybe, just maybe," the author and economist Umair Haque conjectures, "banks need people a lot more than people need banks."[11]

Another Form of Taxation

What a contrast with that other strike two years earlier and 3,000 miles away. Where New Yorkers had looked on in desperation as their city deteriorated into a garbage dump, the Irish became their own bankers. Where New York was staring into the abyss after just six days, in Ireland things were still going swimmingly even after six months.

Let's get one thing straight, however. Making money without creating anything of value is anything but easy. It takes talent, ambition, and brains. And the banking world is brimming with clever minds. "The genius of the great speculative investors is to see what others do not, or to see it earlier," explains the economist Roger Bootle. "This is a skill. But so is the ability to stand on tiptoe, balancing on one leg, while holding a pot of tea above your head, without spillage."[12]

In other words, the fact that something is difficult does not automatically make it valuable.

In recent decades those clever minds have concocted all manner of complex financial products that don't create wealth, but destroy it. These products are, essentially, like a tax on the rest of the population. Who do you think is paying for all those custom-tailored suits, sprawling mansions, and luxury yachts? If bankers aren't generating the underlying value themselves, then it has to come from somewhere – or someone – else. The government isn't the only one redistributing wealth. The financial sector does it, too, but without a democratic mandate.

The bottom line is that wealth can be *concentrated* somewhere, but that doesn't also mean that's where it's being *created*. This is just as true for your former feudal landowner as it is for the current CEO of Goldman Sachs. The only difference is that bankers sometimes have a momentary lapse and imagine themselves the great creators of all this wealth. The lord who was proud to live off his peasants' labor suffered no such delusions.

Bullshit Jobs

And to think that things could have been so different.

You will remember that the economist John Maynard Keynes predicted we'd all be working just fifteen hours a week by 2030.[13] That our prosperity would shoot through the roof and we'd exchange a sizable chunk of our wealth for leisure time.

In reality, that's not at all what has happened. We're plenty more prosperous, but we're not exactly swimming in a sea of free time. Quite the reverse. We're all working harder than ever. In the previous chapter, I described how we have sacrificed our free time on the altar of consumerism. Keynes certainly didn't see that coming.

But there's still one puzzle piece that doesn't fit. Most people play no part in the production of iPhone cases in their panoply of colors, exotic shampoos containing botanical extracts, or Mocha Cookie Crumble Frappuccinos. Our addiction to consumption is enabled mostly by robots and Third World wage slaves. And although agricultural and manufacturing production capacity have grown exponentially over the past decades, employment in these industries has dropped. So is it really true that our overworked lifestyle all comes down to out-of-control consumerism?

David Graeber, an anthropologist at the London School of Economics, believes there's something else going on. A few years ago he wrote a fascinating piece that pinned the blame not on the stuff we buy but on the work we do. It is titled, aptly, "On the Phenomenon of Bullshit Jobs."[14]

In Graeber's analysis, innumerable people spend their entire working lives doing jobs they consider to be pointless, jobs like telemarketer, HR manager, social media strategist, PR advisor, and a whole host of administrative positions at hospitals, universities, and government offices. "Bullshit jobs," Graeber calls them. They're the jobs that even the people doing them admit are, in essence, superfluous.

When I first wrote an article about this phenomenon, it unleashed a small flood of confessions. "Personally, I'd prefer to do something that's genuinely useful," responded one stockbroker, "but I couldn't handle the pay cut." He also described his "amazingly talented former classmate with a Ph.D. in physics" who develops cancer-detection technologies, and "earns so much less than me it's depressing." But of course, that your work happens to serve a weighty public interest and requires lots of talent, intelligence, and perseverance doesn't automatically mean you're raking in the cash.

Or vice versa. Is it any coincidence that the proliferation of well-paid bullshit jobs has coincided with a huge boom in higher education and an economy that revolves around knowledge? Remember, making money without creating anything of value isn't easy. For starters, you have to memorize some very important-sounding but meaningless jargon. (Crucial when attending strategic trans-sector peer-to-peer meetings to brainstorm the value add-on co-creation in the network society.) Almost anybody can collect trash, but a career in banking is reserved for a select few.

In a world that's getting ever richer, where cows produce more milk and robots produce more stuff, there's more room for friends, family, community service, science, art, sports, and all the other things that make life worthwhile. But there's also more room for bullshit. As long as we continue to be obsessed with work, work, and more work (even as useful activities are further automated or outsourced), the number of superfluous jobs will only continue to grow. Much like the number of managers in the developed world, which has grown over the last thirty years without making us a dime richer. On the contrary, studies show that countries with more managers are actually *less* productive and innovative.[15] In a survey of 12,000 professionals by the *Harvard Business Review*, half said they felt their job had no "meaning and significance," and an equal number were unable to relate to their company's mission.[16] Another recent poll revealed that as many as 37% of British workers think they have a bullshit job.[17]

By no means are all these new service sector jobs pointless – far from it. Look at healthcare, education, fire services, and the police and you'll find lots of people who go home every day knowing, despite their modest paychecks, they've made the world a better place. "It's as if they are being told," Graeber writes, "You get to have real jobs! And on top of that you have the nerve to also expect middle-class pensions and health care?"

There is Another Way

What makes all this especially shocking is that it's happening in a capitalist system, a system founded on capitalist values like efficiency and productivity. While politicians endlessly stress the need to downsize government, they remain largely silent as the number of bullshit jobs goes right on growing. This results in scenarios where, on the one hand, governments cut back on useful jobs in sectors like healthcare, education, and infrastructure – resulting in unemployment – while on the other investing millions in the unemployment industry of training and surveillance whose effectiveness has long been disproven.[18]

The modern marketplace is equally uninterested in usefulness, quality, and innovation. All that really matters is profit. Sometimes that leads to marvelous contributions, sometimes not. From telemarketers to tax consultants, there's a rock-solid rationale for creating one bullshit job after another: You can net a fortune without ever producing a thing.

In this situation, inequality only exacerbates the problem. The more wealth is concentrated at the top, the greater the demand for corporate attorneys, lobbyists, and high-frequency traders. Demand doesn't exist in a vacuum, after all; it's the product of a constant negotiation, determined by a country's laws and institutions, and, of course, by the people who control the purse strings.

Maybe this is also a clue as to why the innovations of the past thirty years – a time of spiraling inequality – haven't quite lived up to our expectations. "We wanted flying cars, instead we got 140 characters," mocks Peter Thiel, Silicon Valley's self-described resident intellectual.[19] If the postwar era gave us fabulous inventions like the washing machine, the refrigerator, the space shuttle, and the pill, lately it's been slightly improved iterations of the same phone we bought a couple years ago.

In fact, it has become increasingly profitable *not* to innovate. Imagine just how much progress we've missed out on because thousands of bright minds have frittered away their time dreaming up hypercomplex financial products that are ultimately only destructive. Or spent the best years of their lives duplicating existing pharmaceuticals in a way that's infinitesimally different enough to warrant a new patent application by a brainy lawyer so a brilliant PR department can launch a brand-new marketing campaign for the not-so-brand-new drug.

Imagine that all this talent were to be invested not in *shifting* wealth around, but in *creating* it. Who knows, we might already have had jetpacks, built submarine cities, or cured cancer.

A long time ago, Friedrich Engels described the "false consciousness" to which the working classes of his day – the "proletariat" – had fallen victim. According to Engels, the nineteenth-century factory worker didn't rise up against the landed elite because his worldview was clouded by religion and nationalism. Maybe society is stuck in a comparable rut today, except this time at the very top of the pyramid. Maybe some of those people have had their vision clouded by all the zeros on their paychecks, the hefty bonuses, and the cushy retirement plans. Maybe a fat billfold triggers a similar false consciousness: the conviction that you're producing something of great value *because* you earn so much.

Whatever the case, the way things are is not the way they have to be. Our economy, our taxes, and our universities can all be reinvented to make real innovation and creativity pay off. "We do not have to wait patiently for slow cultural change," the maverick economist William Baumol declared more than twenty years ago.[20] We don't have to wait until gambling with other people's money is no longer profitable; until sanitation workers, police agents, and nurses earn a decent wage; and until math whizzes once again start dreaming of building colonies on Mars instead of starting their own hedge funds.

We can take a step toward a different world, and we can start, as such steps so often do, with taxes. Even utopias need a tax clause. For example, we could start with a transactions tax to rein in the financial industry. Back in 1970, American stocks were still held for an average of five years; forty years later, it's a mere five days.[21] If we imposed a transactions tax – where you would have to pay a fee each time you buy or sell a stock – those high-frequency traders who contribute almost nothing of social value would no longer profit from split-second buying and selling of financial assets. In fact, we would save on frivolous expenditures that aid and abet the financial sector. Take the fiber-optic cable laid to speed transmissions between financial markets in London and New York in 2012. Price tag: $300 million. Time gain: a whole 5.2 milliseconds.

More to the point though, these taxes would make all of us richer. Not only would they give everyone a more equal share of the pie, but the whole pie would be bigger. Then the whiz kids who pack off to Wall Street could go back to becoming teachers, inventors, and engineers.

What has happened in recent decades is exactly the opposite. A study conducted at Harvard found that Reagan-era tax cuts sparked a mass career switch among the country's brightest minds, from teachers and engineers to bankers and accountants. Whereas in 1970 twice as many male Harvard grads were still opting for a life devoted to research over banking, twenty years later the balance had flipped, with one and a half times as many alumni employed in finance.

The upshot is that we've all gotten poorer. For every dollar a bank earns, an estimated equivalent of 60 cents is destroyed elsewhere in the economic chain. Conversely, for every dollar a researcher earns, a value of at least $5 – and often much more – is pumped back into the economy.[22] Higher taxes for top earners would serve, in Harvard science-speak, "to reallocate talented individuals from professions that cause negative externalities to those that cause positive externalities."

In plain English: Higher taxes would get more people to do work that's useful.

Trend Watchers

If there were ever a place where the quest for a better world ought to start, it's in the classroom.

Though it may have bolstered the phenomenon of bull-shit jobs, education has also been a source of new and tangible prosperity. If you were to draw up a list of the most influential professions, teacher would likely rank among the highest. This isn't because teachers accrue rewards like money, power, or status, but because teaching shapes something much bigger – the course of human history.

That may sound dramatic, but take an ordinary elementary school teacher. Forty years at the head of a class of twenty-five children amounts to influencing the lives of 1,000 children. Moreover, that teacher is molding pupils at an age when they're at their most malleable. They're still just children, after all. He or she not only equips them for the future, but in the process also has a direct hand in shaping that future.

If there's one place, then, where we can intervene in a way that will pay dividends for society down the road, it's in the classroom.

Yet that's barely happening. All the big debates in education are about format. About delivery. About didactics. Education is consistently presented as a means of adaptation – as a lubricant to help you glide more effortlessly through life. On the education conference circuit, an endless parade of trend watchers prophesy about the future and essential twenty-first-century skills, the buzzwords being "creative," "adaptable," and "flexible."

The focus, invariably, is on competencies, not values. On didactics, not ideals. On "problem-solving ability," but not which problems need solving. Invariably, it all revolves around the question: Which knowledge and skills do today's students need to get hired in tomorrow's job market – the market of 2030?

Which is precisely the wrong question.

In 2030, there will likely be a high demand for savvy accountants untroubled by a conscience. If current trends hold, countries like Luxembourg, the Netherlands, and Switzerland will become even bigger tax havens, enabling multinationals to dodge taxes even more effectively, leaving developing countries with an even shorter end of the stick. If the aim of education is to roll with these kinds of trends rather than upend them, then egotism is set to be the quintessential twenty-first-century skill. Not because the law or the market or technology demand it, but solely because that, apparently, is how we prefer to earn our money.

Instead, we should be posing a different question altogether: Which knowledge and skills do we *want* our children to have in 2030? Then, instead of anticipating and adapting, we'd be focusing on steering and creating. Instead of wondering what we *need* to do to make a living in this or that bullshit job, we could ponder how we *want* to make a living. This is a question no trend watcher can answer. How could they? They only follow the trends, they don't make them. That part is up to us.

To answer this question, we'll need to examine ourselves and our personal ideals. What do we want? More time for friends, for example, or family? For volunteer work? Art? Sports? Future education would have to prepare us not only for the job market but, more fundamentally, for life. Do we want to rein in the financial sector? Then maybe we should give budding economists some instruction in philosophy and morals. Do we want more solidarity across race, sex, and socioeconomic groups? Start in social studies class.

If we restructure education around our new ideals, the job market will happily tag along. Let's imagine we were to incorporate more art, history, and philosophy into the school curriculum. You can bet there will be a lift in demand for artists, historians, and philosophers. It's like the dream of 2030 that John Maynard Keynes had back in 1930. Increased prosperity – and the increased robotization of work – would finally enable us to "value ends above means and prefer the good to the useful." The purpose of a shorter workweek is not so we can all sit around doing nothing, but so we can spend more time on the things that genuinely matter to us.

In the end, it's not the market or technology that decides what has real value, but society. If we want this century to be one in which all of us get richer, then we'll need to free ourselves of the dogma that all work is meaningful. And, while we're at it, let's also get rid of the fallacy that a higher salary is automatically a reflection of societal value.

Then we might realize that in terms of value creation, it just doesn't pay to be a banker.

New York City, Fifty Years Later

Half a century after the strike, the Big Apple seems to have learned its lesson. "EVERYONE IN NYC WANTS TO BE GARBAGE COLLECTOR," read a recent newspaper headline. These days, the people who pick up after the megacity earn an enviable salary. After five years on the payroll, they can take home as much as $70,000 plus overtime and perks. "They keep the city running," a Sanitation Department spokesperson explained in the article. "If they were to stop working, however briefly, all of New York City would come to a standstill."[23]

The paper also interviewed a city sanitation worker. In 2006, Joseph Lerman, then twenty, got a call from the city informing him that he could report for duty as a collector. "I felt like I'd won the jackpot," he recounts. Nowadays, Lerman gets up at 4 every morning to haul garbage bags for shifts of up to twelve hours. To his fellow New Yorkers, it's only logical that he is well paid for his labors. "Honest," the city spokesperson smiles, "these men and women aren't known as the heroes of New York City for nothing."

The goal of the future is full unemployment,
so we can play.

Arthur C. Clarke (1917–2008)

8

Race Against the Machine

This wouldn't be the first time. At the start of the twentieth century, machines were already rendering a time-honored occupation obsolete. While England still counted more than one million of these jobs in 1901, they had all but disappeared just decades later.[1] Slowly but surely, the advent of motorized vehicles ate away at their earnings until they couldn't even pay for their own food.

I'm referring, naturally, to the draft horse.

And the inhabitants of the Land of Plenty have every reason to fear for their jobs, too, with the breakneck development of driving robots, reading robots, talking, writing, and – most importantly – calculating robots. "The role of humans as the most important factor of production is bound to diminish," Nobel laureate Wassily Leontief wrote back in 1983, "in the same way that the role of horses in agricultural production was first diminished and then eliminated by the introduction of tractors."[2]

Robots. They have become one of the strongest arguments in favor of a shorter workweek and a universal basic income. In fact, if current trends hold, there is really just one other alternative: structural unemployment and growing inequality. "Machinery . . . is a thief and would rob thousands," fulminated an English craftsman by the name of William Leadbeater at a meeting in Huddersfield in 1830. "We shall find that it shall be the destruction of this country."[3]

It started with our paychecks. In the United States, the real salary of the median nine-to-fiver *declined* 14% between 1969 and 2009.[4] In other developed countries, too, from Germany to Japan, wage growth has been stagnating in most occupations for years even as productivity continues to grow. The foremost reason for this is simple: Labor is becoming less and less scarce. Technological advances are putting the inhabitants of the Land of Plenty in direct competition with billions of working people across the world, and in competition with machines themselves.

Obviously, people aren't horses. There's only so much you can teach a horse. People, on the other hand, can learn and grow. So we pump more money into education and give three cheers for the knowledge economy.

There's just one problem. Even people with a framed piece of paper on their wall have cause for concern. William Leadbeater was well trained in his job when it was supplanted by a mechanized loom in 1830. The point is not that he wasn't educated, but that suddenly his skills were superfluous. This is an experience awaiting more and more people. "In the end, I will venture to say, it will be the destruction of the universe," William warned.

Welcome to the race against the machine.

The Chip and the Box

In the spring of 1965, Gordon Moore, a technician at IBM, received a letter from *Electronics Magazine* asking him to write a piece on the future of the computer chip in honor of the magazine's thirty-fifth anniversary. In those days, even the best prototypes had just thirty transistors. Transistors are the basic building blocks of every computer and, back then, transistors were big and computers were slow.

So Moore began gathering some figures and discovered something that surprised him. The number of transistors per chip had been doubling every year since 1959. Naturally, this got him thinking: What if this trend continues? By 1975, he was disconcerted to realize, there would be a whopping 60,000 transistors per chip. Before long, computers might be able to do sums better than all the smartest university mathematicians combined![5] The title of Moore's paper pretty much said it all: "Cramming More Components onto Integrated Circuits." These crammed chips would bring us "such wonders as home computers," as well as "portable communications equipment," and perhaps even "automatic controls for automobiles."

It was a shot in the dark, Moore knew. But forty years later, the world's largest chip producer, Intel, would offer $10,000 to anybody who could dig up an original issue of that *Electronics Magazine*. The shot in the dark went down in history as a law — Moore's Law, to be precise.

"Several times along the way, I thought we reached the end of the line," its namesake reported in 2005. "Things taper off."[6] But they haven't tapered off. Not yet. In 2013, the new Xbox One video game console relied on a chip that contained an incredible five *billion* transistors. How much longer this will continue, no one can say, but for now Moore's Law is still tearing ahead.[7]

Enter *the box*.

In the same way that transistors became the standard unit of information in the late 1950s, shipping containers once upon a time became the standard unit of transport.[8] Now, a rectangular steel box may not sound quite as revolutionary as chips and computers, but consider this: Before shipping containers, goods were all loaded onto ships, trains, or trucks one by one. All this loading, unloading, and reloading could add days to each leg of the journey.

By contrast, you only need to pack and unpack a shipping container once. In April 1956, the first container ship set out from New York City to Houston. Fifty-eight boxes were brought ashore in mere hours, and a day later the vessel was making its way back with another full load of

FIGURE 10   Moore's Law

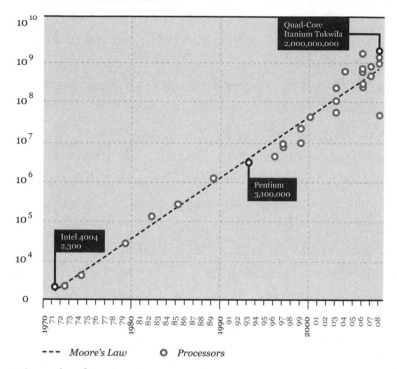

--- *Moore's Law*   ○ *Processors*

The number of transistors in processors 1970–2008

Source: Wikimedia Commons

cargo. Before the invention of the steel box, ships might spend four to six days in port, fully 50% of their time. A couple years later, just 10%.

The advent of the chip and the box made the world shrink as goods, services, and capital circled the globe ever more rapidly.[9] Technology and globalization advanced hand in hand and faster than ever. Then something happened – something that nobody had imagined possible.

Labor vs. Capital

Something happened that, according to the textbooks, *could not* happen.

Back in 1957 the economist Nicholas Kaldor outlined his six famous "facts" of economic growth. The first was: "The shares of national income that go toward labor and capital are constant over long periods of time." The constant being that two-thirds of a country's income goes into the paychecks of laborers and one-third goes into the pockets of the owners of capital – that is, the people who own the stock shares and the machines. Generations of young economists had it drilled into their heads that "the ratio of capital to labor is constant." Period.

But it's not.

Things were already beginning to change thirty years ago, and today only 58% of industrialized nations' wealth goes to pay people's salaries. It may sound like a fractional difference, but in fact it's a shift of seismic proportions. Various factors are involved, including the decline of labor unions, the growth of the financial sector, lower taxes on capital, and the rise of the Asian giants. But the most important cause? Technological progress.[10]

Take the iPhone. It's a miracle of technology, certainly inconceivable without the chip and the box. It's a phone constructed out of parts made in the U.S., Italy, Taiwan, and Japan that are screwed into place in China and then sent the world over. Or, take an ordinary jar of Nutella chocolate spread. The Italian brand is made in factories in Brazil, Argentina, Europe, Australia, and Russia with chocolate sourced from Nigeria, palm oil from Malaysia, vanilla flavoring from China, and sugar from Brazil.

We may be living in the age of individualism, but our societies have never been more dependent on one another.

The big question is: Who's profiting? Innovations in Silicon Valley trigger mass layoffs elsewhere. Just take webshops like Amazon. The emergence of online sellers led to the loss of millions of jobs in retail. The British

FIGURE 11   Where a Jar of Nutella Comes From

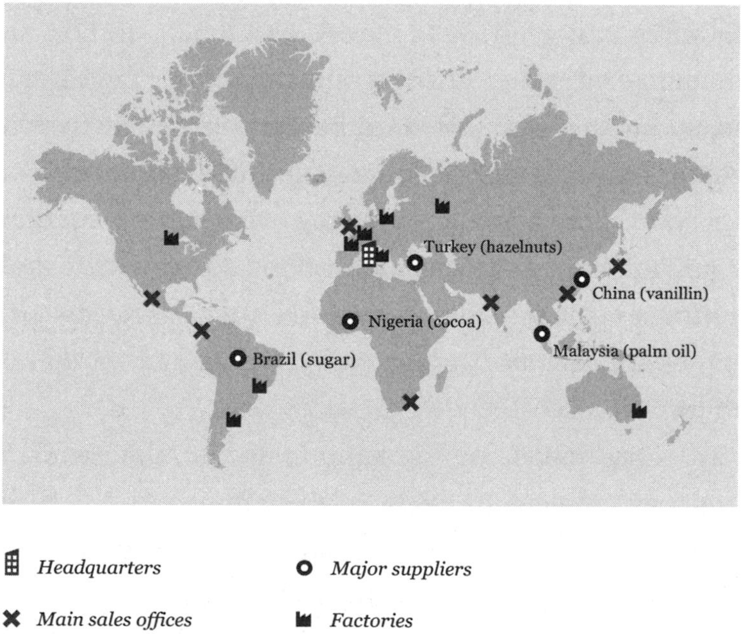

Headquarters   Major suppliers

Main sales offices   Factories

Source: OECD

economist Alfred Marshall already noted this dynamic back in the late nineteenth century: The smaller the world gets, the fewer the number of winners. In his own day, Marshall observed a shrinking oligopoly on the production of grand pianos. With each new road that was paved and each new canal that was dug, the costs of transport dropped another notch, making it increasingly easy for piano builders to export their wares. With their marketing clout and economies of scale, the big producers quickly overran small local suppliers. And as the world contracted further, the minor league players were driven from the field.

That same process has changed the face of sports, music, and publishing, which are now similarly dominated by a handful of heavy hitters. In the age of the chip, the box, and Internet retail, being just fractionally better than the rest means you've not only won the battle, you've won the war. Economists call this phenomenon the "winner-take-all society."[11] From small accountancy firms that are undercut by tax software to corner bookshops struggling to hold their own against online megastores – in one sector after another the giants have grown even as the world has shrunk.

By now, inequality is ballooning in almost every developed country. In the U.S., the gap between rich and poor is already wider than it was in ancient Rome – an economy founded on slave labor.[12] In Europe, too, there's a growing divide between the haves and the have-nots.[13]

Even the World Economic Forum, a clique of entrepreneurs, politicos, and pop stars, has described this escalating inequality as the biggest threat facing our global economy.

Granted, it all happened very fast. Whereas in 1964 each of the four largest American companies still had an average workforce of about 430,000 people, by 2011 they employed only a quarter that number, despite being worth twice as much.[14] Or take the tragic fate of Kodak, inventor of the digital camera and a company that in the late 1980s had 145,000 people on its payroll. In 2012, it filed for bankruptcy, while Instagram – the free online mobile photo service staffed by 13 people at the time – was sold to Facebook for $1 billion.

The reality is that it takes fewer and fewer people to create a successful business, meaning that when a business succeeds, fewer and fewer people benefit.

Automation of Knowledge Work

Back in 1964, Isaac Asimov was already predicting, "Mankind will . . . become largely a race of machine tenders." But that turns out to have been a little optimistic. Now, robots are threatening even the jobs of the tenders.[15] To quote a joke popular among economists: "The factory of the future will have only two employees, a man and a dog. The man will be there to feed the dog. The dog will be there to keep the man from touching the equipment."[16]

By now it's no longer just the Silicon Valley trend watchers and techno-prophets who are apprehensive. Scholars at Oxford University estimate that no less than 47% of all American jobs and 54% of all those in Europe are at a high risk of being usurped by machines.[17] And not in a hundred years or so, but in the next twenty. "The only real difference between enthusiasts and skeptics is a time frame," a New York University professor notes. "But a century from now, nobody will much care about how *long* it took, only what happened next."[18]

I admit, we've heard it all before. Employees have been worrying about the rising tide of automation for 200 years now, and for 200 years employers have been assuring them that new jobs will naturally materialize to take their place. After all, if you look at the year 1800, some 74% of all Americans were farmers, whereas by 1900 this figure was down to 31%, and by 2000 to a mere 3%.[19] Yet this hasn't led to mass unemployment. And look at Keynes writing in the 1930s about the "new disease" of "technological unemployment" that would soon be making headlines; when he died in 1946, everything still was peachy.

Over the 1950s and 1960s the American automotive industry experienced successive waves of automation, yet wages and work opportunities both continued their steady rise. A study conducted in 1963 demonstrated that though new technologies had wiped out thirteen million jobs over the previous decade, they had also created twenty million new ones. "Instead of being alarmed about growing

FIGURE 12   Productivity and Jobs in the United States, 1947–2011

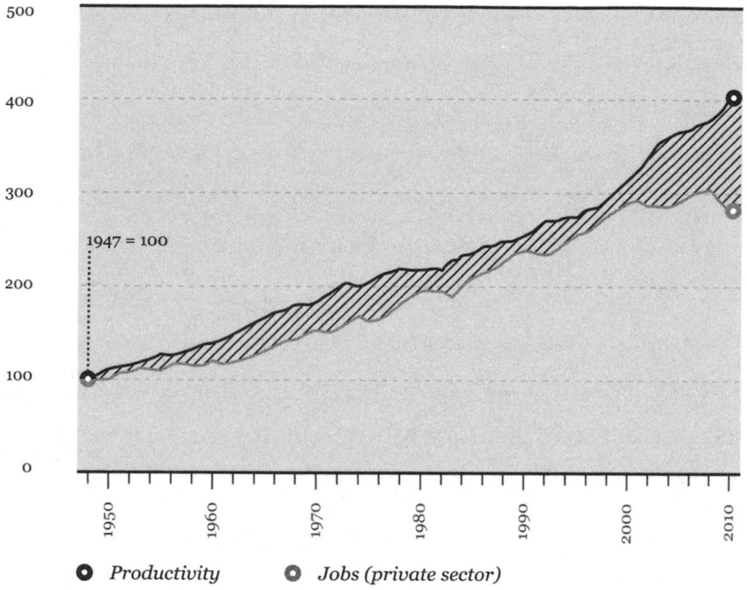

● Productivity   ○ Jobs (private sector)

Source: U.S. Department of Labor, Bureau of Labor Statistics

automation, we ought to be cheering it on," remarked one of the researchers.[20]

But that was 1963.

Over the course of the twentieth century, productivity growth and job growth ran more or less parallel. Man and machine marched along side by side. Now, as we step out into a new century, the robots have suddenly picked up the pace. It began around the year 2000, with what two MIT economists called "the great decoupling." "It's the great paradox of our era," said one. "Productivity is at record levels, innovation has never been faster, and yet at the same time, we have a falling median income and we have fewer jobs."[21]

Today, new jobs are concentrated mostly at the bottom of the pyramid – at supermarkets, fast-food chains, and nursing homes. Those are the jobs that are still safe. For the moment.

When People Still Mattered

A hundred years ago, computers were still folks like you and me. I'm not kidding: Back then, the word "computer" was just a job title. Computers were workers – mostly women – who did simple sums all day. It didn't take long though before their task could be performed by calculators, the first in a long line of jobs swallowed up by computers of the automated variety.

In 1990 the techno-prophet Ray Kurzweil predicted that a computer would even be able to outplay a chess master by 1998. He was wrong, of course. It was in 1997 that Deep Blue defeated chess legend Garry Kasparov. The world's fastest computer at that time was the ASCI Red, developed by the American military and offering a peak performance speed of one teraflop. It was the size of a tennis court and cost $55 million. Sixteen years later, in 2013, a new supercomputer came on the market that easily clocked two teraflops and at just a fraction of the price: the PlayStation 4.

By 2011, computers were even appearing as contestants on TV game shows. In that year, the two brightest minds in trivia, Ken Jennings and Brad Rutter, pitted their wits against "Watson" on the quiz show *Jeopardy!* Jennings and Rutter had already amassed winnings of more than \$3 million, but their computerized opponent slaughtered them. Stuffed to the gills with 200 million pages of information, including a complete copy of Wikipedia, Watson gave more correct responses than Jennings and Rutter put together. "'Quiz show contestant' may be the first job made redundant by Watson," Jennings observed, "but I'm sure it won't be the last."[22]

The new generations of robots are proxies not only for our muscle power, but for our mental capacity, too. Welcome, my friends, to the Second Machine Age, as this brave new world of chips and algorithms is already being called. The first began with the Scottish inventor James Watt, who during a stroll in 1765 came up with an idea for improving the efficiency of the steam engine. It being a Sunday, the pious Watt had to wait another day before putting his idea into action, but by 1776, he'd built a machine able to pump sixty feet of water out of a mine in just sixty minutes.[23]

At a time when nearly everyone everywhere was still poor, hungry, dirty, afraid, stupid, sick, and ugly, the line of technological development began to curve. Or rather, to skyrocket, at an angle of around ninety degrees. Whereas in 1800, water power still supplied England with three times the amount of energy as steam, seventy years later English steam engines were generating the power equivalent of forty million grown men.[24] Machine power was replacing muscle power on a massive scale.

Now, two centuries later, our brains are next. And it's high time, too. "You can see the computer age everywhere but in the productivity statistics," the economist Bob Solow said in 1987. Computers could already do some pretty neat things, but their economic impact was minimal. Like the steam engine, the computer needed time to, well, gather steam. Or compare it to electricity: All the major technological innovations happened in the 1870s, but it wasn't until around 1920 that most factories actually switched to electric power.[25]

Fast forward to today, and chips are doing things that even ten years ago were still deemed impossible. In 2004 two prominent scientists authored a chapter suggestively titled "Why People Still Matter."[26] Their argument? Driving a car is something that could never be automated. Six years later, Google's robo-cars had already covered a million miles.

Futurologist Ray Kurzweil is convinced that by 2029 computers will be just as intelligent as people. In 2045 they might even be a billion times smarter than all human brains put together. According to the techno-prophets, there simply is no limit to the exponential growth of machine computing power. Of course, Kurzweil is equal parts genius and mad. And it's worth bearing in mind that computing power is not the same thing as intelligence.

But still – we dismiss his predictions at our peril. After all, it wouldn't be the first time that we underestimated the power of exponential growth.

This Time is Different

The million-dollar question is: What should we do? What new jobs will the future bring? And, more importantly, will we want to do those new jobs?

Employees of companies like Google will be well cared for, of course, with finger-licking food, daily massages, and generous paychecks. But to get hired in Silicon Valley you'll need inordinate talent, ambition, and luck. That's one side of what economists call "labor market polarization," or the widening gap between "lousy jobs" and "lovely jobs." Though the share of highly skilled and unskilled jobs has remained fairly stable, work for the average-skilled is on a decline.[27] Slowly but surely, the bedrock of modern democracy – the middle class – is crumbling. And while the U.S. is leading this process, other developed nations aren't far behind.[28]

Some people in our modern Land of Plenty have even found themselves completely sidelined, despite being hale and hearty and eager to roll up their sleeves. Similar to the English draft horses at the turn of the twentieth century, they won't find employers willing to hire them at any wage. Asian, African, or robot labor will always come cheaper.

And while it's still often more efficient to outsource work cheaply to Asia and Africa,[29] the moment wages and technologies in those countries start to catch up, robots will win out even there. In the end, outsourcing is just a stepping-stone. Eventually, even the sweatshops in Vietnam and Bangladesh will be automated.[30]

Robots don't get sick, don't take time off, and never complain, but if they wind up forcing masses of people into poorly paid, dead-end jobs, well that's just asking for trouble. The British economist Guy Standing has predicted the emergence of a new, dangerous "precariat" – a surging social class of people in low-wage, temporary jobs and with no political voice. Their frustrations sound eerily like those of William Leadbeater. This English craftsman who was afraid that machines would destroy his country – or, indeed, the entire universe – was a part of such a dangerous class, and of a movement that laid the foundations of capitalism.

Meet the Luddites.

The Battle of Rawfolds Mill

April 11, 1812 – Some 100 to 200 masked men have gathered on a darkened plot of land near Huddersfield, between Manchester and Leeds in England. They've congregated around a stone column known as Dumb Steeple, armed to the teeth with hammers, axes, and pistols.

Their leader is a charismatic young cropper by the name of George Mellor. He raises his long pistol – brought from Russia, some say – up high for all to see. Their target is Rawfolds Mill, a factory owned by one William Cartwright. A wealthy businessman, Cartwright has just introduced a new type of power-loom that can do the work of four skilled weavers. Since then, unemployment among the Yorkshire Luddites, as these masked men call themselves, has soared.

But Cartwright has been tipped off. He has called in soldiers, and they are lying in wait. Twenty minutes, 140 bullets, and two deaths later, Mellor and his men are forced to retreat. Judging by the bloodstains found as far as four miles away, dozens of men have been hit.

Two weeks pass before William Horsfall, a mill owner enraged by the attack on Rawfolds Mill, rides from Huddersfield to the nearby village of Marsden swearing he'll soon "ride up to his saddle in Luddite blood." What he doesn't know is that four Luddites, including Mellor, are plotting an ambush. Horsfall is dead before noon, felled by a bullet fired from the barrel of a Russian pistol.

In the months that follow, all Yorkshire is up in arms. A committee headed by the energetic magistrate Joseph Radcliff is appointed to investigate the Battle at Rawfolds Mill and the murder of William Horsfall. They launch a manhunt. Soon Benjamin Walker, one of the men responsible for luring Horsfall into the trap, turns himself in to Radcliff, hoping to save his own skin and claim the promised £2,000 reward. Walker identifies his co-conspirators as William Thorpe, Thomas Smith, and their leader George Mellor.

Not long thereafter, all three are swinging from a scaffold.

Luddites in the Right

"Not one of the prisoners shed a tear," reported the *Leeds Mercury* on the day following the executions. Mellor had prayed and begged forgiveness for his sins, but made no reference to his Luddite activities. Walker, the traitor, was spared the gallows but never got his reward. He is said to have ended his days impoverished on the streets of London.

Two hundred years later, Rawfolds Mill is long gone, but there is still a rope works nearby where the workers like to tell of Luddite ghosts roaming the fields at night.[31] And they're right; the specter of Luddism remains with us to this day. It was at the beginning of the First Machine Age that textile workers in central and northern England rose up in rebellion, taking their name from the movement's mythical leader Ned Ludd, who was supposed to have smashed two looms in a fit of rage in 1779. Because labor unions were outlawed, the Luddites opted for what the historian Eric Hobsbawm calls "negotiation by riot." Advancing from factory to factory, the activists left a trail of destruction in their wake.

Of course, the laborer William Leadbeater may have been exaggerating slightly when he predicted that machines would be the "destruction of the universe," but the Luddites' concerns were far from unfounded. Their wages were plummeting and their jobs were disappearing like dust in the wind. "How are those men, thus thrown out of employ to provide for their families?" wondered the late eighteenth-century clothworkers of Leeds. "Some say, Begin and learn some other business. Suppose we do; who will maintain our families, whilst we undertake the arduous task; and when we have learned it, how do we know we shall be any better for all our pains; for . . . another machine may arise, which may take away that business also."[32]

The Luddite rebellion, at its height around 1811, was brutally crushed. More than 100 men were hanged. They had declared a war on machines, but it was the machines that won. As a result, this episode is generally treated as something of a minor hiccup in the march of progress. Ultimately, after all, machines generated so many new jobs that there were still enough to go around even after the twentieth-century population explosion. According to the radical freethinker Thomas Paine, "every machine for the abridgment of labor is a blessing to the great family of which we are part."[33]

And so they are. The word "robot" actually comes from the Czech *robota*, meaning "toil." Humans created robots to do precisely those things they'd rather not do themselves. "Machinery must work for us in coal mines," Oscar

Wilde enthused in 1890. Machines should "be the stoker of steamers, and clean the streets, and run messages on wet days, and do anything that is tedious or distressing." According to Wilde, the ancient Greeks had known an uncomfortable truth: Slavery is a prerequisite for civilization. "On mechanical slavery, on the slavery of the machine, the future of the world depends."[34]

However, there's something else that is equally vital to the future of our world, and that's a mechanism for redistribution. We have to devise a system to ensure that everybody benefits from this Second Machine Age, a system that compensates the losers as well as the winners. For 200 years that system was the labor market, which ceaselessly churned out new jobs and, in so doing, distributed the fruits of progress. But for how much longer? What if the Luddites' fears were premature, but ultimately prophetic? What if most of us are doomed, in the long run, to lose the race against the machine?

What can be done?

Remedies

Not much, according to many economists. The trends are clear. Inequality will continue to increase and everybody who hasn't managed to learn a skill that machines cannot or will not be able to master will be sidelined. "Making high earners feel better in just about every part of their lives will be a major source of job growth in the future," writes the American economist Tyler Cowen.[35] Though the lower classes might have access to new amenities like cheap solar power and free Wi-Fi, the gap between them and the ultra-rich will be wider than ever.

Beyond that, the rich and well educated will continue to close ranks even as peripheral villages and towns grow more impoverished. We're already seeing this happen in Europe, where Spanish techies can more easily find jobs in Amsterdam than in Madrid, and Greek engineers are pulling up stakes and heading for cities like Stuttgart and Munich. People with a college education are moving to live closer to other people with a college education. In the 1970s, the most learned American city (in terms of the percentage of residents with four-year degrees) was 16 percentage points more educated than the least educated city. Today, this difference has doubled.[36] If people used to judge each other on their parentage, now it's the diplomas on their wall. As long as machines can't go to college, a degree offers higher returns than ever.

So it's not surprising that our standard response has been to call for more money for education. Rather than outrun the machine, we do our best to keep up with it. After all, massive investments in schools and universities are what enabled us to adapt to the technological tsunamis of the nineteenth and twentieth centuries. But then, not much was needed to boost the earning capacity of a nation of farmers — just basic skills like reading, writing, and arithmetic. Preparing our own children for the new century will be considerably more difficult, however, not to mention expensive. All the low-hanging fruit has already been plucked.

Alternatively, we could take a tip from Dutch chess grandmaster Jan Hein Donner. When asked what his strategy would be if he were pitted against a computer, he didn't have to think long. "I'd bring a hammer." To choose that path would be to follow in the footsteps of someone like Holy Roman Emperor Francis II (1768–1835), who refused to allow the construction of factories and railways. "No, no, I will have nothing to do with it," he declared, "lest the revolution might come into the country."[37] His resistance meant that, far into the nineteenth century, Austrian trains continued to be drawn by horses.

Anyone who wants to continue plucking the fruits of progress will have to come up with a more radical solution. Just as we adapted to the First Machine Age through a revolution in education and welfare, so the Second Machine Age calls for drastic measures. Measures like a shorter workweek and universal basic income.

The Future of Capitalism

For us today, it is still difficult to imagine a future society in which paid labor is not the be-all and end-all of our existence. But the inability to imagine a world in which things are different is evidence only of a poor imagination, not of the impossibility of change. In the 1950s we couldn't conceive that the advent of refrigerators, vacuum cleaners, and, above all, washing machines would help prompt women to enter the workplace in record numbers, and yet they did.

Nevertheless, it is not technology itself that determines the course of history. In the end, it is we humans who decide how we want to shape our destiny. The scenario of radical inequality that is taking shape in the U.S. is not our only option. The alternative is that at some point during this century, we reject the dogma that you have to work for a living. The richer we as a society become, the less effectively the labor market will be at distributing prosperity. If we want to hold onto the blessings of technology, ultimately there's only one choice left, and that's redistribution. Massive redistribution.

Redistribution of money (basic income), of time (a shorter working week), of taxation (on capital instead of labor), and, of course, of robots. As far back as the nineteenth century, Oscar Wilde looked forward to the day when everybody would benefit from intelligent machines that were "the property of all."[38] Technological progress may make a society more prosperous in aggregate, but there's no economic law that says everyone will benefit.

Not long ago, the French economist Thomas Piketty had people up in arms with his contention that if we continue down our current path we'll soon find ourselves back in the rentier society of the Gilded Age. People who owned capital (stocks, houses, machines) enjoyed a much higher standard of living than folks who merely worked hard. For hundreds of years the return on capital was 4–5%, while annual economic growth lagged behind at under 2%. Barring a resurgence of strong, inclusive growth (rather unlikely), high taxation on capital (equally improbable), or World War III (let's hope not), inequality could develop to frightening proportions once again.

All the standard options – more schooling, regulation, austerity – will be a drop in the bucket. In the end, the only solution is a worldwide, progressive tax on wealth, says Professor Piketty, though he acknowledges this is merely a "useful utopia." And yet, the future is not carved in stone. All throughout history, the march toward equality has always been steeped in politics. If a law of common progress fails to manifest itself of its own accord, there is nothing to stop us from enacting it ourselves. Indeed, the absence of such a law may well imperil the free market itself. "We have to save capitalism from the capitalists," Piketty concludes.[39]

This paradox is neatly summed up by an anecdote from the 1960s. When Henry Ford's grandson gave labor union leader Walter Reuther a tour of the company's new, automated factory, he jokingly asked, "Walter, how are you going to get those robots to pay your union dues?" Without missing a beat, Reuther answered, "Henry, how are you going to get them to buy your cars?"

The future is already here —
it's just not very evenly distributed.

William Gibson (b. 1948)

9

Beyond the Gates of the Land of Plenty

A nd then there's that nagging sense of guilt.
Here we are in the Land of Plenty, philosophizing about decadent utopias with free cash and fifteen-hour workweeks, while hundreds of millions of people still have to survive on a dollar a day. Shouldn't we instead be tackling the single biggest challenge of our times: to afford every person on Earth the joys of the Land of Plenty?

Well, we've tried. The Western world spends $134.8 billion a year, $11.2 billion a month, $4,274 a second on foreign development aid.[1] Over the past fifty years, that brings us to a grand total of almost $5 trillion.[2] Sound like a lot? Actually, the wars in Iraq and Afghanistan cost about the same.[3] And let's not forget that developed countries spend twice as much annually on subsidizing domestic agriculture as they do on foreign aid.[4] But, sure, it's a lot. Frankly, $5 trillion is an astronomical sum.

So then the question is: Has it helped?

Here's where it gets tricky. There's really only one way to answer this: Nobody knows.

Quite literally, we have no idea. Relatively speaking, the 1970s were the heyday of humanitarian aid, but then again, the situation in Africa was downright dire. Now we have cut back on aid and things are getting better. Is there a connection? Who knows? Without Band Aid and Bono, it might have all been a hundred times worse. Or not. According to a study done by the World Bank, 85% of all Western aid in the twentieth century was used differently than intended.[5]

So was it all for nothing?

We have no idea.

What we do have, of course, are economic models that tell us how people will act based on the assumption that humans are purely rational beings. We have retrospective surveys that show how a school, village, or country changed after it got a pile of money. We have case studies offering heartwarming or heartrending anecdotes about aid that did – or didn't – help. And we have gut feelings. Lots of gut feelings.

Esther Duflo, a professor at MIT with a strong French accent, likens all this research on development aid to medieval bloodletting.[6] The once popular medical practice involved placing leeches on patients' veins in order to rebalance their bodily humors. If the patient returned to health, the physician could pat himself on the back. If the patient died, it was clearly God's will. Though those doctors acted with the best of intentions, nowadays we realize that bloodletting cost millions of lives. Even in

1799, the year Alessandro Volta invented the electric battery, President George Washington was relieved of several pints of blood to treat a sore throat. Two days later, he died.

Bloodletting, in other words, is a case where the remedy is worse than the disease. The question is, does the same apply to development aid? According to Professor Duflo, both remedies certainly share one key feature, which is the fundamental lack of scientific proof.

In 2003, Duflo helped found MIT's Poverty Action Lab, which today employs 150 researchers who have conducted over 500 studies in fifty-six countries. Their work has turned the world of development aid on its head.

Once Upon a Time There was a Control Group

Our story begins in Israel, some time in the 7th century B.C. Nebuchadnezzar, the king of Babylon, has just conquered Jerusalem and orders his head eunuch to escort several Israelite nobles to his palace. Among them is Daniel, a man known for his piety. Upon his arrival, Daniel asks the head eunuch to let him abstain from eating "the king's food and wine" since he and his men have their own religious diet. The eunuch is taken aback and objects. "I am afraid of my lord the king," he says, "who has decided what you shall eat and drink. If the king sees you looking worse than the other young men your age, he would have my head because of you."

So Daniel devises a stratagem. "Test your servants for ten days: Give us nothing but vegetables to eat and water to drink. Then compare our appearance with that of the young men who eat the royal food, and decide what to do with us based on how we look." The Babylonian agrees. After ten days, Daniel and his friends look "healthier and better nourished" than the other courtiers, and from that moment on they are no longer served the royal delicacies and wine but a diet of pure vegetables. *Quod erat demonstrandum.*

This is the first written record of a comparative experiment in which a hypothesis is tested and a control group is used. A few centuries later, these events would be immortalized in the biggest bestseller ever: the Bible (see Daniel 1:1–16). But it would still be several hundred years before this kind of comparative research came to be considered the scientific gold standard. These days, we would call this a randomized controlled trial, or RCT. If you were a medical researcher, you would proceed as follows: Using a lottery system, you divide people with the same health problem into two groups. One gets the medicine you want to test and the other gets a placebo.[7]

In the case of bloodletting, the first comparative experiment was published in 1836 by the French doctor Pierre Louis, who had treated some pneumonia sufferers by immediately relieving them of a few pints of blood and others by holding off on the leeches for a few days. In the first group, 44% died; in the second, 25%.[8] In essence, Dr. Louis had carried out the first-ever clinical trials, and bloodletting came out looking pretty dicey.

Bizarrely, the first RCT of foreign development aid didn't happen until 1998. Not until more than a century and a half after Dr. Louis had banished bloodletting to history's dustbin did a young American professor named Michael Kremer have the insight to investigate the effects of free textbooks on Kenyan grade-school pupils. The books were supposed to curb truancy and raise test scores — at least, in theory. There was a ton of academic literature that said as much and the World Bank had enthusiastically recommended a free book-distribution program just a few years before, in 1991.[9]

There was one small problem. None of those earlier studies had checked for other variables.

Kremer threw himself into the project. Joining forces with a humanitarian organization, he selected fifty schools, twenty-five of which got free textbooks while the others went empty-handed. Setting up an RCT in a country where the communication infrastructure was poor, roads were deplorable, and famine was a fact of life was by no means easy, but after four years, the data was in.

The free books had made no difference. Test scores showed no improvement.[10]

Kremer's was a landmark experiment. Since then, a veritable randomization industry has grown up around development aid, led by the aptly nicknamed "random-istas." These are researchers who have had enough of the intuition, gut feelings, and ideological bickering of ivory-tower scholars about the needs of people struggling in Africa and elsewhere. What the randomistas want is numbers – incontrovertible data to show which aid helps, and which doesn't.

And the chief randomista? She's a petite professor with a strong French accent.

A Pile of Money and a Good Plan

Not so long ago I was a college student taking a course on development aid. Our assigned reading included books by Jeffrey Sachs and William Easterly, both leading thinkers on the topic. In 2005, Sachs published a book titled *The End of Poverty* (with a preface by Bono, the pop star), in which the American professor argued that extreme poverty could be wiped out completely before 2025. All we need is a pile of money and a good plan. *His* plan, mind you.

Easterly responded by lambasting Sachs' ideas, accusing him of post-colonial messianic do-goodism and arguing that developing countries can only be changed from the bottom up – that is, through local democracy and, crucially, the marketplace. According to Easterly, "The best plan is to have no plan at all."

Reviewing my old lecture notes, one name I didn't see was Esther Duflo. That's not especially surprising, considering that she steers well clear of the high-flown intellectual posturing of academic types like Sachs and Easterly. Her ambition, in a nutshell, is to "take the guesswork out of policy-making."[11]

Take malaria. Every year, hundreds of thousands of children die of this disease, which can be prevented by mosquito nets that we can produce, ship, distribute, and teach people to use for all of $10 apiece. In a 2007 paper titled "The $10 Solution," Sachs wrote, "We should bring forth armies of Red Cross volunteers to distribute bed nets and to offer village-based training for tens of thousands of villages across Africa."

To Easterly, it was obvious where all this was heading. Sachs and his buddy Bono would organize a charity concert, rake in a couple million, and then drop thousands of mosquito nets over Africa. In no time, the local net retailers would all be out of business, while the surfeit of nets would soon be doing duty as fishing gear or wedding veils. A few years after Sachs the Redeemer's campaign, when the gift nets had worn out, the number of children dying of malaria would be higher than ever.

Sound plausible? Sure.

But Esther Duflo isn't interested in theory-mongering or in what *sounds* plausible. If you want to know whether it would be better to hand out mosquito nets or to sell them, you can armchair-philosophize till you're blue in the

face . . . or you can go out and do the research. Two scholars at Cambridge University decided to do just that. They
set up an RCT in Kenya in which one group of people got
a net for free and the other only got a discount. As soon as
people had to pay for the nets, sales plummeted; at $3,
fewer than 20% of people bought them. Conversely, almost
everybody in the group offered free nets took up the offer.
More important, 90% of the time the nets were used
precisely as intended regardless of whether they came free
or not.[12]

But that's not all. A year later the trial participants were
given the option to buy another net, this time for $2.
Anybody who has read Easterly's books would expect that
people who had been in the "free" group before would
be averse to paying now since they'd become accustomed
to being spoiled. It sounds like a plausible theory.
Unfortunately though, it lacks something crucial: evidence. The people who got nets at no charge actually
proved twice as likely to purchase a new net as those who
paid $3 the first time around.

"People do not get used to handouts," Duflo succinctly
points out. "They get used to nets."

A Miraculous Method?

This is nothing less than a whole new approach to economics. The randomistas don't think in terms of models. They

don't believe humans are rational actors. Instead, they assume we are quixotic creatures, sometimes foolish and sometimes astute, and by turns afraid, altruistic, and self-centered. And this approach appears to yield considerably better results.

So why did it take so long to figure this out?

Well, several reasons. Doing randomized controlled trials in poverty-stricken countries is difficult, time consuming, and expensive. Often, local organizations are less than eager to cooperate, not least because they're worried the findings will prove them ineffective. Take the case of microcredit. Development aid trends come and go, from "good governance" to "education" to the ill-fated "microcredit" at the start of this century. Microcredit's reckoning came in the form of our old friend Esther Duflo, who set up a fatal RCT in Hyderabad, India, and demonstrated that, all the heartwarming anecdotes notwithstanding, there is no hard evidence that microcredit is effective at combating poverty and illness.[13] Handing out cash works way better. As it happens, cash handouts may be the most extensively studied anti-poverty method around. RCTs across the globe have shown that over both the long and short term and on both a large and small scale, cash transfers are an extremely successful and efficient tool.[14]

And yet, RCTs aren't a silver bullet. Not everything is measurable. And findings can't always be generalized. Who can say whether distributing free textbooks will have the same effect in western Kenya as in northern Bangladesh? And there are also the ethics to consider. Say that after a natural disaster, your study provides aid to half the victims but leaves a control group in the lurch. At best, that's pretty iffy, morally speaking. Yet this objection is moot when it comes to structural development aid. Since there's never enough money to fix all the problems anyway, the best method is to do whatever seems to work. It's like with new pharmaceuticals: You would never just market them untested.

Or take school attendance. Everybody seems to have different ideas on how to raise it. We should pay for uniforms. Advance school fees on credit. Offer free meals. Install toilets. Raise public awareness of the value of education. Hire more teachers. And on and on. All of these suggestions sound perfectly logical. Thanks to RCTs, however, we know that $100 worth of free meals translates into an additional 2.8 years of educational attainment — three times as much as free uniforms. Speaking of proven impact, deworming children with intestinal complaints has been shown to yield 2.9 years of additional schooling for the absurdly small investment of $10 worth of treatment. No armchair philosopher could have predicted that, but since this finding was revealed, tens of millions of children have been dewormed.

In point of fact, few intuitions hold up against the evidence from RCTs. Traditional economists would say that the poor would get treated for worms of their own accord, given the obvious benefits — and innate human rationality. But that's a fallacy. In a piece in the *New Yorker* a few years ago, Duflo recounted a well-known joke about an economist who sees a $100 bill in the street. Being a rational person, he doesn't pick it up, because how could it be anything but a fake?

For randomistas like Duflo, the sidewalk is littered with these $100 bills.

The Three I's

The time has come to put paid to what Duflo calls the three I's of development aid: Ideology, Ignorance, and Inertia. "I don't have many opinions to start with," she said in an interview a few years ago. "I have one opinion — one should evaluate things — which is strongly held. I'm never unhappy with the results. I haven't yet seen a result I didn't like."[15] Many a would-be do-gooder could learn from this attitude. Duflo is an example of how to combine big ideals with a thirst for knowledge, for how to be idealist without becoming ideological.

And yet.

And yet development aid, no matter how effective, is always just a drop in the bucket. Major dilemmas such as how to structure a democracy or what a country needs to prosper can't be answered by an RCT, let alone solved by throwing some cash at the problem. To fixate on all those clever studies is to forget that the most effective anti-poverty measures happen elsewhere in the economic food chain. The OECD estimates that poor countries lose three times as much to tax evasion as they receive in foreign aid.[16] Measures against tax havens, for example, could potentially do far more good than well-meaning aid programs ever could.

We could even think on a bigger scale than that. Imagine there was a single measure that could wipe out all poverty everywhere, raising everybody in Africa above our Western poverty line, and in the process put a few extra months' salary in *our* pockets too. Just imagine. Would we take that measure?

No. Of course not. After all, this measure has been around for years. It's the best plan that never happened.

I'm talking about open borders.

Not just for bananas, derivatives, and iPhones, but for one and all – for knowledge workers, for refugees, and for ordinary people in search of greener pastures.

Of course, we've all learned the hard way by now that economists are no fortune tellers (the economist John Kenneth Galbraith once quipped that the only purpose of economic forecasts is to give astrology a better image), but on this point their views are remarkably consistent. Four different studies have shown that, depending on the level of movement in the global labor market, the estimated growth in "gross worldwide product" would be in the range of 67% to 147%.[17]

Effectively, open borders would make the whole world *twice* as rich.

This has led one New York University researcher to conclude that we're currently leaving "trillion-dollar bills on the sidewalk."[18] An economist at the University of Wisconsin has calculated that open borders would boost the income of an average Angolan by about $10,000 a year, and of a Nigerian by $22,000 annually.[19]

So why bother quibbling over the crumbs of development aid – Duflo's $100 bills – when instead we could simply throw open the gates of the Land of Plenty?

$65,000,000,000,000

As plans go, it sounds a little outrageous. Then again, the world's borders were still as good as open only a century ago. "Passports are only good for annoying honest folks," the detective in Jules Verne's novel *Around the World in 80 Days* (1874) remarks to the British consul in Suez. "You know that a visa is useless, and that no passport is required?" the consul says when the protagonist, Phileas Fogg, asks for a stamp.

On the eve of World War I, borders existed mostly as lines on paper. Passports were rare and the countries that did issue them (like Russia and the Ottoman Empire) were seen as uncivilized. Besides, that wonder of nineteenth-century technology, the train, was poised to erase borders for good.

And then the war broke out. Suddenly, borders were sealed to keep spies out and everybody needed for the war effort in. At a 1920 conference in Paris, the international community came to the first ever agreements on the use of passports. These days, anyone retracing Phileas Fogg's journey would have to apply for dozens of visas, pass through hundreds of security checkpoints, and get frisked more times than you could count. In this era of "globalization," only 3% of the world's population lives outside their country of birth.

Oddly though, the world is wide open for everything but people. Goods, services, and stocks crisscross the globe. Information circulates freely, Wikipedia is available in 300 languages and counting, and the NSA can easily check which games John in Texas is playing on his smartphone.

Sure, we still have a few trade barriers. In Europe, for example, we have tariffs on chewing gum (€1.20 per kilo) and the U.S. taxes imported live goats ($0.68 a head),[20] but if we scrapped such barriers, the global economy would grow only a few percentage points.[21] According to the International Monetary Fund, lifting the remaining restrictions on capital would free up at most $65 billion.[22] Pocket change, according to Harvard economist Lant Pritchett. Opening borders to labor would boost wealth by much more — *one thousand times more*.

In numbers: $65,000,000,000,000. In words: sixty-five trillion dollars.

Borders Discriminate

Economic growth isn't a cure-all, of course, but out beyond the gates of the Land of Plenty, it's still the main driver of progress. In the hinterlands there are still countless mouths to feed, children to educate, and homes to build.

Ethics, too, favors open borders. Say John from Texas is dying of hunger. He asks me for food, but I refuse. If John dies, is it my fault? Arguably, I merely *allowed* him to die, which while not exactly benevolent, isn't exactly murder either.

Now imagine that John doesn't ask for food, but goes off to the market, where he'll find plenty of people willing to exchange their goods for work that he can do in return. This time though, I hire a couple of heavily armed baddies to block his way. John dies of starvation a few days later.

Can I still claim innocence?

The story of John is the story of our "everything except labor" brand of globalization.[23] Billions of people are forced to sell their labor at a fraction of the price that they would get for it in the Land of Plenty, all because of borders. Borders are the single biggest cause of discrimination in all of world history. Inequality gaps between people living in the same country are nothing in comparison to those between separated global citizenries. Today, the richest 8% earn half of all the world's income,[24] and the richest 1% own more than half of all wealth.[25] The poorest billion people account for just 1% of all consumption; the richest billion, 72%.[26]

From an international perspective, the inhabitants of the Land of Plenty aren't merely rich, but filthy rich. A person living at the poverty line in the U.S. belongs to the richest 14% of the world population; someone earning a median wage belongs to the richest 4%.[27] At the very top, the comparisons get even more skewed. In 2009, as the credit crunch was gathering momentum, the employee bonuses paid out by investment bank Goldman Sachs were equal to the combined earnings of the world's 224 million poorest people.[28] And just eight people – the richest people on Earth – own the same as the poorest *half* of the whole world.[29]

FIGURE 13   Which Countries are the Richest?

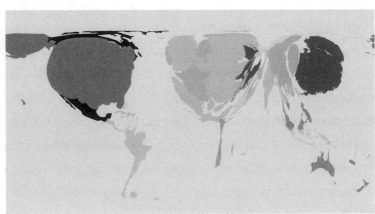

This map shows which countries have the highest per capita GDP. The bigger the country is on the map, the richer it is.

Source: Sasi Group, University of Sheffield (2005)

That's right, a mere sixty-two people are richer than 3.5 billion put together.

Our Location Bonus

No wonder, then, that millions of people have come knocking on the gates of the Land of Plenty. In developed countries, employees are expected to be flexible. If you want a job, you have to follow the money. But when ultra-flexible labor heads our way from the world's developing countries, we suddenly see them as economic freeloaders. Those seeking asylum are allowed to stay only if they have reason to fear persecution at home based on their religion or birth.

If you think about it, that's downright bizarre.

Take a Somalian toddler. She has a 20% probability of dying before reaching the age of five. Now compare: American frontline soldiers had a mortality rate of 6.7% in the Civil War, 1.8% in World War II, and 0.5% in the Vietnam War.[30] Yet we won't hesitate to send that Somalian toddler back if it turns out her mother isn't a "real" refugee. Back to the Somalian child-mortality front.

In the nineteenth century, inequality was still a matter of class; nowadays, it's a matter of location. "Workers of the world, unite!" was the rallying cry back when all the poor everywhere were more or less equally miserable. But now, as the World Bank's lead economist Branko

Milanovic notes, "Proletarian solidarity is then simply dead because there is no longer such a thing as the global proletariat."[31] In the Land of Plenty, the poverty line is seventeen times higher than in the wilds beyond Cockaigne.[32] Even food-stamp recipients in the U.S. live like royalty compared to the poorest people in the world.

Still, we mostly reserve our outrage for the injustices that happen inside our own national borders. We're indignant that men get paid more than women for doing the same work, and that white Americans earn more than black Americans. But even the 150% racial income gap of the 1930s pales in comparison to the injustices inflicted by our borders. A Mexican citizen living and working in the U.S. earns more than twice as much as a

FIGURE 14   Where Do the Most Children Die?

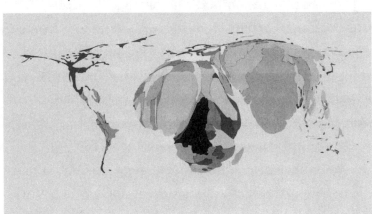

This map shows where child mortality (up to age five) is highest. The bigger the country, the higher its child mortality rate.

Source: Sasi Group (University of Sheffield) and Mark Newman (University of Michigan), 2012

compatriot still living in Mexico. An American earns nearly three times as much for the same work as a Bolivian, even when they are of the same skill level, age, and sex. With a comparable Nigerian, the difference is a factor of 8.5 – and that's adjusted for purchasing power in the two countries.[33]

"[T]he U.S. border effect on the wages of equal intrinsic productivity workers is greater than *any* form of wage discrimination (gender, race, or ethnicity) that has *ever* been measured," observe three economists. It's apartheid on a global scale. In the twenty-first century, the real elite are those born not in the right family or the right class but in the right country.[34] Yet this modern elite is scarcely aware of how lucky it is.

Falsifying the Fallacies

Esther Duflo's deworming treatments are child's play compared to expanding the opportunities for immigration. Opening up our borders, even just a crack, is by far the most powerful weapon we have in the global fight against poverty. But sadly, it's an idea that keeps getting beaten back by the same old faulty arguments.

(1) They're all terrorists
If you follow the news, you couldn't be blamed for thinking so. Because the news consists of what happened

today (BREAKING NEWS: TERROR ATTACK IN PARIS) and not what happens every day (BREAKING NEWS: THE WORLD'S TEMPERATURE RISES BY 0.00005 °C) many believe that terrorism is the biggest threat we face. Yet between 1975 and 2015, the annual odds of being killed in the U.S. in an attack by foreigners or immigrants was just 1 in 3,609,709. In thirty of those forty-one years, no one was killed in such an attack, and apart from the 2,983 people who died in the September 11 terrorist attack, only forty-one other people, an average of one a year, were killed by a foreign-born terrorist in those years.[35]

New research from the University of Warwick on migration flows between 145 countries shows that immigration is actually associated with a *decline* in terrorist acts. "When migrants move from one country to another they take new skills, knowledge and perspectives," the lead researcher writes. "If we subscribe to the belief that economic development is linked to a decrease in extremism then we should expect an increase in migration to have a positive effect."[36]

(2) They're all criminals
Not according to the data. As it happens, people making a new life in the U.S. commit fewer offenses and less frequently end up in prison than the native population. Even as the number of illegal immigrants tripled between 1990 and 2013 to over eleven million, the crime rate reversed

dramatically.[37] The same is true for the U.K.: a few years ago, researchers from the London School of Economics reported that the crime rate had fallen significantly in areas that had experienced mass immigration from Eastern Europe.[38]

So then what about the kids of immigrants? In the U.S. they, too, are less likely than those with established American roots to enter a life of crime. In Europe, it's a different story. To take my native Netherlands as an example, the children of Moroccan immigrants more frequently run afoul of the law. The question, of course, is why? For a long time, research into this question was put off limits by the dictates of political correctness. But in 2004 the first extended study exploring the connection between ethnicity and youth crime got under way in Rotterdam. Ten years later, the results were in. The correlation between ethnic background and crime, it turns out, is precisely zero. None, nothing, *nada*. Youth crime, the report stated, has its origins in the neighborhood where kids grow up. In poor communities, kids from Dutch backgrounds are every bit as likely to engage in criminal activity as those from ethnic minorities.[39]

Subsequent study after study has clinched these findings. In fact, if you adjust for sex, age, and income, ethnicity and criminality prove to be unconnected. "What is more," Dutch researchers wrote in a recent article, "asylum-immigrants are actually underrepresented relative to the native population."[40]

Not that anybody paid much attention to these findings. The new brand of political correctness holds that crime and ethnicity are linked at every level.

(3) They will undermine social cohesion

It looked like a distinctly inconvenient truth, when the famous sociologist Robert Putnam conducted a study in 2000 which revealed that diversity undermines cohesion in communities. Specifically, he found that it makes people less trustful of each other and less inclined to form friendships or do voluntary work. Basically, as Putnam concluded on the basis of a staggering 30,000 interviews, it makes them "pull in like a turtle."[41]

Shocked, he put off releasing his findings for years. When they were finally published in 2007, the effect was – predictably – akin to dropping a bombshell. Hailed as one of the most influential sociological studies of the century, Putnam's research was cited in countless newspapers and reports, and up until this very day he's the go-to source for politicians who doubt the benefits of a multicultural society.

There's only one problem. Putnam's findings were debunked years ago.

A later retrospective analysis of ninety studies found no correlation whatsoever between diversity and social cohesion.[42] Not only that, as sociologists Maria Abascal at Princeton University and Delia Baldassarri at New York University discovered, Putnam had made a critical error. He hadn't taken account of the fact that African Americans and Latinos report lower levels of trust, regardless of where they live.[43] When you adjust for this, Putnam's shocking discovery crumbles to dust.

So, if diversity isn't to blame for the lack of cohesion in modern-day society, what is? The answer is simple: poverty, unemployment, and discrimination. "It is not the diversity of a community that undermines trust," conclude Abascal and Baldassarri, "but rather the disadvantages that people in diverse communities face."

(4) They'll take our jobs

We've all heard this one before. When a huge number of women suddenly entered the labor market in the 1970s, the papers were filled with predictions that the flood of cheaper working women would displace male breadwinners. There is a stubborn misconception that the job market is like a game of musical chairs. It's not. Productive women, seniors, or immigrants won't displace men, young adults, or hardworking citizens from their jobs. In fact, they create *more* employment opportunities. A bigger workforce means more consumption, more demand, more jobs. If we insist on comparing the job market to musical chairs, then it's a version where new party animals keep showing up with more chairs.[44]

(5) Cheap immigrant labor will force our wages down

To disprove this fallacy, we can turn to a study by the Center for Immigration Studies – a think tank that *opposes* immigration – which found that immigration has virtually no effect on wages.[45] Other research even shows that new arrivals lead to an uptick in the earnings of the domestic workforce.[46] Hardworking immigrants boost productivity, which brings paycheck payoffs to everybody.

And that's not all. In an analysis of the period between 1990 and 2000, researchers at the World Bank found that *emigration out of a country* had a negative effect on wages in Europe.[47] Low-skilled workers got the shortest end of the stick. Over these same years, immigrants were more productive and better educated than typically assumed, even serving to motivate less skilled natives to measure up. All too often, moreover, the alternative to hiring immigrants is to outsource work to other countries. And that, ironically, does force wages down.[48]

(6) They're too lazy to work

It is true that in the Land of Plenty we pay people more to put their feet up than they might earn working outside our gates, but there's no evidence that immigrants are more likely to apply for assistance than native citizens. Nor do countries with a strong social safety net attract a higher share of immigrants. In reality, if you correct for income and job status, immigrants actually take *less* advantage of public assistance.[49] Overall, the net value of immigrants is almost wholly positive. In countries like Austria, Ireland, Spain, and England, they even bring in more tax revenue per capita than the native population.[50]

Still not reassured? Countries could also decide not to give immigrants the right to government assistance, or not until after a minimum number of years, or not until they've paid, say, $50,000 in taxes. And you could set up similar parameters if you're concerned they form a political threat or won't integrate. You can create language and culture tests. You can withhold the right to vote. And you can send them back if they don't find a job.

Unfair? Perhaps so. Yet isn't the alternative of keeping people out altogether exponentially more unfair?

(7) They'll never go back

This brings us to a fascinating paradox: Open borders *promote* immigrants' return.[51] Take the border between Mexico and the U.S. In the 1960s, seventy million Mexicans crossed it, but in time 85% returned home. Since the 1980s, and especially since 9/11, the U.S. side of the border has been heavily militarized, with a 2,000-mile wall secured by cameras, sensors, drones, and 20,000 border patrol agents. Nowadays, only 7% of illegal Mexican immigrants ever go back.

"We annually spend billions of taxpayer dollars on border enforcement that is worse than useless – it is counterproductive," observes a sociology professor at Princeton University. "Migrants quite rationally responded to the increased costs and risks by minimizing the number of times they crossed the border."[52] Little wonder that the number of Mexicans who are in the U.S. illegally grew to seven million by 2007 – seven times as many as in 1980.

Get a Move On, Get Rich

Even in a world without border patrols, lots of poor people will stay right where they are. After all, most people feel strong ties to their country, their home, and their family. Furthermore, travel is expensive, and few people in very poor countries can afford to emigrate. Finances aside though, a recent poll revealed that, given the opportunity, 700 million people would prefer to move to a different country.[53]

Opening our borders is not something we can do overnight, of course – nor should it be. Unchecked migration would certainly corrode social cohesion in the Land of Plenty. But we do need to remember one thing: In a world of insane inequality, migration is the most powerful tool for fighting poverty. How do we know? Experience. When life in 1850s Ireland and in 1880s Italy took a dramatic downturn, most poor farmers left; so did 100,000 Dutch people in 1830–80. All of them set their sights across the ocean on the land where opportunity seemed unlimited. The richest country in the world, the United States, is a nation built on immigration.

Now, a century and a half later, hundreds of millions of people around the world are living in veritable open-air prisons. Three-quarters of all border walls and fences were erected after the year 2000. Thousands of miles of barbed wire run between India and Bangladesh. Saudi Arabia is fencing off the entire country. And even as the European

Union continues to open borders between its member states, it is allocating millions to head off flimsy boats on the Mediterranean Sea. This policy hasn't made a dent in the flood of would-be immigrants but is helping human traffickers do a brisk business and is claiming the lives of thousands in the process. Here we are, twenty-five years after the fall of the Berlin Wall, and from Uzbekistan to Thailand, from Israel to Botswana, the world has more barriers than ever.[54]

Humans didn't evolve by staying in one place. Wanderlust is in our blood. Go back a few generations and almost everybody has an immigrant in the family tree. And look at modern China, where twenty years ago the biggest migration in world history led to the influx of hundreds of millions of Chinese from the countryside into its cities. However disruptive, migration has time and again proven to be one of the most powerful drivers of progress.

Open the Gates

Which brings us back to that $134.8 billion a year, $11.2 billion a month, $4,274 a second. It sounds like a vast sum, but it's not. The grand total of global development aid adds up to about what a small European country like the Netherlands spends on healthcare alone. The average American thinks their federal government spends more than a quarter of the national budget on foreign aid, but the real figure is less than 1%.[55] Meanwhile, the gates of the

Land of Plenty remain locked and barred. Hundreds of millions of people are thronging outside this gated community, just like paupers once pounded on the gates of walled cities. Article 13 of the Universal Declaration of Human Rights says everyone has the right to leave their country, but guarantees no one the right to move to the Land of Plenty. And as those who apply for asylum soon discover, the procedure is even more riddled with red tape, more maddening, and more hopeless than applying for public assistance. These days, if you want to get to Cockaigne, you have to work your way not through miles of rice pudding but through a mountain of paperwork.

Perhaps in a century or so we'll look back on these boundaries the way we look back on slavery and apartheid today. One thing is certain however: If we want to make the world a better place, there's no getting around migration. Even just cracking the door would help. If all the developed countries would let in just 3% more immigrants, the world's poor would have $305 billion more to spend, say scientists at the World Bank.[56] That's the combined total of all development aid – times three.

As Joseph Carens, one of the leading advocates of open borders, wrote in 1987, "Free migration may not be immediately achievable, but it is a goal toward which we should strive."[57]

The difficulty lies, not in the new ideas,
but in escaping from the old ones.

John Maynard Keynes (1883–1946)

10

How Ideas Change the World

In the late summer of 1954, a brilliant young psychologist was reading the newspaper when his eye fell on a strange headline on the back page:

PROPHECY FROM PLANET CLARION

CALL TO CITY: FLEE THAT FLOOD.

IT'LL SWAMP US ON DEC 21,

OUTER SPACE TELLS SUBURBANITE.

His interest piqued, the psychologist, whose name was Leon Festinger, read on. "Lake City will be destroyed by a flood from Great Lake just before dawn, Dec. 21." The message came from a homemaker in a Chicago suburb who had received it, she reported, from superior beings on another planet: "These beings have been visiting the earth, she says, in what we call flying saucers."

It was precisely what Festinger had been waiting for. This was a chance to investigate a simple but thorny question that he had been puzzling over for years: What happens

233

when people experience a severe crisis in their convictions? How would this homemaker respond when no flying saucers came to rescue her? What happens when the great flood doesn't materialize? With a little digging, Festinger discovered that the woman, one Dorothy Martin, wasn't the only one convinced that the world was ending on December 21, 1954. Around a dozen of her followers – all intelligent, upstanding Americans – had quit their jobs, sold their possessions, or left their spouses on the strength of their conviction.

Festinger decided to infiltrate the Chicago sect. Right off, he noticed that its members made little effort to persuade other people that the end was near. Salvation was reserved for them, the chosen few. On the morning of December 20, 1954, Mrs. Martin was beamed a new message from above: "At the hour of midnight you shall be put into parked cars and taken to a place where ye shall be put aboard a porch [flying saucer]."

The excited group settled in to await their ascendency to the heavens.

The Evening of December 20, 1954

11:15 p.m.: Mrs. Martin receives a message telling the group to put on their coats and prepare.

12:00 a.m.: Nothing happens.

12:05 a.m.: One of the believers notices another clock in

the room reads 11:55 p.m. The group agrees it is not yet midnight.

12:10 a.m.:   Message from aliens: The flying saucers are delayed.

12:15 a.m.:   The telephone rings several times: journalists calling to check if the world has ended yet.

2:00 a.m.:   One of the younger followers, who expected to be a couple light years away by now, recalls that his mother was planning to call the police if he wasn't home by 2 a.m. The others assure him that his departure is a worthy sacrifice to save the group, and he leaves.

4:00 a.m.:   One of the believers says: "I've burned every bridge. I've turned my back on the world. I can't afford to doubt. I have to believe."

4:45 a.m.:   Mrs. Martin gets another message: God has decided to spare the Earth. Together, the small group of believers has spread so much "light" on this night that the Earth is saved.

4:50 a.m.:   One last message from above: The aliens want the good news "to be released immediately to the newspapers." Armed with this new mission, the believers inform all the local papers and radio stations before daybreak.

When Prophecies Fail

"A man with a conviction is a hard man to change." So opens Leon Festinger's account of these events in *When Prophecy Fails*, first published in 1956 and a seminal text in social psychology to this day. "Tell him you disagree and he turns away," Festinger continues. "Show him facts or figures and he questions your sources. Appeal to logic and he fails to see your point."

It's easy to scoff at the story of Mrs. Martin and her believers, but the phenomenon Festinger describes is one that none of us is immune to. "Cognitive dissonance," he termed it. When reality clashes with our deepest convictions, we'd rather recalibrate reality than amend our worldview. Not only that, we become even more rigid in our beliefs than before.[1]

Mind you, we tend to be quite flexible when it comes to practical matters. Most of us are even willing to accept advice on how to remove a grease stain or chop a cucumber. No, it's when our political, ideological, or religious ideas are at stake that we get the most stubborn. We tend to dig in our heels when someone challenges our opinions about criminal punishment, premarital sex, or global warming. These are ideas to which people tend to get attached, and that makes it difficult to let them go. Doing so affects our sense of identity and position in social groups – in our churches or families or circles of friends.

One factor that certainly is *not* involved is stupidity. Researchers at Yale University have shown that educated people are more unshakable in their convictions than anybody.[2] After all, an education gives you tools to defend your opinions. Intelligent people are highly practiced in finding arguments, experts, and studies that underpin their preexisting beliefs, and the Internet has made it easier than ever to be consumers of our own opinions, with another piece of evidence always just a mouse-click away.

Smart people, concludes the American journalist Ezra Klein, don't use their intellect to obtain the correct answer; they use it to obtain what they *want* to be the answer.[3]

When My Clock Struck Midnight

I have something to confess. In the course of writing the sixth chapter of this book ("A Fifteen-Hour Workweek"), I stumbled across an article titled "Shorter Workweek May Not Increase Well-Being."[4] It was a piece in the *New York Times* about a South Korean study which claimed that a 10% shorter workweek had not made employees happier. Additional Googling led me to an article in the London *Telegraph* which suggested that working less might be downright bad for our health.[5]

Suddenly I was Dorothy Martin and my clock had struck midnight. Immediately, I mobilized my defense mechanisms. To begin with, I had my doubts about the source: The *Telegraph* is a conservative newspaper, so how seriously should I take that article? Plus, there was that "may" in the *New York Times* headline. How conclusive were the study findings really? Even my stereotypes kicked in: Those South Koreans, they're such workaholics – they probably kept working off the clock even when they reported fewer hours. Moreover, *happiness*? How exactly do you measure that?

Satisfied, I pushed the study aside. I'd convinced myself it couldn't be relevant.[6]

I'll give you another example. In Chapter 2, I laid out the arguments in favor of universal basic income. This is a conviction in which I have invested a lot over the past few years. The first article I wrote on the topic garnered nearly a million views and was picked up by the *Washington Post*. I gave lectures about universal basic income and made a case for it on Dutch television. Enthusiastic emails poured in. Not long ago, I even heard someone refer to me as "Mr. Basic Income." Slowly but surely, my opinion has come to define my personal and professional identity. I do earnestly believe that a universal basic income is an idea whose time has come. I've researched the issue extensively, and that's the direction the evidence points in. But, if I'm being honest, I sometimes wonder if I'd even let myself notice if the evidence were pointing another way. Would I be observant enough – or brave enough – to have a change of heart?

The Power of an Idea

"Keep building your castles in the sky," a friend quipped a while back after I sent him a couple of my articles on a shorter workweek and a universal basic income. I could understand where he was coming from. After all, what's the point of crazy new ideas when politicians can't even manage to balance a budget?

That's when I began to ask myself whether new ideas can genuinely change the world.

Now, your (very reasonable) gut response might be: They can't – people will stubbornly stick to the old ideas that they're comfortable with. The thing is, we know that ideas have changed over time. Yesterday's avant-garde is today's common sense. Simon Kuznets willed the idea of the GDP into being. The randomistas upset the apple cart of foreign aid by forcing it to prove its efficacy. The question is not *can* new ideas defeat old ones; the question is *how*.

Research suggests that sudden shocks can work wonders. James Kuklinski, a political scientist at the University of Illinois, discovered that people are most likely to change their opinions if you confront them with new and disagreeable facts as directly as possible.[7] Take the recent success of right-wing politicians who were already warning of "the Islamic threat" back in the 1990s, but didn't get much attention until the shocking destruction of the Twin Towers on September 11, 2001. Viewpoints that had once been fringe suddenly became a collective obsession.

If it is true that ideas don't change things gradually but in fits and starts – in shocks – then the basic premise of our democracy, our journalism, and our education is all wrong. It would mean, in essence, that the Enlightenment model of how people change their opinions – through information-gathering and reasoned deliberation – is really a buttress for the status quo. It would mean that those who swear by rationality, nuance, and compromise fail to grasp how ideas govern the world. A worldview is not a Lego set where a block is added here, removed there. It's a fortress that is defended tooth and nail, with all possible reinforcements, until the pressure becomes so overpowering that the walls cave in.

Over the same months that Leon Festinger was infiltrating Mrs. Martin's sect, the American psychologist Solomon Asch demonstrated that group pressure can even cause us to ignore what we can plainly see with our own eyes. In a now-famous experiment, he showed test subjects three lines on a card and asked them which one was longest. When the other people in the room (all Asch's coworkers, unbeknown to the subject) gave the same answer, the subject did, too – even when it was clearly erroneous.[8]

It's no different in politics. Political scientists have established that how people vote is determined less by their perceptions about their own lives than by their conceptions of society. We're not particularly interested in what government can do for us personally; we want to know what it can do for us all. When we cast our vote, we do so not just for ourselves, but for the group we want to belong to.

But Solomon Asch made another discovery. A single opposing voice can make all the difference. When just one other person in the group stuck to the truth, the test subjects were more likely to trust the evidence of their own senses. Let this be an encouragement to all those who feel like a lone voice crying out in the wilderness: Keep on building those castles in the sky. Your time will come.

Long Was the Night

In 2008, it seemed as if that time had finally come when we were confronted with the biggest case of cognitive dissonance since the 1930s. On September 15, the investment bank Lehman Brothers filed for bankruptcy. Suddenly, the whole global banking sector seemed poised to tumble like a row of dominoes. In the months that followed, one free-market dogma after another crashed and burned.

Former Federal Reserve Chair Alan Greenspan, once dubbed the "Oracle" and the "Maestro," was gobsmacked. "Not only have individual financial institutions become less vulnerable to shocks from underlying risk factors," he had confidently asserted in 2004, "but also the financial system as a whole has become more resilient."[9] When

Greenspan retired in 2006, everyone assumed he would be immortalized in history's financial hall of fame.

In a House Committee hearing two years later, the broken banker admitted that he was "in a state of shocked disbelief." Greenspan's faith in capitalism had taken a severe beating. "I have found a flaw. I don't know how significant or permanent it is. But I have been very distressed by that fact."[10] When a congressman asked him if he had been misled by his own ideas, Greenspan replied, "That's precisely the reason I was shocked because I'd been going for 40 years or so with considerable evidence that it was working exceptionally well."

The lesson of December 21, 1954 is that everything centers on that one moment of crisis. When the clock strikes midnight, what happens next? A crisis can provide an opening for new ideas, but it can also shore up old convictions.

So what happened after September 15, 2008? The Occupy movement briefly galvanized people, but quickly ebbed. Meanwhile, left-leaning political parties lost elections across most of Europe. Greece and Italy more or less canned democracy altogether and rolled out neoliberal-tinted reforms to please their creditors, trimming government and boosting labor market flexibility. In northern Europe, too, governments proclaimed a new age of austerity.

And Alan Greenspan? When, a few years later, a reporter asked him if there had been any error in his ideas, his reply was resolute: "Not at all. I think that there is no alternative."[11]

Fast forward to today: Fundamental reform of the banking sector has yet to happen. On Wall Street, bankers are seeing the highest bonus payments since the crash.[12] And the banks' capital buffers are as minuscule as ever. Joris Luyendijk, a journalist at the *Guardian* who spent two years looking under the hood of London's financial sector, summed up the experience in 2013 as follows: "It's like standing at Chernobyl and seeing they've restarted the reactor but still have the same old management."[13]

You have to wonder: Was the cognitive dissonance from 2008 even big enough? Or was it *too* big? Had we invested too much in our old convictions? Or were there simply no alternatives?

This last possibility is the most worrying of all.

The word "crisis" comes from ancient Greek and literally means to "separate" or "sieve." A crisis, then, should be a moment of truth, the juncture at which a fundamental choice is made. But it almost seems that back in 2008 we were unable to make that choice. When we suddenly found ourselves facing the collapse of the entire banking sector, there were no real alternatives available; all we could do was keep plodding down the same path.

Perhaps, then, crisis isn't really the right word for our current condition. It's more like we're in a coma. That's ancient Greek, too. It means "deep, dreamless sleep."

Capitalist Resistance Fighters

It's all deeply ironic, if you think about it.

If there were ever two people who dedicated their lives to building castles in the sky with preternatural certainty that they would someday be proven right, it was the founders of neoliberal thought. I'm an admirer of them both: the slippery philosopher Friedrich Hayek and the public intellectual Milton Friedman.

Nowadays, "neoliberal" is a put-down leveled at anybody who doesn't agree with the left. Hayek and Friedman, however, were proud neoliberals who saw it as their duty to reinvent liberalism.[14] "We must make the building of a free society once more an intellectual adventure," Hayek wrote. "What we lack is a liberal Utopia."[15]

Even if you believe them to be villains who made greed fashionable and are to blame for the financial crisis that left millions of people in dire straits — even then, there's a lot you can learn from Friedrich Hayek and Milton Friedman.

One was born in Vienna, the other in New York. Both were firm believers in the power of ideas. For many years, both belonged to a small minority, a sect almost, that existed outside the cocoon of mainstream thought. Together, they tore apart that cocoon, upending the world in a way dictators and billionaires can only dream of. They set about shredding the life's work of their archrival, the British economist John Maynard Keynes. Seemingly the only thing they had in common with Keynes was the belief that the ideas of economists and philosophers are stronger forces than the vested interests of business leaders and politicians.

This particular story begins on April 1, 1947, not quite a year after Keynes' death, when forty philosophers, historians, and economists converged in the small village of Mont Pèlerin in Switzerland. Some had traveled for weeks, crossing oceans to get there. In later years, they would be known as the Mont Pèlerin Society.

All forty thinkers who came to this Swiss village were encouraged to speak their minds, and together they formed a corps of capitalist resistance fighters against socialist supremacy. "There are, of course, very few people left today who are not socialists," Hayek, the event's initiator, had once lamented. At a time when the provisions of the New Deal had pushed even the United States toward more socialistic policies, a defense of the free market was still seen as downright revolutionary, and Hayek felt "hopelessly out of tune with his time."[16]

Milton Friedman was also at the meeting of minds. "Here I was, a young, naive provincial American," Friedman later recalled, "meeting people from all over the world, all dedicated to the same liberal principles as we were; all beleaguered in their own countries, yet among them scholars, some already internationally famous, others destined to be."[17] In fact, no fewer than eight members of the Mont Pèlerin Society would go on to win Nobel Prizes.

However, in 1947 no one could have predicted such a star-studded future. Large swaths of Europe lay in ruins. Reconstruction efforts were colored by Keynesian ideals: employment for all, curbing the free market, and regulation of banks. The war state became the welfare state. Yet it was during those same years that neoliberal thought began gaining traction thanks to the efforts of the Mont Pèlerin Society, a group that would go on to become one of the leading think tanks of the twentieth century. "Together, they helped precipitate a global policy transformation with implications that will continue to reverberate for decades," says the historian Angus Burgin.[18]

In the 1970s, Hayek handed the presidency of the Society over to Friedman. Under the leadership of this diminutive, bespectacled American whose energy and enthusiasm surpassed even that of his Austrian predecessor, the society radicalized. Essentially, there wasn't a problem around that Friedman didn't blame on government. And the solution, in every case, was the free market. Unemployment? Get rid of the minimum wage. Natural disaster? Get corporations to organize a relief effort. Poor schools? Privatize education. Expensive healthcare? Privatize that, too, and ditch public oversight while we're at it. Substance abuse? Legalize drugs and let the market work its magic.

Friedman deployed every means possible to spread his ideas, building a repertoire of lectures, op-eds, radio interviews, TV appearances, books, and even a documentary.

In the preface to his bestselling *Capitalism and Freedom*, he wrote that it is the duty of thinkers to keep offering alternatives. Ideas that seem "politically impossible" today may one day become "politically inevitable."

All that remained was to await the critical moment. "Only a crisis – actual or perceived – produces real change," Friedman explained. "When that crisis occurs, the actions that are taken depend on the ideas that are lying around."[19] The crisis came in October 1973, when the Organization of Arab Petroleum Exporting Countries raised oil prices by 70% and imposed an oil embargo on the U.S. and The Netherlands. Inflation went through the roof and the Western economies spiraled into recession. "Stagflation," as this effect was called, wasn't even possible in Keynesian theory. Friedman, however, had predicted it.

For the rest of his life, Friedman never stopped emphasizing that his success would have been inconceivable without the groundwork laid since 1947. The rise of neoliberalism played out like a relay race, with think tanks passing the baton to journalists, who handed it off to politicians. Running the anchor leg were two of the most powerful leaders in the Western world, Ronald Reagan and Margaret Thatcher. When asked what she considered to be her greatest victory, Thatcher's reply was "New Labour": Under the leadership of neoliberal Tony Blair, even her social democratic rivals in the Labour Party had come around to her worldview.

In less than fifty years, an idea once dismissed as radical and marginal had come to rule the world.

The Lesson of Neoliberalism

Some argue that these days it hardly matters any more who you vote for. Though we still have a right and a left, neither side seems to have a very clear plan for the future. In an ironic twist of fate, the neoliberalist brainchild of two men who devoutly believed in the power of ideas has now put a lockdown on the development of new ones. It would seem that we have arrived at "the end of history," with liberal democracy as the last stop and the "free consumer" as the terminus of our species.[20]

By the time Friedman was named president of the Mont Pèlerin Society in 1970, most of its philosophers and historians had already decamped, the debates having become overly technical and economic.[21] In hindsight, Friedman's arrival marked the dawn of an era in which economists would become the leading thinkers of the Western world. We are still in that era today.[22]

We inhabit a world of managers and technocrats. "Let's just concentrate on solving the problems," they say. "Let's just focus on making ends meet." Political decisions are continually presented as a matter of exigency — as neutral and objective events, as though there were no other choice. Keynes observed this tendency emerging even in his own day. "Practical men, who believe themselves to be quite exempt from any intellectual influences," he wrote, "are usually the slaves of some defunct economist."[23]

When Lehman Brothers collapsed on September 15, 2008, and inaugurated the biggest crisis since the 1930s, there were no real alternatives to hand. No one had laid the groundwork. For years, intellectuals, journalists, and politicians had all firmly maintained that we'd reached the end of the age of "big narratives" and that it was time to trade in ideologies for pragmatism.

Naturally, we should still take pride in the liberty that generations before us fought for and won. But the question is, what is the value of free speech when we no longer have anything worthwhile to say? What's the point of freedom of association when we no longer feel any sense of affiliation? What purpose does freedom of religion serve when we no longer believe in anything?

On the one hand, the world is still getting richer, safer, and healthier. Every day, more and more people are arriving in Cockaigne. That's a huge triumph. On the other hand, it's high time that we, the inhabitants of the Land of Plenty, staked out a new utopia. Let's rehoist the sails. "Progress is the realisation of Utopias," Oscar Wilde wrote many years ago.[24] A fifteen-hour workweek, universal basic income, and a world without borders . . . They're all crazy dreams – but for how much longer?

People now doubt that "human ideas and beliefs are the main movers of history," as Hayek argued back when neoliberalism was still in its infancy. "We all find it so difficult to imagine that our belief [*sic*] might be different from what they in fact are."[25] It could easily take a generation, he asserted, before new ideas prevail. For this very reason, we need thinkers who not only are patient, but also have "the courage to be 'utopian.'"

Let this be the lesson of Mont Pèlerin. Let this be the mantra of everyone who dreams of a better world, so that we don't once again hear the clock strike midnight and find ourselves just sitting around, empty-handed, waiting for an extraterrestrial salvation that will never come.

Ideas, however outrageous, have changed the world, and they will again. "Indeed," wrote Keynes, "the world is ruled by little else."[26]

Utopia is on the horizon. I move two steps closer;
it moves two steps further away. I walk another ten
steps and the horizon runs ten steps further away.
As much as I may walk, I'll never reach it. So
what's the point of utopia? The point is this: to
keep walking.

Eduardo Galeano (1940–2015)

Epilogue

For the last time, then: how do we make utopia *real*? How do we take these ideas and implement them?

The path from the ideal to the real is one that never ceases to fascinate me. As the Prussian statesman Otto von Bismarck famously said, "Politics is the art of the possible." That impression certainly seems to hold if you follow the news from places like Washington and Westminster. But there's another form of politics that is much more important. I'm talking about Politics with a capital P, one that's not about rules, but about revolution. Not about the art of the possible, but about making the impossible inevitable.

This political arena has room for many more politicians, from garbage men to bankers, from scientists to shoemakers, from writers to you, reading this book. And this Politics is diametrically opposed to politics with a lowercase p. Where politics acts to reaffirm the status quo, Politics breaks free.

The Window of Overton

It was Joseph Overton, an American lawyer, who first explained the mechanisms of uppercase Politics in the 1990s. He began with a simple question: Why is it that so many good ideas don't get taken seriously?

Overton realized that politicians, provided they want to be reelected, can't permit themselves viewpoints that are seen as too extreme. In order to hold power, they have to keep their ideas within the margins of what's acceptable. This window of acceptability is populated by schemes that are rubber-stamped by the experts, tallied up by statistics services, and have good odds of making it into the law books.

FIGURE 15   The Overton Window

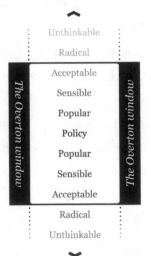

Source: 'Overton Window' by Hydrargyrum is licensed under CC BY-SA 2.0

Anybody who forays outside the "Overton window" faces a rocky road. He or she will quickly be branded as "unrealistic" or "unreasonable" by the media, the fearsome gatekeepers of the window. Television, for example, offers little time or space to present fundamentally different opinions. Instead, talk shows feed us an endless merry-go-round of the same people saying the same things.

And yet, despite all this, a society can change completely in a few decades. The Overton window can shift. A classic strategy for achieving this is to proclaim ideas so shocking and subversive that anything less radical suddenly sounds sensible. In other words, to make the radical reasonable, you merely have to stretch the bounds of the radical.

Donald Trump in the U.S., Boris Johnson in the U.K., and the Islamophobic Geert Wilders in my own country have all mastered this art to perfection. If they are not always taken seriously, they have certainly pulled the Overton window into their camps. In fact, for several decades now this window has been migrating to the right on both economic and cultural issues. With neoliberal economists having bagged the economic debate, the right has reached out to take control of the discourse on religion and migration, too.

What we are witnessing is a colossal change in course. Historically, Politics was the preserve of the left. *Be realistic, demand the impossible!* rang the rallying cry of the Paris demonstrators in 1968. The end of slavery, the emancipation of women, the rise of the welfare state – all were progressive ideas that started out as crazy and "irrational" but were ultimately accepted as basic common sense.

These days, however, the left seems to have forgotten the art of Politics. Worse, many left-wing thinkers and politicians attempt to quell radical sentiments among their own rank and file in their terror of losing votes. This attitude is one I've begun to think of in recent years as the phenomenon of "underdog socialism."

It's an international phenomenon, observable across the globe among legions of left-wing thinkers and movements, from trade unions to political parties, from columnists to college professors. The worldview of the underdog socialist is that the neoliberals have mastered the game of reason, judgment, and statistics, leaving the left with emotion. Its heart is in the right place. Underdog socialists have a surfeit of compassion and find prevailing policies deeply unfair. Seeing the welfare state crumbling to dust, they rush in to salvage what they can. But when push comes to shove, the underdog socialist caves in to the arguments of the opposition, always accepting the premise on which the debate takes place.

"National debt is out of control," they concede, "but we can make more programs income-dependent."

"Fighting poverty is terribly expensive," reason the underdog socialists, "but it's part of being a civilized nation."

"Taxes are high," they lament, "but each according to his ability."

The underdog socialist forgets that the real problem isn't the national debt, but overextended households and businesses. He forgets that fighting poverty is an investment that pays off in spades. And he forgets that, all the while, the bankers and the lawyers are polishing turds at the expense of waste collectors and nurses.

Reining in and restraining the opposition, that's the sole remaining mission of the underdog socialist. Anti-privatization, anti-establishment, anti-austerity. Given everything that they're against, one is left to wonder, what are underdog socialists actually *for?*

Time and again, they side with society's unfortunates: poor people, dropouts, asylum seekers, the disabled, and the discriminated against. They decry Islamophobia, homophobia, and racism. They obsess over the proliferation of "rifts" dividing the world into blue-collar and white-collar, poverty and wealth, ordinary people and the one-percenters, and vainly seek to "reconnect" with a constituency that has long since packed its bags.

But the underdog socialists' biggest problem isn't that they're wrong. Their biggest problem is that they are dull. Dull as a doorknob. They've got no story to tell, nor even any language to convey it in.

And, too often, it seems as if those on the left actually like losing. As if all the failure, the doom, and the atrocities mainly serve to prove they were right all along. "There's a kind of activism," Rebecca Solnit remarks in her book *Hope in the Dark*, "that's more about bolstering identity than achieving results." One thing Donald Trump understands very well is that most people prefer to be on the winning side. ("We're going to win so much. You're going to get tired of winning.") Most people resent the pity and paternalism of the Good Samaritan.

Sadly, the underdog socialist has forgotten that the story of the left ought to be a narrative of hope and progress. By that I don't mean a narrative that only excites a few hipsters who get their kicks philosophizing about "post-capitalism" or "intersectionality" after reading some long-winded tome. The greatest sin of the academic left is that it has become fundamentally aristocratic, writing in bizarre jargon that makes simple matters dizzyingly complex. If you can't explain your ideal to a fairly intelligent twelve-year-old, after all, it's probably your own fault. What we need is a narrative that speaks to millions of ordinary people.

It all starts with reclaiming the language of progress.

Reforms? Hell, yes. Let's give the financial sector a real overhaul. Force banks to build bigger buffers so they don't topple as soon as another crisis rolls around. Break them up, if need be, so that next time taxpayers won't be left footing the bill because the banks are "too big to fail." Expose and destroy all tax havens, so that the rich can finally be made to cough up their fair share and their accountants can do something worthwhile.

Meritocracy? Bring it on. Let's finally pay people according to their real contributions. Waste collectors, nurses, and teachers would get a substantial raise, obviously, while quite a few lobbyists, lawyers, and bankers would see their salaries dive into the negatives. If you want to do a job that hurts the public, go right ahead. But you'll have to pay for the privilege with a heftier tax.

Innovation? Totally. Even now, a vast amount of talent is going wasted. If Ivy League grads once went on to jobs in science, public service, and education, these days they're far more likely to opt for banking, law, or ad proliferators like Google and Facebook. Stop for a moment to ponder the billions of tax dollars being pumped into training society's best brains, all so they can learn how to exploit other people as efficiently as possible, and it makes your head spin. Imagine how different things might be if our generation's best and brightest were to double down on the greatest challenges of our times. Climate change, for example, and the aging population, and inequality . . . Now that would be real innovation.[1]

Efficiency? That's the whole point. Think about it: every dollar invested in a homeless person returns triple or more in savings on healthcare, police, and court costs. Just imagine what the eradication of child poverty might achieve. Solving these kinds of problems is a whole lot more efficient than "managing" them, which costs significantly more in the long run.

Cut the nanny state? Spot on. Let's ax those senseless, overweening reemployment courses for the out of work (the ones that actually *prolong* unemployment) and let's quit drilling and degrading benefit recipients. Let's give everybody a basic income – venture capital for the people – empowering us to plot the course of our *own* lives.

Freedom? Sing it, sister. As we speak, upwards of a third of the workforce is stuck in "bullshit jobs" considered meaningless by the people doing them. Not long ago I gave a talk to a few hundred consultants about the rise of pointless work. To my amazement, there was no hissing from the audience. Not only that, over drinks afterwards more than one person confided to me that some high-paying inconsequential assignment had actually given them the financial freedom to do a less lucrative yet worthwhile engagement.

These stories reminded me of all the freelance journalists who get sucked into doing PR pieces for companies they despise to subsidize their critical investigative work (on precisely the same sorts of companies). Has the world been turned on its head? Apparently, in modern capitalism we finance the things we find genuinely fulfilling with . . . bullshit.

The time has come to redefine our concept of "work." When I call for a shorter workweek, I'm not pushing for long, lethargic weekends. I'm calling for us to spend more time on the things that truly matter to us. A few years ago, Australian writer Bronnie Ware published a book titled *The Top Five Regrets of the Dying*, about patients she had tended during her nursing career.[2] And guess what? No one said he or she would have liked to pay closer attention to coworkers' PowerPoint presentations or to have brain-stormed a little more on disruptive co-creation in the network society. The biggest regret was: "I wish I'd had the courage to live a life true to myself, not the life others expec-ted of me." Number two: "I wish I didn't work so hard."

Across the spectrum from left to right we're hearing about the need for more work and more jobs. For most politicians and economists, employment is morally neutral: the more, the better. I'd argue that it's time for a new labor movement. One that fights not only for more jobs and higher wages, but more importantly for work that has intrinsic value. Then we'll see unemployment *rise* when we spend more time on mind-numbing market-ing, asinine administration, and polluting junk, and *drop* when we start investing more time in the things that fulfill us.

Two Final Pieces of Advice

But first, the underdog socialists will have to stop wallow-ing in their moral superiority and outdated ideas. Everyone who reckons themselves progressive should be a beacon of not just energy but ideas, not only indignation but hope, and equal parts ethics and hard sell. Ultimately, what the underdog socialist lacks is the most vital ingredient for political change: the conviction that there truly is a better way. That utopia really is within reach.

I don't mean to suggest that it will be easy, mastering Politics with a capital P. Quite the reverse. The first and major hurdle lies in being taken seriously at all. This has been my own experience over the last three years as I argued the case for a universal basic income, a shorter working week, and the eradication of poverty. Time after time, I was told that these ideas were unrealistic, unaffordable, or downright dumb.

It took a while before I realized that my so-called lack of realism had little to do with actual flaws in my reasoning. Calling my ideas "unrealistic" was simply a shorthand way of saying they didn't fit the status quo. And the best way to shut people up is to make them feel silly. It's even better than censorship, because people are almost guaranteed to hold their tongues.

When I first began writing about basic income, most people had never heard of it. But now, just three years later, the idea is everywhere. Finland and Canada have both announced large experiments. It's catching on in a big way in Silicon Valley. GiveDirectly (the organization mentioned in Chapter 2) is launching a major basic income study in Kenya. And in my own country, the Netherlands, no fewer than twenty municipalities are putting basic income into action.

The impetus for this sudden flurry of interest was a referendum held in Switzerland on June 5, 2016. Perhaps only a couple of hundred Swiss knew what basic income was five years ago, but today it's a whole different story.

Of course, the proposal was voted down by a sizable majority, but let's not forget that as recently as 1959 the greater share of Swiss men also voted no on another bizarre utopian proposition: women's right to vote. When a second referendum came around in 1971, most were in favor.

My point is this: the Swiss referendum is not the end of this discussion, but the beginning. Since the first Dutch edition of my book was published, I have talked about it in Paris, in Montreal, in New York, in Dublin, and in London. Everywhere I went I encountered an enthusiasm for basic income that is born of precisely the same factors. Since the global financial crash of 2008 and the dawning era of Brexit and Trump, more and more people are hungry for a real, radical antidote to both xenophobia and inequality. For a whole new map of the world. For a new source of hope. In short, for a new Utopia.

So, in closing, I'd like to offer two final pieces of advice for everybody who is ready to put the ideas proposed in these pages into action. First, realize that there are more people out there like you. Lots and lots of people. I've met countless readers who told me that while they believe absolutely in the ideas from this book, they see the world as a corrupt and greedy place. My answer to them was this: turn off the TV, look around you, and *organize*. Most people really do have their hearts in the right place.

And second, my advice is to cultivate a thicker skin. Don't let anyone tell you what's what. If we want to change the world, we need to be unrealistic, unreasonable, and impossible. Remember: those who called for the abolition of slavery, for suffrage for women, and for same-sex marriage were also once branded lunatics. Until history proved them right.

NOTES

CHAPTER I THE RETURN OF UTOPIA

1   Extreme poverty means living on less than $1.25 a day, which is
    just enough to survive. See François Bourguignon and Christian
    Morrisson, "Inequality among World Citizens: 1820–1992,"
    American Economic Review (September 2002). http://piketty.pse
    .ens.fr/files/BourguignonMorrisson2002.pdf.

2   In the Netherlands, someone who is homeless receives around
    $10,000 a year in government assistance. The per capita GNP of
    1950s Holland, corrected for purchasing power and inflation, was
    $7,408 (according to figures from gapminder.org). From 1600 to
    1800, it was between $2,000 and $2,500.

3   See the figures presented by the historians Angus Maddison,
    J. Bolt, and J. L. van Zanden, "The First Update of the Maddison
    Project; Re-Estimating Growth Before 1820," *Maddison Project
    Working Paper 4* (2013). http://www.ggdc.net/maddison/
    maddison-project/home.htm.

4   Herman Pleij, *Dromen van Cocagne. Middeleeuwse fantasieën over
    het volmaakte leven* (1997), p. 11.

5   World Health Organization, "Obesity and overweight," Fact
    sheet No. 311 (March 2013). http://www.who.int/mediacentre/
    factsheets/fs311/en/.

6   Manuel Eisner, "Long-Term Historical Trends in Violent
    Crime," University of Chicago (2003), table 2. http://www.vrc
    .crim.cam.ac.uk/vrcresearch/paperdownload/manuel-eisner-
    historical-trends-in-violence.pdf.

7   World Bank, "An update to the World Bank's estimates
    of consumption poverty in the developing world" (2012).

http://siteresources.worldbank.org/INTPOVCALNET/
Resources/Global_Poverty_Update_2012_02-29-12.pdf.

8   J.O.'s, "Development in Africa: Growth and other good things,"
    Economist (May 1, 2013). http://www.economist.com/blogs/
    baobab/2013/05/development-africa.

9   UN News Centre, "Deputy UN chief calls for urgent action to
    tackle global sanitation crisis" (March 21, 2013). http://www
    .un.org/apps/news/story.asp?NewsID=44452.

10 According to figures from Internet Live Stats. See: http://www
    .internetlivestats.com.

11 According to the World Health Organization, the average life
    expectancy in Africa for those born in 2000 was fifty years.
    In 2012, it was fifty-eight years. http://www.who.int/gho/
    mortality_burden_disease/life_tables/situation_trends_
    text/en/.

12 According to figures from the World Bank: http://apps.who.int/
    gho/data/view.main.700?lang=en.

13 The individual average daily caloric intake rose from 2,600 in
    1990 to 2,840 in 2012 (in sub-Saharan Africa from 2,180 to
    2,380). Miina Porka et al., "From Food Insufficiency towards
    Trade Dependency: A Historical Analysis of Global Food
    Availability," *Plos One* (December 18, 2013). http://www.ncbi
    .nlm.nih.gov/pubmed/24367545.

14 Bjørn Lomborg, "Setting the Right Global Goals," *Project
    Syndicate* (May 20, 2014). https://www.project-syndicate
    .org/commentary/bj-rn-lomborg-identifies-the-areas-in-
    which-increased-development-spending-can-do-the-most-
    good.

15 One is Audrey de Grey of Cambridge University, who gave a
    TED Talk on this topic: http://www.ted.com/talks/aubrey_
    de_grey_says_we_can_avoid_aging.

16 Peter F. Orazem, "Challenge Paper: Education," Copenhagen
    Consensus Center (April 2014). http://copenhagenconsensus
    .com/publication/education.

17 "Where have all the burglars gone?" *Economist* (July 18, 2013).
    http://www.economist.com/news/briefing/21582041-rich-world-
    seeing-less-and-less-crime-even-face-high-unemployment-and-
    economic.

18   Francis Fukuyama, "The End of History?" *National Interest* (Summer 1989). http://ps321.community.uaf.edu/files/2012/10/Fukuyama-End-of-history-article.pdf.

19   Andrew Cohut et al., *Economies of Emerging Markets Better Rated During Difficult Times. Global Downturn Takes Heavy Toll; Inequality Seen as Rising*, Pew Research (May 23, 2013), p. 23. http://www.pewglobal.org/files/2013/05/Pew-Global-Attitudes-Economic-Report-FINAL-May-23-20131.pdf.

20   Lyman Tower Sargent, *Utopianism. A Very Short Introduction* (2010), p. 12. Take this Buddhist variation on the Land of Plenty: "Whenever they wish to take nourishment, they have only to place this rice upon a certain great stone, from which a flame instantly issues, [and] dresses their food."

21   Ian C. Storey (trans.), *Fragments of Old Comedy*, Vol. III: *Philonicus to Xenophon. Adespota.* Loeb Classical Library, 515 (2011), p. 291. https://www.loebclassics.com/view/telecides-testimonia_fragments/2011/pb_LCL515.291.xml.

22   Russell Jacoby, *Picture Imperfect. Utopian Thought for an Anti-Utopian Age* (2005). Also see my last (Dutch) book, *De geschiedenis van de vooruitgang* (2013), in which I discuss Jacoby's distinction between the two forms of utopian thought.

23   George Kateb, quoted in: Lyman Tower Sargent, *Utopianism. A Very Short Introduction* (2010), p. 107. Even so, anyone who dips into Thomas More's utopia will come away unpleasantly surprised. More described a thoroughly authoritarian society, whose inhabitants were sold into slavery for even relatively minor missteps. Yet it's crucial to realize that all this would have seemed like a breath of fresh air to the medieval peasant. Slavery was positively lenient compared to the customary repertoire of hanging, quartering, and burning at the stake. But it's also worth noting that many commentators didn't catch on to More's intended irony because they didn't read his book in the original Latin. Our tour guide in More's utopia, for example, is named Hythlodaeus, which translates as "speaker of nonsense."

24   Branko Milanovic, "Global Inequality: From Class to Location, from Proletarians to Migrants," World Bank Policy Research Working Paper (September 2011). http://elibrary.worldbank.org/doi/book/10.1596/1813-9450-5820.

25 On the U.S., see: Bryan Caplan, "How Dems and Reps Differ: Against the Conventional Wisdom," *Library of Economics and Liberty* (September 7, 2008). http://econlog.econlib.org/archives/2008/09/how_dems_and_re.html. On England, see: James Adams, Jane Green, and Caitlin Milazzo, "Has the British Public Depolarized Along with Political Elites? An American Perspective on British Public Opinion," *Comparative Political Studies* (April 2012). http://cps.sagepub.com/content/45/4/507.

26 See Alain de Botton, *Religion for Atheists* (2012), Chapter 3.

27 Which is not to say it's by choice: Study upon study has demonstrated that the vast majority of the populations of all developed countries are concerned about materialism, individualism, and the harsh modern-day culture. In the U.S., a nationwide poll showed that most Americans want society to "move away from greed and excess toward a way of life more centred on values, community and family." Quoted in: Richard Wilkinson and Kate Pickett, *The Spirit Level. Why Equality Is Better for Everyone* (2010), p. 4.

28 Paraphrased from the movie *Fight Club*, Professor of Sustainable Development Tim Jackson, and hundreds of other variations on this quote.

29 Quoted in: Don Peck, "How a New Jobless Era Will Transform America," *Atlantic* (March 2010). http://www.theatlantic.com/magazine/archive/2010/03/how-a-new-jobless-era-will-transform-america/307919/.

30 Wilkinson and Pickett, *The Spirit Level*, p. 34.

31 World Health Organization, "Health for the World's Adolescents. A second chance in the second decade' (June 2014). http://apps.who.int/iris/bitstream/10665/112750/1/WHO_FWC_MCA_14.05_eng.pdf?ua=1.

32 Wilkinson and Pickett, *The Spirit Level*, p. 36. This specifically concerns young adults in North America, but the same trend is visible in other developed countries.

33 Quoted in: Ashlee Vance, "This Tech Bubble Is Different," *Bloomberg Businessweek* (April 14, 2011). http://www.business-week.com/magazine/content/11_17/b4225060960537.htm.

34 John Maynard Keynes, "Economic Possibilities for our Grandchildren" (1930), *Essays in Persuasion*. http://www.econ.yale.edu/smith/econ116a/keynes1.pdf.

35   Bertrand Russell, *Philosophy and Politics* (1947), p. 14.
36   Bertrand Russell, *Political Ideals* (1917), Chapter 1.

CHAPTER 2   WHY WE SHOULD GIVE FREE MONEY TO EVERYONE

1   This is a very conservative estimate. A study conducted by the British government put the amount at £30,000 per homeless person per year (for social services, police, legal costs, etc.). In this case the amount would have been much higher as they were the most notorious vagrants. The study cites sums as high as £400,000 for a single homeless person per year. See: Department for Communities and Local Government, "Evidence Review of the Costs of Homelessness" (August 2012). https://www.gov.uk/government/uploads/system/uploads/attachment_data/file/7596/2200485.pdf.

2   The recipients were generally not told the exact amount of money in their "personalised budget," according to the Broadway report; however, as the report goes on to say that one of the homeless suggested lowering it from £3,000 to £2,000, he obviously did know.

3   The homeless were not given the money directly. All their expenditures had to be approved first by the "street population manager," which he always did "promptly." That this scrutiny was limited was also affirmed by one of the social workers in an interview with the *Economist* (see Chapter 2, endnote 6): "We just said, 'It's your life and up to you to do what you want with it, but we are here to help if you want.'" The report also states that "Throughout the interviews, many people used the phrases 'I chose' or 'I made the decision' when discussing their accommodation and the use of their personalised budget, emphasising their sense of choice and control."

4   The Joseph Rowntree Foundation published an extensive report on the experiment, which is the source of all the quotes cited here. See: Juliette Hough and Becky Rice, *Providing Personalised Support to Rough Sleepers. An Evaluation of the City of London Pilot* (2010). http://www.jrf.org.uk/publications/support-rough-sleepers-london.

For another evaluation, see: Liz Blackender and Jo Prestidge, "Pan London Personalised Budgets for Rough Sleepers," *Journal of Integrated Care* (January 2014). http://www.emeraldinsight.com/journals.htm?articleid=17104939&.

5   In 2013, the project was expanded to twenty-eight rough sleepers in London's City, of whom twenty already had a roof over their heads.

6   "Cutting out the middle men," *Economist* (November 4, 2010). http://www.economist.com/node/17420321.

7   Quoted in: Jacob Goldstein, "Is It Nuts to Give to the Poor Without Strings Attached?" *New York Times* (August 13, 2013). http://www.nytimes.com/2013/08/18/magazine/is-it-nuts-to-give-to-the-poor-without-strings-attached.html.

8   Johannes Haushofery and Jeremy Shapiroz, "Policy Brief: Impacts of Unconditional Cash Transfers." https://www.princeton.edu/~joha/publications/Haushofer_Shapiro_Policy_Brief_2013.pdf.

9   The prestigious charity evaluator GiveWell, which has reviewed over 500 charities, ranks GiveDirectly fourth on its list of top charities.

10 Christopher Blattman, Nathan Fiala, and Sebastian Martinez, "Generating Skilled Self-Employment in Developing Countries: Experimental Evidence from Uganda," *Quarterly Journal of Economics* (November 14, 2013). http://papers.ssrn.com/sol3/papers.cfm?abstract_id=2268552.

11 Christopher Blattman et al., *Building Women's Economic and Social Empowerment Through Enterprise. An Experimental Assessment of the Women's Income Generating Support (WINGS) Program in Uganda* (April 2013). https://openknowledge.worldbank.org/bitstream/handle/10986/17862/860590NWP0Box30ySeriesNo10Ugandaohr.pdf?sequence=1&isAllowed=y. See also: Isobel Coleman, "Fighting Poverty with Unconditional Cash," *Council on Foreign Relations* (December 12, 2013). http://blogs.cfr.org/development-channel/2013/12/12/fighting-poverty-with-unconditional-cash/.

12 Christopher Blattman et al., "The Returns to Cash and Microenterprise Support Among the Ultra-Poor: A Field Experiment." http://sites.bu.edu/neudc/files/2014/10/paper_15.pdf.

13   The following is a selection of studies on the effects of conditional and unconditional "cash grants." In South Africa: Jorge M. Agüero and Michael R. Carter, "The Impact of Unconditional Cash Transfers on Nutrition: The South African Child Support Grant," University of Cape Town (August 2006). http://www .ipc-undp.org/pub/IPCWorkingPaper39.pdf.

  In Malawi: W. K. Luseno et al., "A multilevel analysis of the effect of Malawi's Social Cash Transfer Pilot Scheme on school-age children's health," *Health Policy Plan* (May 2013). http://www.ncbi.nlm.nih.gov/pmc/articles/PMC4110449/.

  Also in Malawi: Sarah Baird et al., "The Short-Term Impacts of a Schooling Conditional Cash Transfer Program on the Sexual Behavior of Young Women." http://cega.berkeley.edu/assets/cega_research_projects/40/Short_Term_Impacts_of_a_Schooling_CCT_on_Sexual_Behavior.pdf.

14   Charles Kenny, "For Fighting Poverty, Cash Is Surprisingly Effective," *Bloomberg Businessweek* (June 3, 2013). http://www .bloomberg.com/bw/articles/2013-06-03/for-fighting-poverty-cash-is-surprisingly-effective.

15   Joseph Hanlon et al., *Just Give Money to the Poor* (2010), p. 6.

16   Armando Barrientos and David Hulme, "Just Give Money to the Poor. The Development Revolution from the Global South," Presentation for the OECD. http://www.oecd.org/dev/pgd/46240619.pdf.

17   Christopher Blattman and Paul Niehaus, "Show Them the Money. Why Giving Cash Helps Alleviate Poverty," *Foreign Affairs* (May/June 2014).

18   David McKenzie and Christopher Woodruff, "What Are We Learning from Business Training and Entrepreneurship Evaluations around the Developing World?" World Bank Policy Research Working Paper (September 2012). http://ftp.iza.org/dp6895.pdf.

19   Hanlon et al., *Just Give Money to the Poor*, p. 4. Of course, cash transfers are not a cure-all – they won't build bridges or bring peace. But they do make a huge difference. Cash transfers "are as close as you can come to a magic bullet in development," observes Nancy Birdsall, president of the Center for Global Development in Washington. Quoted in: ibid., p. 61.

20 It should be noted that this decline was not statistically significant, so in most cases cash transfers have no effect on the level of tobacco and alcohol consumption. See: David K. Evans and Anna Popova, "Cash Transfers and Temptation Goods. A Review of Global Evidence," World Bank Policy Research Working Papers (May 2014). http://documents.worldbank.org/curated/en/2014/05/19546774/cash-transfers-temptation-goods-review-global-evidence.

21 Blattman and Niehaus, "Show Them the Money."

22 In 2009 the *Lancet* stated: "Emerging data from cash transfers, conditional or unconditional, largely dispel the counter arguments that these programmes prevent adults from seeking work or create a dependency culture which perpetuates intergenerational poverty." See: The Lancet Editorial, "Cash Transfers for Children. Investing into the Future," *Lancet* (June 27, 2009).

23 Claudia Haarmann et al., "Making the Difference! The BIG in Namibia," Assessment Report (April 2009), p. VII. http://www.bignam.org/Publications/big_Assessment_report_08b.pdf.

24 Including Thomas Paine, John Stuart Mill, H. G. Wells, George Bernard Shaw, John Kenneth Galbraith, Jan Tinbergen, Martin Luther King, and Bertrand Russell.

25 See, for example: Matt Zwolinski, "Why Did Hayek Support a Basic Income?" *Libertarianism.org* (December 23, 2013). http://www.libertarianism.org/columns/why-did-hayek-support-basic-income.

26 Robert van der Veen and Philippe van Parijs, "A Capitalist Road to Communism," *Theory & Society* (1986). https://www.ssc.wisc.edu/~wright/ERU_files/PVP-cap-road.pdf.

27 A quote by the conservative proponent of basic income, Charles Murray, in: Annie Lowrey, "Switzerland's Proposal to Pay People for Being Alive," *New York Times* (November 12, 2013). http://www.nytimes.com/2013/11/17/magazine/switzerlands-proposal-to-pay-people-for-being-alive.html.

28 Quoted in: Zi-Ann Lum, 'A Canadian City Once Eliminated Poverty and Nearly Everyone Forgot About It', *Huffington Post*. http://www.huffingtonpost.ca/2014/12/23/mincome-in-dauphin-manitoba_n_6335682.html.

29 Quoted in: Lindor Reynolds, "Dauphin's Great Experiment," *Winnipeg Free Press* (March 12, 2009). http://www.winnipeg-freepress.com/local/dauphins-great-experiment.html.

30 Here and in the section that follows, all references are to U.S. dollars.

31 Quoted in: Vivian Belik, "A Town Without Poverty?" *Dominion* (September 5, 2011). http://www.dominionpaper.ca/articles/4100. "For a lot of economists, the issue was that you would disincentivize work," observed Wayne Simpson, another Canadian economist who has studied Mincome. "The evidence showed that it was not nearly as bad as some of the literature had suggested." Quoted in: Lowrey, "Switzerland's Proposal to Pay People for Being Alive."

32 Quoted from a lecture on Vimeo: http://vimeo.com/56648023.

33 Evelyn Forget, "The town with no poverty," University of Manitoba (February 2011). http://public.econ.duke.edu/~erw/197/forget-cea %282%29.pdf.

34 Allan Sheahen, *Basic Income Guarantee. Your Right to Economic Security* (2012), p. 108.

35 Dylan Matthews, "A Guaranteed Income for Every American Would Eliminate Poverty – And It Wouldn't Destroy the Economy," *Vox.com* (July 23, 2014). http://www.vox.com/2014/7/23/5925041/guaranteed-income-basic-poverty-gobry-labor-supply.

36 Quoted in: Allan Sheahen, "Why Not Guarantee Everyone a Job? Why the Negative Income Tax Experiments of the 1970s Were Successful." USBIG Discussion Paper (February 2002). http://www.usbig.net/papers/013-Sheahen.doc.
    The researchers thought people might eventually even work *more*, provided the government created additional jobs. "Any reduction in work effort caused by cash assistance would be more than offset by the increased employment opportunities provided in public service jobs."

37 Matthews, "A Guaranteed Income for Every American Would Eliminate Poverty."

38 "Economists Urge Assured Income," *New York Times* (May 28, 1968).

39 Brian Steensland, *The Failed Welfare Revolution. America's Struggle over Guaranteed Income Policy* (2008), p. 123.

40   Quoted in: Sheahen, *Basic Income Guarantee*, p. 8.

41   Steensland, *The Failed Welfare Revolution*, p. 69.

42   Quoted in: Peter Passell and Leonard Ross, "Daniel Moynihan and President-Elect Nixon: How Charity Didn't Begin at Home," *New York Times* (January 14, 1973). http://www.nytimes.com/books/98/10/04/specials/moynihan-income.html.

43   Quoted in: Leland G. Neuberg, "Emergence and Defeat of Nixon's Family Assistance Plan," USBIG Discussion Paper (January 2004). http://www.usbig.net/papers/066-Neuberg-FAP2.doc.

44   Bruce Bartlett, "Rethinking the Idea of a Basic Income for All," *New York Times Economix* (December 10, 2013). http://economix.blogs.nytimes.com/2013/12/10/rethinking-the-idea-of-a-basic-income-for-all.

45   Steensland, *The Failed Welfare Revolution*, p. 157.

46   Glen G. Cain and Douglas Wissoker, "A Reanalysis of Marital Stability in the Seattle–Denver Income Maintenance Experiment," Institute for Research on Poverty (January 1988). http://www.irp.wisc.edu/publications/dps/pdfs/dp85788.pdf.

47   According to a poll conducted by Harris in 1969. Mike Alberti and Kevin C. Brown, "Guaranteed Income's Moment in the Sun," *Remapping Debate*. http://www.remappingdebate.org/article/guaranteed-income's-moment-sun.

48   Matt Bruenig, "How a Universal Basic Income Would Affect Poverty," *Demos* (October 3, 2013). http://www.demos.org/blog/10/3/13/how-universal-basic-income-would-affect-poverty.

49   Linda J. Bilmes, "The Financial Legacy of Iraq and Afghanistan: How Wartime Spending Decisions Will Constrain Future National Security Budgets," Faculty Research Working Paper Series (March 2013). https://research.hks.harvard.edu/publications/getFile.aspx?Id=923.

50   Try this for a thought experiment: A basic income of $1.25 a day for everyone on Earth would cost an annual $3 trillion, or 3.5% of global GDP. The same cash assistance to the world's 1.3 billion poorest inhabitants would require less than $600 billion, or

approximately 0.7% of global GDP, and would completely eliminate extreme poverty.

51 Walter Korpi and Joakim Palme, "The Paradox of Redistribution and Strategies of Equality: Welfare State Institutions, Inequality and Poverty in the Western Countries," *American Sociological Review* (October 1998). http://citeseerx.ist.psu.edu/viewdoc/download?doi=10.1.1.111.2584&rep=rep1&type=pdf.

52 Wim van Oorschot, "Globalization, the European Welfare State, and Protection of the Poor," in: A. Suszycki and I. Karolewski (eds), *Citizenship and Identity in the Welfare State* (2013), pp. 37–50.

53 Alaska is the best example of this, as the only political entity to have a universal, unconditional basic income (just over $1,000 a year), financed by oil revenues. Support is virtually unanimous. According to University of Alaska in Anchorage professor Scott Goldsmith, for a politician to question this program would be political suicide. It is thanks in part to this small basic income that Alaska has the lowest inequality of any U.S. state. See: Scott Goldsmith, "The Alaska Permanent Fund Dividend: An Experiment in Wealth Distribution," 9th International Congress BIEN (September 12, 2002). http://www.basicincome.org/bien/pdf/2002Goldsmith.pdf.

54 Studies of the behavior of lottery winners shows that even hitting the jackpot rarely makes people quit their jobs, and if they do it's to spend more time with their children or find other work. See this famous study: Roy Kaplan, "Lottery Winners: The Myth and Reality," *Journal of Gambling Behavior* (Fall 1987), pp. 168–78.

55 Prison inmates are a good example. Given food and a roof over their heads, they can just enjoy kicking back, you might think. Yet in prison the withholding of work is actually used as a punishment. If an inmate misbehaves, he's barred from the shop floor or kitchen. Almost everyone wants to make some sort of contribution, though what we mean by "work" and "unemployment" is subject to change. Indeed, we place far too little emphasis on the huge amount of unpaid work that people already do.

56 She said this on Canadian TV. Watch the clip here: https://youtu.be/EPRTUZsiDYw?t=45m30s.

CHAPTER 3   THE END OF POVERTY

1   Jessica Sedgwick, "November 1997: Cherokee Casino Opens" (November 1, 2007). https://blogs.lib.unc.edu/ncm/index.php/2007/11/01/this_month_nov_1997/.

2   James H. Johnson Jr., John D. Kasarda, and Stephen J. Appold, "Assessing the Economic and Non-Economic Impacts of Harrah's Cherokee Casino, North Carolina" (June 2011). https://www.kenan-flagler.unc.edu/~/media/Files/kenaninstitute/UNC_KenanInstitute_Cherokee.pdf.

3   Money for children under eighteen is paid into a fund that is released when they reach their majority.

4   Jane Costello et al., "Relationships Between Poverty and Psychopathology. A Natural Experiment," *Journal of the American Medical Association* (October 2003). http://jama.jamanetwork.com/article.aspx?articleid=197482.

5   Quoted in: Moises Velasquez-Manoff, "What Happens When the Poor Receive a Stipend?" *New York Times* (January 18, 2014). http://opinionator.blogs.nytimes.com/2014/01/18/what-happens-when-the-poor-receive-a-stipend/.

6   William Copeland and Elizabeth J. Costello, "Parents' Incomes and Children's Outcomes: A Quasi-Experiment," *American Economic Journal: Applied Economics* (January 2010). http://www.ncbi.nlm.nih.gov/pmc/articles/pmc2891175/.

7   Quoted in: Velasquez-Manoff, "What Happens When the Poor Receive a Stipend?" According to Costello, it was the cash transfers – and not the new facilities (school, hospital) – that made the real difference, since the improvements in the Cherokees' lives were discernible from the moment the money arrived, long before the new facilities were available.

8   Costello et al., "Relationships Between Poverty and Psychopathology," p. 2029.

9   Richard Dowden, "The Thatcher Philosophy," *Catholic Herald* (December 22, 1978). http://www.margaretthatcher.org/document/103793.

10 Sendhil Mullainathan and Eldar Shafir, *Scarcity: Why Having Too Little Means So Much* (2013).

11 Velasquez-Manoff, "What Happens When the Poor Receive a Stipend?"

12   Donald Hirsch, "An estimate of the cost of child poverty in 2013," Centre for Research in Social Policy. http://www.cpag .org.uk/sites/default/files/Cost of child poverty research update (2013).pdf.

13   Donald Hirsch, "Estimating the costs of child poverty," Joseph Rowntree Foundation (October 2008). http://www.jrf.org.uk/ sites/files/jrf/2313.pdf.

14   See for example: Harry J. Holzer et al., "The Economic Costs of Poverty in the United States. Subsequent Effects of Children Growing Up Poor," Center for American Progress (January 2007). https://www.americanprogress.org/issues/poverty/ report/2007/01/24/2450/the-economic-costs-of-poverty.

15   I've rounded off these numbers. See: Greg J. Duncan, "Economic Costs of Early Childhood Poverty," Partnership for America's Economic Success, Issue Brief #4 (February 2008). http:// ready-nation.s3.amazonaws.com/wp-content/uploads/ Economic-Costs-Of-Early-Childhood-Poverty-Brief.pdf.

16   Valerie Strauss, "The cost of child poverty: $500 billion a year," *Washington Post* (July 25, 2013). http://www.washingtonpost. com/blogs/answer-sheet/wp/2013/07/25/the-cost-of-child-poverty-500-billion-a-year/.

17   Daniel Fernandes, John G. Lynch Jr., and Richard G. Netemeyer, "Financial Literacy, Financial Education and Downstream Financial Behaviors," *Management Science* (January 2014). http://papers.ssrn.com/sol3/papers.cfm?abstract_id=2333898.

18   That is to say, average life expectancy. Naturally there are always sizable health differences between rich and poor in any given country. But this does not detract from the fact that economic growth fairly quickly ceases to impact on average national life expectancy.

19   Quoted in: Rutger Bregman, "99 problemen, 1 oorzaak," *De Correspondent*. https://decorrespondent.nl/388/99-problemen-1oorzaak/14916660-5a5eee06.

20   Also see: Brian Nolan et al., *Changing Inequalities and Societal Impacts in Rich Countries: Thirty Countries' Experien*ces (2014). This report on a major study conducted by more than 200 researchers throughout Europe, the U.S., Australia, Canada, Japan, and South Korea found strong links between inequality

and reduced happiness, social mobility, and election turnouts and greater desire for status. Correlations between crime and social participation are less clear cut; poverty has a higher adverse effect across the board than inequality.

21 Ironically, people in countries where equality is high, like Germany and Norway, are the least likely to take personal credit for success. In the U.S., by contrast, people are less likely (as the World Values Survey shows) to consider their successes a product of luck or circumstance.

22 Jonathan D. Ostry, Andrew Berg, and Charalambos G. Tsangarides, "Redistribution, Inequality, and Growth," IMF (April 2014). http://www.imf.org/external/pubs/ft/sdn/2014/sdn1402.pdf.

23 Wilkinson and Pickett's findings caused quite a stir, but since the publication of *The Spirit Level* there have been dozens more studies confirming their thesis. In 2011, the Joseph Rowntree Foundation conducted an independent analysis of their evidence, and concluded that there is indeed wide scientific consensus on the correlation between inequality and social problems. And, crucially, there is also a sizable share of data to support causality. See: Karen Rowlingson, "Does income inequality cause health and social problems?" (September 2011). http://www.jrf.org.uk/sites/files/jrf/inequality-income-social-problems-full.pdf.

Inversely, in countries with a more extensive welfare regime, rich and poor tend to be happier and experience less of these social problems. For an in-depth study on this, see: Patrick Flavin, Alexander C. Pacek, and Benjamin Radcliff, "Assessing the Impact of the Size and Scope of Government on Human Well-Being," *Social Forces* (June 2014). http://sf.oxfordjournals.org/content/92/4/1241.

24 Jan-Emmanuel De Neve and Nattavudh Powdthavee, "Income Inequality Makes Whole Countries Less Happy," *Harvard Business Review* (January 12, 2016). https://hbr.org/2016/01/income-inequality-makes-whole-countries-less-happy.

25 See Matthew 26:11, Mark 14:7, and John 12:8.

26 Quoted in: Emily Badger, "Hunger Makes People Work Harder, and Other Stupid Things We Used to Believe About Poverty,"

Atlantic Cities (July 17, 2013). http://www.theatlanticcities.com/
jobs-andeconomy/2013/07/hunger-makes-people-work-harder-
and-other-stupid-things-we-used-believe-about-poverty/6219/.

27 Bernard de Mandeville, *The Fable of the Bees, or, Private Vices,
Publick Benefits* (1714).

28 Samuel Johnson, Letter to James Boswell, 7th December 1782.

29 Quoted in: Kerry Drake, "Wyoming can give homeless a place to
live, and save money," *Wyofile* (December 3, 2013). http://www
.wyofile.com/column/wyoming-homelessness-place-live-
save-money/.

30 A Florida study has demonstrated that a person living on the
street costs $31,000 annually, while providing them with a house
and a social worker would cost the state only $10,000. A
Colorado study calculated the costs at $43,000 versus $17,000
annually. See: Kate Santich, "Cost of homelessness in Central
Florida? $31K per person," *Orlando Sentinel* (May 21, 2014).
http://articles.orlandosentinel.com/2014-05-21/news/os-cost-of-
homelessness-orlando-20140521_1_homeless-individuals-central-
florida-commission-tulsa.

   And Scott Keyes, "Colorado Proves Housing the Homeless Is
Cheaper Than Leaving Them on the Streets," *Think Progress*
(September 5, 2013). http://thinkprogress.org/economy/
2013/09/05/2579451/coloradohomeless-shelter.

31 Malcolm Gladwell wrote a brilliant essay about this. See: http://
gladwell.com/million-dollar-murray.

32 Birgit Kooijman, "Rotterdam haalt daklozen in huis," *Binnenlands
Bestuur* (August 28, 2009). http://www.binnenlandsbestuur.nl/
sociaal/achtergrond/achtergrond/rotterdam-haalt-daklozen-
inhuis.127589.lynkx.

33 Plan van aanpak Maatschappelijke Opvang Fase II, "Van de straat
naar een thuis." http://www.utrecht.nl/fileadmin/uploads/
documenten/5.sociaal-maatschappelijk/Zorg_voor_sociaal_
kwetsbaren/ocw_Plan_van_Aanpak_MO_fase2_
samenvatting_1_.pdf.

34 In 2006 there were about 10,000 homeless in the four major cities,
according to the Action Plan. In 2009 their number had declined
to some 6,500, but in 2012 it had ricocheted to 12,400. See:
Statistics Netherlands Statline, "Daklozen; persoonskenmerken."

http://statline.cbs.nl/StatWeb/publication/?VW=T&DM=SL
NL&PA=80799NED&LA=L.

35 Cebeon, "Kosten en baten van Maatschappelijke opvang.
Bouwstenen voor effectieve inzet van publieke middelen" (2011).
http://www.opvang.nl/site/item/kosten-en-baten-van-maat-
schappe-lijke-opvang-bouwstenen-voor-effectieve.

36 Ruper Neate, "Scandal of Europe's 11m empty homes," *Guardian*
(February 23, 2014). http://www.theguardian.com/
society/2014/feb/23/europe-11m-empty-properties-enough-
house-homeless-continent-twice.

37 Richard Bronson, "Homeless and Empty Homes – An American
Travesty," *Huffington Post* (August 24, 2010). http://www
.huffingtonpost.com/richard-skip-bronson/post_733_b_692546
.html.

38 Quoted in: John Stoehr, "The Answer to Homelessness,"
American Conservative (March 20, 2014). http://www
.theamericanconservative.com/articles/the-answer-to-
homelessness.

39 Quoted in: Velasquez-Manoff, "What Happens When the Poor
Receive a Stipend?"

CHAPTER 4 THE BIZARRE TALE OF PRESIDENT NIXON AND
HIS BASIC INCOME BILL

1   The British writer L. P. Hartley (1895–1972) in his novel *The
Go-Between* (1953).

2   Brian Steensland, *The Failed Welfare Revolution. America's
Struggle Over Guaranteed Income Policy* (2008), p. 93.

3   Ibid., p. 96.

4   Ibid., p. 115.

5   Peter Passell and Leonard Ross, "Daniel Moynihan and
President-elect Nixon: How charity didn't begin at home," *New
York Times* (January 14, 1973). http://www.nytimes.com/
books/98/10/04/specials/moynihan-income.html.

6   Ibid.

7   A recent study conducted at Johns Hopkins University reveals
that over the past thirty years the American welfare state has
focused increasingly on the "wealthy poor" – people who have
jobs, are married, or are elderly and are considered more

"deserving" of support. As a consequence, conditions for the very poorest families, most of them fatherless, have worsened by 35% since 1983. In 2012 nearly 1.5 million households, including 2.8 million children, were living in "extreme poverty" on less than $2 per person per day. See: Gabriel Thompson, "Could You Survive on $2 a Day?", *Mother Jones* (December 13, 2012). http://www.motherjones.com/politics/2012/12/extreme-poverty-unemployment-recession-economy-fresno.

8 *Reading Mercury* (May 11, 1795). http://www1.umassd.edu/ir/resources/poorlaw/p1.doc.

9 See: Thomas Malthus, "An Essay on the Principle of Population" (1798). http://www.esp.org/books/malthus/population/malthus.pdf.

10 For simplicity's sake I refer to David Ricardo as an "economist," but in his own day he was considered a "political economist." As the chapter on GDP explains, modern economists are a twentieth-century invention.

11 *Report from His Majesty's Commissioners for Inquiring into the Administration and Practical Operation of the Poor Laws* (1834), pp. 257–61. http://www.victorianweb.org/history/poorlaw/endallow.html.

12 Polanyi had a different take on its ostensive failure than his predecessors, however. He assumed that the Speenhamland system had depressed wages by undermining workers' collective action.

13 Boyd Hilton, *A Mad, Bad & Dangerous People? England 1783–1846* (2006), p. 594.

14 Fred Block and Margaret Somers, "In the Shadow of Speenhamland: Social Policy and the Old Poor Law," *Politics & Society* (June 2003), p. 287.

15 In Bangladesh, for example, women still averaged seven children in 1970, a quarter of whom died before the age of five. Nowadays, Bengal women have just two children and child mortality is down to 4%. Everywhere in the world, as soon as poverty declines, child mortality follows suit and population growth slows.

16 Frances Coppola, "An Experiment With Basic Income," *Pieria* (January 12, 2014). http://www.pieria.co.uk/articles/an_experiment_with_basic_income. Also see: Walter I. Trattner,

From Poor Law to Welfare State. A History of Social Welfare in America (1999), pp. 48–9.

17   Hilton, *A Mad, Bad & Dangerous People?*, p. 592.

18   The gold standard is a monetary system in which the value of money is based on a fixed quantity of gold. The return to the pre-war value of the pound in 1819 caused deflation (the pound rose in value). This was great news for those who already had a lot of money, but not for the rest of Britain. Wheat prices kept falling, farmers found it increasingly difficult to get a loan, and unemployment soared. A hundred years later, Keynes realized that Western governments were repeating Ricardo's mistake when they continued to uphold the gold standard following the Great Depression. The same thing happened after the financial crisis hit in 2008, with Europe holding on to a euro that, for southern countries, was like a gold standard (when they couldn't devalue their currency, their competitive position deteriorated and unemployment soared). Just like in 1834, there were a fair number of politicians in 1930 and 2010 who ascribed the consequences of this macroeconomic policy (poverty, unemployment, etc.) to the so-called laziness of workers and a too-generous welfare state.

19   B. A. Holderness, "Prices, Productivity and Output," in *The Agrarian History of England and Wales*, vol. 6: 1750–1850, ed. G.E. Mingay (1989), p. 140.

20   Joseph Hanlon et al., *Just Give Money to the Poor* (2010), pp. 17–18.

21   Block and Somers, "In the Shadow of Speenhamland," p. 312.

22   Mark Blaug, "The Poor Law Report Reexamined," *Journal of Economic History* (June 1964), pp. 229–45. http://journals.cambridge.org/action/displayAbstract?fromPage=online&aid=7548748.

23   Hanlon et al., *Just Give Money to the Poor*, pp. 16–17.

24   In the same year, the historian Gertrude Himmelfarb published *The Idea of Poverty*, in which she too recycled the criticisms of Malthus, Bentham, and de Tocqueville on the Speenhamland system.

25   Matt Bruenig, "When pundits blamed white people for a 'culture of poverty,'" *The Week* (April 1, 2014). http://theweek.com/

article/index/259055/when-pundits-blamed-white-people-for-a-culture-of-poverty.

26 "I am shocked to look at these findings and say we scientists were wrong," Moynihan told Congress. One of the reasons that he, a conservative Republican, had always believed in a basic income was that it would reinforce the institution of marriage. See: R. A. Levine, "A Retrospective on the Negative Income Tax Experiments: Looking Back at the Most Innovative Field Studies in Social Policy," USBIG Discussion Paper (June 2004). http://www.usbig.net/papers/086-Levine-et-al-NIT-session.doc.

27 Quoted in: Steensland, *The Failed Welfare Revolution*, p. 216.

28 Barbara Ehrenreich, "Rediscovering Poverty: How We Cured 'The Culture of Poverty,' Not Poverty Itself," *Economic Hardship Project* (March 15, 2012). http://www.tomdispatch.com/blog/175516/tomgram%3A_barbara_ehrenreich,_american_poverty,_50_years_later/.

29 Austin Stone, "Welfare: Moynihan's Counsel of Despair," *First Things* (March 1996). http://www.firstthings.com/article/1996/03/001-welfare-moynihans-counsel-of-despair.

30 Daniel Patrick Moynihan, "Speech on Welfare Reform" (September 16, 1995). http://www.j-bradford-delong.net/politics/danielpatrickmoynihansspee.html.

31 Beyond this, Nixon's plan, once implemented, would have been difficult to repeal as it would have rapidly garnered widespread support. "New policies create new politics," writes Steensland, *The Failed Welfare Revolution*, p. 220.

32 Ibid., p. 226.

33 Ibid., p. x.

34 In a large meta-analysis of ninety-three European programs, no or negative effects were found in at least half. See: Frans den Butter and Emil Mihaylov, "Activerend arbeidsmarktbeleid is vaak niet effectief," *ESB* (April 2008). http://personal.vu.nl/f.a.g.den.butter/activerend arbmarktbeleid2008.pdf.

35 Stephen Kastoryano and Bas van der Klaauw, "Dynamic Evaluation of Job Search Assistance," *IZA Discussion Papers* (June 15, 2011). http://www.roa.nl/seminars/pdf2012/BasvanderKlaauw.pdf.

36　The cynical thing is that claimants often aren't even allowed to do purposeful work in exchange for their benefits because that would lead to fewer paid jobs.

37　Deborah Padfield, "Through the eyes of a benefits adviser: a plea for a basic income," *Open Democracy* (October 5, 2011). http://www.opendemocracy.net/ourkingdom/deborah-padfield/through-eyes-of-benefits-adviser-plea-for-basic-income.

38　David Graeber, "On the Phenomenon of Bullshit Jobs," *Strike! Magazine* (August 17, 2013). http://www.strikemag.org/bullshit-job.

CHAPTER 5　NEW FIGURES FOR A NEW ERA

1　Tim Webb, "Japan's economy heads into freefall after earthquake and tsunami," *Guardian* (March 13, 2011). http://www.theguardian.com/world/2011/mar/13/japan-economy-recession-earthquake-tsunami.

2　Merijn Knibbe, "De bestedingsgevolgen van de watersnoodramp: een succesvolle 'Keynesiaanse' schok," *Lux et Veritas* (April 1, 2013). http://www.luxetveritas.nl/blog/?p=3006.

3　Frédéric Bastiat, "Ce qu'on voit et ce qu'on ne voit pas" (1850). http://bastiat.org/en/twisatwins.html.

4　Quoted in: Diane Coyle, *GDP. A Brief But Affectionate History* (2014), p. 106.

5　OECD (2011), "Cooking and Caring, Building and Repairing: Unpaid Work around the World," *Society at a Glance 2011*, p. 25. http://www.oecd-ilibrary.org/social-issues-migration-health/society-at-a-glance-2011/cooking-and-caring-building-and-repairing_soc_glance-2011-3-en. Also see: Coyle, *GDP*, p. 109.

6　Coyle, *GDP*, p. 108.

7　J. P. Smith, "'Lost milk?': Counting the economic value of breast milk in gross domestic product," *Journal of Human Lactation* (November 2013). http://www.ncbi.nlm.nih.gov/pubmed/23855027.

8　According to the International Institute for Strategic Studies, China spent $112 billion on its military in 2013.

9　Statisticians do try to factor in product advancements, but it's extremely difficult to do. Improvements in some technical devices, such as lamps and computers, are only fractionally reflected in

GDP. See: Diane Coyle, *The Economics of Enough. How to Run the Economy as if the Future Matters* (2012), p. 37.

10 Robert Quigley, "The Cost of a Gigabyte Over the Years," *Geeko-system* (March 8, 2011). http://www.geekosystem.com/gigabyte-cost-over-years.

11 Erik Brynjolfsson and Andrew McAfee, *The Second Machine Age* (2014), p. 112.

12 Clifford Cobb, Ted Halstead, and Jonathan Rowe, "If the GDP is Up, Why is America Down?" *Atlantic Monthly* (October 1995). http://www.theatlantic.com/past/politics/ecbig/gdp.htm.

13 Jonathan Rowe, "The Gross Domestic Product." Testimony before the U.S. Senate Committee on Commerce, Science and Transportation (March 12, 2008). http://jonathanrowe.org/the-gross-domestic-product.

14 If the GDP were to be corrected for this, the financial industry share would drop by one-fifth to one-half. See: Coyle, *GDP*, p. 103.

15 David Pilling, "Has GDP outgrown its use?" *Financial Times* (July 4, 2014). http://www.ft.com/intl/cms/s/2/dd2ec158-023d-11e4-ab5b-00144feab7de.html – axzz39szhgwni.

16 Quoted in: European Systemic Risk Board, "Is Europe Overbanked?" (June 2014), p. 16.

17 Oscar Wilde, *The Soul of Man under Socialism* (1891).

18 Quoted in: Coyle, *GDP*, p. 10.

19 Quoted in: J. Steven Landefeld, "GDP: One of the Great Inventions of the 20th Century," Bureau of Economic Analysis. http://www.bea.gov/scb/account_articles/general/0100od/maintext.htm.

20 Maarten van Rossem, *Drie Oorlogen. Een kleine geschiedenis van de 20ᵉ eeuw* (2008), p. 120.

21 Quoted in: Landefeld, "GDP: One of the Great Inventions of the 20th Century."

22 Timothy Shenk, "The Long Shadow of Mont Pèlerin," *Dissent* (Fall 2013). http://www.dissentmagazine.org/article/the-long-shadow-of-mont-pelerin.

23 Quoted in: Jacob Goldstein, "The Invention of 'The Economy,'" *Planet Money* (February 28, 2014). http://www.npr.org/blogs/money/2014/02/28/283477546/the-invention-of-the-economy.

24 Coyle, *GDP*, p. 25.

25 Listen to the speech in which Kennedy said it here: https://www
    .youtube.com/watch?v=5P6b9688K2g.

26 John Stuart Mill, *Utilitarianism* (1863), Chapter 2.

27 Oscar Wilde, *A Woman of No Importance* (1893), Act II.

28 See: William Baumol, *The Cost Disease. Why Computers Get
    Cheaper and Health Care Doesn't* (2012).

29 Attempts are made, of course. For example in education, with
    standardized testing using multiple-choice questions, online lectures,
    and larger classes. But these efficiency gains come at the cost of
    quality.

30 Susan Steed and Helen Kersley, "A Bit Rich: Calculating the Real
    Value to Society of Different Professions," *New Economics
    Foundation* (December 14, 2009). http://www.neweconomics.
    org/publications/entry/a-bit-rich.

31 Kevin Kelly, "The Post-Productive Economy," *Technium*
    (January 1, 2013). http://kk.org/thetechnium/2013/01/
    the-post-produc.

32 Simon Kuznets, "National Income, 1929–1932," National Bureau
    of Economic Research (June 7, 1934). http://www.nber.org/
    chapters/c2258.pdf.

33 Coyle, *GDP*, p. 14.

34 Simon Kuznets, "How to Judge Quality," *New Republic* (October
    20, 1962).

CHAPTER 6 A FIFTEEN-HOUR WORKWEEK

1   John Maynard Keynes, "Economic Possibilities for our
    Grandchildren" (1930), *Essays in Persuasion*. http://www.econ.
    yale.edu/smith/econ116a/keynes1.pdf.

2   John Stuart Mill, *Principles of Political Economy with Some of Their
    Applications to Social Philosophy* (1848), Book IV, Chapter VI.
    http://www.econlib.org/library/Mill/mlP61.html.

3   Quoted from Bertrand Russell's essay, "In Praise of Idleness"
    (1932). http://www.zpub.com/notes/idle.html.

4   Benjamin Kline Hunnicutt, "The End of Shorter Hours," *Labor
    History* (Summer 1984), pp. 373–404.

5   Ibid.

6   Samuel Crowther, "Henry Ford: Why I Favor Five Days' Work
    With Six Days' Pay," *World's Work*. https://en.wikisource.org/

wiki/HENRY_FORD:Why_I_Favor_Five_Days'_
Work_With_Six_Days'_Pay.

7   Andrew Simms and Molly Conisbee, "National Gardening
    Leave," in: Anna Coote and Jane Franklin (eds), *Time on
    Our Side. Why We All Need a Shorter Workweek* (2013),
    p. 155.

8   "Nixon Defends 4-Day Week Claim," *Milwaukee Sentinel*
    (September 25, 1956).

9   Jared Cohen, *Human Robots in Myth and Science* (1966).

10 Hillel Ruskin (ed.), *Leisure. Toward a Theory and Policy* (1984),
    p. 152.

11 Isaac Asimov, "Visit to the World's Fair of 2014," *New York
    Times* (August 16, 1964). http://www.nytimes.com/
    books/97/03/23/lifetimes/asi-v-fair.html.

12 Quoted in: Daniel Akst, "What Can We Learn from Past Anxiety
    Over Automation?" *Wilson Quarterly* (Summer 2013). http://
    wilsonquarterly.com/quarterly/summer-2014-where-have-all-
    the-jobs-gone/theres-much-learn-from-past-anxiety-over-
    automation/.

13 This scene from *The Jetsons* was in series 1, episode 19.

14 Quoted in: Matt Novak, '50 Years of the Jetsons: Why the Show
    Still Matters,' *Smithsonian* (September 19, 2012). http://www
    .smithsonianmag.com/history/50-years-of-the-jetsons-why-
    the-show-still-matters-43459669/

15 Sangheon Lee, Deirdre McCann, and Jon C. Messenger, *Working
    Time Around the World. Trends in Working Hours, Laws and
    Policies in a Global Comparative Perspective* (2007). http://www
    .ilo.org/wcmsp5/groups/public/@dgreports/@dcomm/@
    publ/documents/publication/wcms_104895.pdf.

16 Rasmussen Reports, "Just 31% Work a 40-Hour Week"
    (December 13, 2013). http://www.rasmussenreports.com/
    public_content/lifestyle/general_lifestyle/december_2013/
    just_31_work_a_40_hour_week.

17 Wall Street Journal Staff, *Here Comes Tomorrow! Living and
    Working in the Year 2000* (1967).

18 Hanna Rosin, "The End of Men," *Atlantic* (July/August 2010).
    http://www.theatlantic.com/magazine/archive/2010/07/
    the-end-of-men/308135/2/.

19 New Economics Foundation, *21 Hours. Why a Shorter Working Week Can Help Us All to Flourish in the 21st Century*, p. 10. http://www.neweconomics.org/publications/entry/21-hours.

20 Quoted in: Mirjam Schöttelndreier, "Nederlanders leven vooral om te werken," *De Volkskrant* (January 29, 2001).

21 D'Vera Cohn, "Do Parents Spend Enough Time With Their Children?", *Population Reference Bureau* (January 2007). http://www.prb.org/Publications/Articles/2007/DoParentsSpendEnoughTimeWithTheirChildren.aspx.

22 Rebecca Rosen, "America's Workers: Stressed Out, Overwhelmed, Totally Exhausted," *Atlantic* (March 2014). http://www.theatlantic.com/business/archive/2014/03/americas-workers-stressed-out-overwhelmed-totally-exhausted/284615/.

23 Netherlands Institute for Social Research, *Nederland in een dag. Tijdsbesteding in Nederland vergeleken met die in vijftien andere Europese landen* (2011).

24 Dutch National Working Conditions Survey (*Nationale Enquête Arbeidsomstandigheden*) 2012. http://www.monitorarbeid.tno.nl/dynamics/modules/SFIL0100/view.php?fil_Id=53.

25 Derek Thompson, "Are We Truly Overworked? An Investigation – In 6 Charts," *Atlantic* (June 2013). http://www.theatlantic.com/magazine/archive/2013/06/are-we-truly-overworked/309321/.

26 Yoon Ja-young, "Smartphones leading to 11 hours' extra work a week," *Korea Times*. http://www.koreatimes.co.kr/www/news/biz/2016/06/488_207632.html.

27 These calculations were made using the http://www.gapminder.org website.

28 Quoted in: Herman Pleij, *Dromen van Cocagne. Middeleeuwse fantasieën over het volmaakte leven* (1997), p. 49.

29 Juliet Schor, *The Overworked American. The Unexpected Decline of Leisure* (1992), p. 47. It's worth noting that hunters and gatherers probably worked even less. Archeologists estimate their workweek at no more than twenty hours.

30 Benjamin Kline Hunnicutt, *Kellogg's Six-Hour Day* (1996), p. 35.

31 In his classic work *The Wealth of Nations*, Adam Smith wrote: "The man who works so moderately as to be able to work

constantly, not only preserves his health the longest, but in the course of the year, executes the greatest quantity of works."

32 Kline Hunnicutt, *Kellogg's Six-Hour Day* (1996), p. 62.

33 Kellogg's workday was briefly back at eight hours during World War II, but after the war a large majority of his employees voted to resume the six-hour workday; it wasn't until Kellogg's cornflake-factory managers were allowed to set hours themselves that, one by one, they ramped workdays up to eight hours again. But according to Professor Benjamin Kline Hunnicutt of the University of Iowa, it was ultimately the external pressure to work and consume at the same pace as the Joneses that most undermined the six-hour workday. Nevertheless, it was only in 1985 that the last 530 cornflake workers gave up their six-hour shifts.

34 New Economics Foundation, *21 Hours*, p. 11.

35 A recent analysis of experiments with independent working since the early twentieth century concluded that autonomy and control are far more significant than the number of hours we work. People who can organize their own time are more motivated and achieve better results. See: M. Travis Maynard, Lucy L. Gilson, and John E. Mathieu, "Empowerment – Fad or Fab? A Multilevel Review of the Past Two Decades of Research," *Journal of Management* (July 2012). http://jom.sagepub.com/content/38/4/1231.

36 Sara Robinson, "Bring back the 40-Hour work week," *Salon* (March 14, 2012). http://www.salon.com/2012/03/14/bring_back_the_40_hour_work_week.

37 For an overview, see: Nicholas Ashford and Giorgos Kallis, "A Four-day Workweek: A Policy for Improving Employment and Environmental Conditions in Europe," *European Financial Review* (April 2013). http://www.europeanfinancialreview.com/?p=902.

38 Christian Kroll and Sebastian Pokutta, "Just a Perfect Day? Developing a Happiness Optimised Day Schedule," *Journal of Economic Psychology* (February 2013). http://www.sciencedirect.com/science/article/pii/S0167487012001158.

39 David Rosnick, *Reduced Work Hours as a Means of Slowing Climate Change* (Center for Economic and Policy Research).

http://www.cepr.net/documents/publications/climate-change-workshare-2013-02.pdf.

40 Kyle Knight, Eugene A. Rosa, and Juliet B. Schor, "Reducing Growth to Achieve Environmental Sustainability: The Role of Work Hours." http://www.peri.umass.edu/fileadmin/pdf/working_papers/working_papers_301-350/4.2KnightRosaSchor.pdf.

41 One study showed that hospital interns make five times as many diagnostic errors when working excessively long weeks compared to normal workweeks. Christopher P. Landrigan et al., "Effect of Reducing Interns' Work Hours on Serious Medical Errors in Intensive Care Units," *New England Journal of Medicine* (October 2004). http://www.nejm.org/doi/full/10.1056/nejmoa041406. There is also a mountain of research attesting that working too hard is bad for health. See the meta-analysis: Kate Sparks et al., "The Effects of Hours of Work on Health: A Meta-Analytic Review," *Journal of Occupational and Organizational Psychology* (August 2011). http://onlinelibrary.wiley.com/doi/10.1111/j.2044-8325.1997.tb00656.x/abstract.

42 Jon C. Messenger and Naj Ghosheh, "Work Sharing during the Great Recession" (International Labour Organization). http://www.ilo.org/wcmsp5/groups/public/---dgreports/---dcomm/---publ/documents/publication/wcms_187627.pdf.

43 In Germany, which has come out of the crisis stronger than the rest of Europe, this has saved hundreds of thousands of jobs. See also: Nicholas Ashford and Giorgos Kallis, "A Four-day Workweek." http://www.europeanfinancialreview.com/?p=902.

44 Andreas Kotsadam and Henning Finseraas, "The State Intervenes in the Battle of the Sexes: Causal Effects of Paternity Leave," *Social Science Research* (November 2011). http://www.sciencedirect.com/science/article/pii/S0049089X11001153.

45 Ankita Patnaik, 'Merging Spheres: The Role of Policy in Promoting Dual-Earner Dual-Carer Households,' Population Association of America 2014 Annual Meeting. https://www.researchgate.net/publication/255698124_Merging_Separate_Spheres_The_Role_of_Policy_in_Promoting_'Dual-Earner_Dual-Carer'_Households.

46 Rutger Bregman, 'Zo krijg je mannen achter het aanrecht,' *De Correspondent*. https://decorrespondent.nl/685/Zo-krijg-je-mannen-achter-het-aanrecht/26334825-a492b4c6.

47 Niels Ebdrup, "We Should Only Work 25 Hours a Week, Argues Professor," *Science Nordic* (February 3, 2013). http://sciencenordic.com/we-should-only-work-25-hours-week-argues-professor.

48 Erik Rauch, "Productivity and the Workweek." http://groups.csail.mit.edu/mac/users/rauch/worktime.

49 For an overview of attitudes in various countries, see: Robert Skidelsky and Edward Skidelsky, *How Much Is Enough? The Love of Money and the Case for the Good Life* (2012), pp. 29–30.

50 For an overview, see: Jonathan Gershuny and Kimberly Fisher, "Post-Industrious Society: Why Work Time Will Not Disappear for Our Grandchildren," *Sociology Working Papers* (April 2014). http://www.sociology.ox.ac.uk/working-papers/post-industrious-society-why-work-time-will-not-disappear-for-our-grandchildren.html.

51 Richard Layard, *Happiness* (2005), p. 64. See also: Don Peck, "How a New Jobless Era Will Transform America," *Atlantic* (March 2010). http://www.theatlantic.com/magazine/archive/2010/03/how-a-new-jobless-era-will-transform-america/307919/.

52 Juliet Schor, "The Triple Dividend," in: Anna Coote and Jane Franklin (eds), *Time on Our Side. Why We All Need a Shorter Workweek* (2013), p. 14.

53 Carl Honoré, *In Praise of Slow* (2004), Chapter 8.

54 Schor, *The Overworked American*, p. 66.

55 Consider the costs of training, retirement plans, unemployment insurance, and healthcare costs (the latter especially in the U.S.). Most countries have seen these "hour-invariant costs" rise in recent years. See: Schor, "The Triple Dividend," p. 9.

56 Nielsen Company, "Americans Watching More TV Than Ever." http://www.nielsen.com/us/en/insights/news/2009/americans-watching-more-tv-than-ever.html. See also: http://www.statisticbrain.com/television-watching-statistics.

57 Bertrand Russell, *In Praise of Idleness* (1935, 2004), p. 14.

CHAPTER 7 WHY IT DOESN'T PAY TO BE A BANKER

1   This reconstruction of the strike is based on contemporary coverage in the *New York Times*.

2   'Fragrant Days in Fun City', *Time* (2/16/1968).

3   Though officially there were only 12,281 lobbyists registered in Washington in 2014, this misrepresents the situation since an increasing share of lobbyists operates underground. Lee Fang, "Where Have All the Lobbyists Gone?" *Nation* (February 19, 2014). http://www.thenation.com/article/shadow-lobbying-complex/.

4   Jean-Louis Arcand, Enrico Berkes, and Ugo Panizza, "Too Much Finance?" *IMF Working Paper* (June 2012).

5   Scott L. Cummings (ed.), *The Paradox of Professionalism. Lawyers and the Possibility of Justice* (2011), p. 71.

6   Aalt Dijkhuizen, "Hoogproductieve en efficiënte landbouw: een duurzame greep!?" (March 2013). https://www.wageningenur.nl/upload_mm/a/3/9/351079e2-0a56-41ff-8f9c-ece427a42d97_NVTL maart 2013.pdf.

7   Umair Haque, "The Irish Banking Crisis: A Parable," *Harvard Business Review* (November 29, 2010).

8   Ann Crotty, "How Irish pubs filled the banks' role in 1970," *Business Report* (September 18, 2013).

9   Antoin Murphy, "Money in an Economy Without Banks – The Case of Ireland," *Manchester School* (March 1978), pp. 44–5.

10 Donal Buckley, "How six-month bank strike rocked the nation," *Independent* (December 29, 1999).

11 Haque, "The Irish Banking Crisis: A Parable."

12 Roger Bootle, "Why the economy needs to stress creation over distribution," *Telegraph* (October 17, 2009).

13 John Maynard Keynes, "Economic Possibilities for our Grandchildren," (1930), *Essays in Persuasion*. http://www.econ.yale.edu/smith/econ116a/keynes1.pdf.

14 David Graeber, "On the Phenomenon of Bullshit Jobs," *Strike! Magazine* (August 17, 2013). http://www.strikemag.org/bullshit-job.

15 Alfred Kleinknecht, Ro Naastepad, and Servaas Storm, "Overdaad schaadt: meer management, minder productiviteitsgroei," *ESB* (September 8, 2006).

16   See: Tony Schwartz and Christine Poratz, "Why You Hate
      Work," *New York Times* (May 30, 2014). http://www.nytimes
      .com/2014/06/01/opinion/sunday/why-you-hate-work.html?
      _r=1.

17   Will Dahlgreen, "37% of British workers think their jobs are
      meaningless," YouGov (August 12, 2015). https://yougov
      .co.uk/news/2015/08/12/british-jobs-meaningless.

18   As we have seen in Chapter 4, a large meta-analysis of ninety-
      three European 'active labor market' programs found no
      or negative effects in at least half. See: Frans den Butter and
      Emil Mihaylov, "Activerend arbeidsmarktbeleid is vaak niet
      effectief," ESB (April 2008). http://personal.vu.nl/f.a.g.den
      .butter/activerendarbmarktbeleid2008.pdf.

19   Peter Thiel, "What happened to the future?" *Founders Fund*.
      http://www.foundersfund.com/the-future.

20   William Baumol, "Entrepreneurship: Productive, Unproductive,
      and Destructive," *Journal of Political Economy* (1990),
      pp. 893–920.

21   Sam Ro, "Stock Market Investors Have Become Absurdly
      Impatient," Business Insider (August 7, 2012). http://www
      .businessinsider.com/stock-investor-holding-period-2012-8.

22   Benjamin Lockwood, Charles Nathanson, and E. Glen Weyl,
      "Taxation and the Allocation of Talent." http://papers.ssrn
      .com/sol3/papers.cfm?abstract_id=1324424.

23   Stijn Hustinx, "Iedereen in New York wil vuilnisman worden,"
      Algemeen Dagblad (November 12, 2014).

CHAPTER 8   RACE AGAINST THE MACHINE

 1   Categories of horse as reported by the Agricultural Census, *A
      Vision of Britain through Time*. http://www.visionofbritain.org
      .uk/unit/10001043/cube/AGCEN_HORSES_1900.

 2   Quoted in: Erik Brynjolfsson and Andrew McAfee, *The Second
      Machine Age* (2014), p. 175.

 3   Quoted in: *Leeds Mercury* (March 13, 1830).

 4   Michael Greenstone and Adam Looney, "Trends," *Milken
      Institute Review* (Fall 2011). http://www.milkeninstitute.org/
      publications/review/2011_7/08-16MR51.pdf.

 5   Gordon Moore, "Cramming more components onto integrated

circuits," *Electronics Magazine* (April 19, 1965). http://web.eng. fiu.edu/npala/eee6397ex/Gordon_Moore_1965_Article.pdf.

6   Intel, "Excerpts from a Conversation with Gordon Moore: Moore's Law" (2005). http://large.stanford.edu/courses/2012/ ph250/lee1/docs/Excepts_A_Conversation_with_Gordon_ Moore.pdf.

7   In 1965, Moore still assumed that the number of transistors would double every twelve months. In 1970 he adjusted this to twenty-four months. Now, the accepted figure is eighteen.

8   Arthur Donovan and Joseph Bonner, *The Box That Changed the World: Fifty Years of Container Shipping* (2006).

9   An article in the *Atlantic* got me thinking about the parallel emergence of the chip and the box. Of course, globalization and technological development are impossible to separate, since globalization is enabled by technological advancement. See: Charles Davi, "The Mystery of the Incredible Shrinking American Worker," *Atlantic* (February 11, 2013). http://www .theatlantic.com/business/archive/2013/02/the-mystery-of-the-incredible-shrinking-american-worker/273033/.

10   The OECD has estimated that technology (mainly ICT) is responsible for 80% of the decline of the wage share in GDP. This trend is also evident in countries like China and India, where the share of labor has likewise decreased. Also see: Loukas Karabarbounis and Brent Neiman, "The Global Decline of the Labor Share," *Quarterly Journal of Economics* (February 2014). http://qje.oxfordjournals.org/content/129/1/61.abstract.

11   Robert H. Frank and Philip J. Cook, *The Winner-Take-All Society: Why the Few at the Top Get So Much More Than the Rest of Us* (1996).

12   Walter Scheidel and Steven J. Friesen, "The Size of the Economy and the Distribution of Income in the Roman Empire," *Journal of Roman Studies* (November 2009). http://journals.cambridge. org/action/displayAbstract?fromPage=online&aid=7246320&fi leId=S0075435800000071.

13   Kaja Bonesmo Fredriksen, "Income Inequality in the European Union," OECD Working Papers (April 16, 2012). http:// search.oecd.org/officialdocuments/displaydocument-pdf/?cote=eco/wkp(2012)29&docLanguage=En.

14 Derek Thompson, "This Is What the Post-Employee Economy Looks Like," *Atlantic* (April 20, 2011). http://www.theatlantic.com/business/archive/2011/04/this-is-what-the-post-employee-economy-looks-like/237589/.

15 Take radiologists: With more than ten years' training, they're the highest-paid medical specialists around – but for how much longer? They may soon be up against high-tech scanners that can do the same job better, and at a hundredth of the cost. Lawyers are already facing a similar problem. Research that once required well-paid legal scholars to trawl through piles of legal documents can now be done by computers, unhampered by headaches or eyestrain. A large chemical company that recently unleashed its software on work done by its own legal staff in the 1980s and 1990s found an accuracy rate of only 60%. "Think about how much money had been spent to be slightly better than a coin toss," reflected one of the former lawyers. See: John Markoff, "Armies of Expensive Lawyers, Replaced by Cheaper Software," *New York Times* (March 4, 2011). http://www.nytimes.com/2011/03/05/science/05legal.html.

16 Warren G. Bennis first said this. Cited in: Mark Fisher, *The Millionaire's Book of Quotations* (1991), p. 15.

17 Carl Benedikt Frey and Michael A. Osborne, "The Future of Employment: How Susceptible Are Jobs to Computerisation?" Oxford Martin School (September 17, 2013). http://www.oxfordmartin.ox.ac.uk/downloads/academic/The_Future_of_Employment.pdf. For the calculation for Europe, see: http://www.bruegel.org/nc/blog/detail/article/1399-chart-of-the-week-54-percent-of-eu-jobs-atrisk-of-computerisation.

18 Gary Marcus, "Why We Should Think About the Threat of Artificial Intelligence," *New Yorker* (October 24, 2013). http://www.newyorker.com/online/blogs/elements/2013/10/why-we-should-think-about-the-threat-of-artificial-intelligence.html.

19 Susan B. Carter, "Labor Force for Historical Statistics of the United States, Millennial Edition" (September 2003). http://economics.ucr.edu/papers/papers04/04-03.pdf.

20 Yale Brozen, "Automation: The Retreating Catastrophe," *Left & Right* (September 1966). https://mises.org/library/automation-retreating-catastrophe.

21   David Rotman, "How Technology Is Destroying Jobs," *MIT Technology Review* (June 12, 2013). http://www.technology review.com/featuredstory/515926/how-technology-is-destroying-jobs.

22   Quoted in: Brynjolfsson and McAfee, *The Second Machine Age*, p. 27.

23   Ian Morris, *Why the West Rules – For Now* (2010), p. 495.

24   Ibid., p. 497.

25   Diane Coyle, *GDP. A Brief But Affectionate History* (2014), p. 79.

26   Frank Levy and Richard Murnane, *The New Division of Labor* (2004).

27   There are indications that even jobs for the highly skilled have come under pressure since 2000, leading them to snap up the less-skilled jobs. Increasingly, employees are overqualified for their jobs. See: Paul Beaudry, David A. Green, and Ben Sand, "The Great Reversal in the Demand for Skill and Cognitive Tasks," National Bureau of Economic Research (January 2013). http://www.economics.ubc.ca/files/2013/05/pdf_paper_paul-beaudry-great-reversal.pdf.

28   Bas ter Weel, "Banen in het midden onder druk," CPB Netherlands Bureau for Economic Policy Analysis Policy Brief (June 2012). http://www.cpb.nl/sites/default/files/publicaties/download/cpb-policy-brief-2012-06-loonongelijkheid-nederland-stijgt.pdf.

29   Globalization may even have put the brakes on technological progress. After all, for the moment our clothes are being produced not by steel robotic arms or intelligent cyborgs but by fragile children's fingers in Vietnam and China. For many companies, outsourcing work to Asians still beats using robots. This could also be why we're still waiting for so many of the big technological dreams of the twentieth century to materialize. See: David Graeber, "Of Flying Cars and the Declining Rate of Profit," *The Baffler* (2012).

30   Andrew McAfee, "Even Sweatshops Are Getting Automated. So What's Left?" (May 22, 2014). http://andrewmcafee.org/2014/05/mcafee-nike-automation-labor-technology-globalization/.

31 Steven E. Jones, *Against Technology. From the Luddites to Neo-Luddism* (2006), Chapter 2.

32 "Leeds Woollen Workers Petition, 1786," *Modern History Sourcebook*. http://www.fordham.edu/halsall/mod/1786 machines.asp.

33 Quoted in: Robert Skidelsky, "Death to Machines?" *Project Syndicate* (February 21, 2014). http://www.project-syndicate. org/commentary/robert-skidelsky-revisits-the-luddites-- claim-that-automation-depresses-real-wages.

34 Oscar Wilde, 'The Soul of Man under Socialism' (1891).

35 Tyler Cowen, *Average Is Over. Powering America Beyond the Age of the Great Stagnation* (2013), p. 23.

36 Ibid., p. 172.

37 Quoted in: Daron Acemoglu and James A. Robinson, *Why Nations Fail. The Origins of Power, Prosperity and Poverty* (2012), p. 226.

38 Oscar Wilde, 'The Soul of Man under Socialism' (1891).

39 Thomas Piketty, "Save capitalism from the capitalists by taxing wealth," *Financial Times* (March 28, 2014). http://www.ft.com/ intl/cms/s/0/decdd76e-b50e-11e3-a746-00144feabdc0.html- axzz44qTtjlZN.

CHAPTER 9 BEYOND THE GATES OF THE LAND OF PLENTY

1 OECD, "Aid to developing countries rebounds in 2013 to reach an all-time high" (April 8, 2014). http://www.oecd.org/ newsroom/aid-to-developing-countries-rebounds-in-2013-to- reach-an-all-time-high.htm.

2 Owen Barder, "Is Aid a Waste of Money?" *Center for Global Development* (May 12, 2013). http://www.cgdev.org/blog/ aid-waste-money.

3 Linda J. Bilmes, "The Financial Legacy of Iraq and Afghanistan: How Wartime Spending Decisions Will Constrain Future National Security Budgets," Faculty Research Working Paper Series (March 2013). https://research.hks.harvard.edu/publications/getFile. aspx?Id=923. (Also see Chapter 2.)

4 I did this calculation for 2009. See: OECD, "Agricultural Policies in OECD Countries" (2009). http://www.oecd.org/tad/ agricultural-policies/43239979.pdf.

5   Dambisa Moyo, *Dead Aid* (2009), p. 39.

6   Watch Duflo's TED Talk here: http://www.ted.com/talks/
    esther_-duflo_social_experiments_to_fight_poverty.

7   We don't see this "randomization" in the Book of Daniel. Modern
    studies are usually also "double blind," which means neither the
    doctor nor the patients know who is getting which medicine.

8   Alfredo Morabia, "Pierre-Charles-Alexandre Louis and the
    evaluation of bloodletting," *Journal of the Royal Society of
    Medicine* (March 2006). http://www.ncbi.nlm.nih.gov/pmc/
    articles/pmc1383766/pdf/0158.pdf.

9   Jessica Benko, "The Hyper-Efficient, Highly Scientific Scheme to
    Help the World's Poor," *Wired* (December 11, 2013). http://
    www.wired.com/2013/11/jpal-randomized-trials/.

10 Paul Glewwe, Michael Kremer, and Sylvie Moulin, "Textbooks
    and Test Scores: Evidence from a Prospective Evaluation in
    Kenya" (December 1, 1998). http://www.econ.yale.
    edu/~egcenter/infoconf/kremer_paper.pdf.

11 Quoted in: Ian Parker, "The Poverty Lab," *New Yorker* (May 17,
    2010). http://www.newyorker.com/reporting/2010/05/17/
    100517fa_fact_parker.

12 Jessica Cohen and Pascaline Dupas, "Free Distribution or
    Cost-Sharing? Evidence from a Malaria Prevention Experiment,"
    NBER Working Paper Series (October 2008). http://www.nber
    .org/papers/w14406.pdf.

13 See: Abhijit Banerjee, Esther Duflo, Rachel Glennerster, and
    Cynthia Kinnan, "The miracle of microfinance? Evidence from a
    randomized evaluation" (May 30, 2009). http://economics.mit
    .edu/files/4162.

    Jeffrey Sachs also took a hit from Duflo. A few years ago he
    asked her to evaluate his "Millennium Villages" project, in which
    thirteen regions in sub-Saharan Africa became a testing ground
    for the master's ideas. Duflo said it was too late to do a thorough
    RCT and never heard from Sachs again. Then Nina Munk, a
    journalist who spent years researching the Millennium Villages,
    published a widely acclaimed book in 2013. Her verdict? The
    project cost a fortune and accomplished little.

14 Christopher Blattman and Paul Niehaus, "Show Them the
    Money: Why Giving Cash Helps Alleviate Poverty," *Foreign*

Affairs (May/June 2014). https://www.foreignaffairs.com/articles/show-them-money.

15 Quoted in: Parker, "The Poverty Lab."

16 Angel Gurría, "The global dodgers," *Guardian* (November 27, 2008). http://www.theguardian.com/commentisfree/2008/nov/27/comment-aid-development-tax-havens.

17 Michael Clemens, "Economics and Emigration: Trillion-Dollar Bills on the Sidewalk?" Center for Global Development, p. 85. http://www.cgdev.org/sites/default/files/1425376_file_Clemens_Economics_and_Emigration_FINAL.pdf.

18 Ibid.

19 John Kennan, "Open Borders," National Bureau of Economic Research. http://www.nber.org/papers/w18307.pdf.

20 World Trade Organisation, "Tariff Download Facility." http://tariffdata.wto.org/Default.aspx?culture=en-us.

21 Kym Anderson and Will Martin, "Agricultural Trade Reform and the Doha Development Agenda," World Bank (May 2005). http://elibrary.worldbank.org/doi/abs/10.1596/1813-9450-3607.

22 Francesco Caselli and James Feyrer, "The Marginal Product of Capital," IMF. http://personal.lse.ac.uk/casellif/papers/MPK.pdf. Also see: Lant Pritchett, "The Cliff at the Border," in: Ravi Kanbur and Michael Spence, *Equity and Growth in a Globalizing World* (2010), p. 263. http://www.hks.harvard.edu/fs/lpritch/Labor Mobility – docs/cliff at the borders_submitted.pdf.

23 For the original version of John's story, see: Michael Huemer, "Citizenism and open borders." http://openborders.info/blog/citizenism-and-open-borders.

24 Branko Milanovic, "Global Income Inequality by the Numbers: in History and Now," World Bank Policy Research Working Paper. http://heymancenter.org/files/events/milanovic.pdf.

25 Richard Kersley, "Global Wealth Reaches New All-Time High," Credit Suisse. https://publications.credit-suisse.com/tasks/render/file/?fileID=F2425415-DCA7-80B8-EAD989AF9341D47E.

26 United Nations Sustainable Development Knowledge Platform, "A New Global Partnership: Eradicate Poverty and Transform Economies Through Sustainable Development" (2013), p. 4. http://www.un.org/sg/management/pdf/HLP_P2015_Report.pdf.

27 I made these calculations using the tool on the website www
.givingwhatwecan.org, where you see how your wealth compares
to the world population.

28 Branko Milanovic, "Global income inequality: the past two
centuries and implications for the next century" (Autumn, 2011).
http://www.cnpds.it/documenti/milanovic.pdf.

29 "Just 8 men own same wealth as half world," Oxfam (January 16,
2017). https://www.oxfam.org.uk/en/pressroom/
pressreleases/2017-01-16/just-8-men-own-same-wealth-half-
world.

30 Nicholas Hobbes, *Essential Militaria. Facts, Legends, and
Curiosities About Warfare Through the Ages* (2004).

31 Milanovic, "Global Income Inequality by the Numbers."

32 In 2015 the poverty threshold for a single-person household in
the U.S. was about $980 a month. The poverty line as applied
by the World Bank is just over $57 a month, putting the U.S.
threshold almost seventeen times above extreme poverty.

33 Michael A. Clemens, Claudio E. Montenegro, and Lant Pritchett,
"The Place Premium: Wage Differences for Identical Workers
Across the US Border," Harvard Kennedy School (January
2009). https://dash.harvard.edu/bitstream/handle/1/4412631/
Clemens Place Premium. pdf?sequence=1.

34 The vast majority of "rich" people in poor countries don't
actually live in their home country. Four in five Haitians who earn
above $10 a day and are included in the Haitian statistic in reality
live in the United States. Relocating is hands down the best way
to escape poverty. And even those left behind benefit: In 2012,
immigrants transferred $400 billion to their countries of origin
– almost four times as much as all foreign aid combined.

35 Alex Nowrasteh, "Terrorism and Immigration: A Risk Analysis,"
Policy Analysis Cato Institute. https://www.cato.org/
publications/policy-analysis/terrorism-immigration-risk-
analysis.

36 Nicola Jones, "Study indicates immigration not to blame for
terrorism." http://www2.warwick.ac.uk/newsandevents/
pressreleases/study_indicates_immigration/.

37 Walter Ewing, Daniel E. Martínez and Rubén G. Rumbaut, "The
Criminalization of Immigration in the United States," *American*

Immigration Council Special Report (July 2015). https://www
.americanimmigrationcouncil.org/research/criminalization-
immigration-united-states.

38   Brian Bell, Stephen Machin, and Francesco Fasani, "Crime and
Immigration: Evidence from Large Immigrant Waves," *CEP
Discussion Paper No 984*. http://eprints.lse.ac.uk/28732/1/
dp0984.pdf.

39   F.M.H.M. Driessen, F. Duursma and J. Broekhuizen, "De
ontwikkeling van de criminaliteit van Rotterdamse autochtone en
allochtone jongeren van 12 tot 18 jaar," *Politie & Wetenschap*
(2014). https://www.piresearch.nl/files/1683/driessen+e.a.+
(2014)+de+ontwikkeling+van+de+criminaliteit+van.pdf.

40   Godfried Engbersen, Jaco Dagevos, Roel Jennissen, Linda
Bakker and Arjen Leerkes, "Geen tijd verliezen: van opvang naar
integratie van asielmigranten," *WRR Policy Brief* (December
2015). http://www.wrr.nl/publicaties/publicatie/article/geen-tijd-
verliezen-van-opvang-naar-integratie-van-asielmigranten-4/.

41   Michael Jonas, "The downside of diversity," *The Boston Globe*
(August 15, 2007). http://archive.boston.com/news/globe/
ideas/articles/2007/08/05/the_downside_of_diversity/.

42   Tom van der Meer and Jochem Tolsma, "Ethnic Diversity and Its
Effects on Social Cohesion," *Annual Review of Sociology* (July,
2014). http://www.annualreviews.org/doi/abs/10.1146/annurev-
soc-071913-043309.

43   Maria Abascal and Delia Baldassarri, "Don't Blame Diversity for
Distrust," *New York Times* (May 20, 2016). http://www.nytimes.
com/2016/05/22/opinion/sunday/dont-blame-diversity-
for-distrust.html?_r=1.

44   Immigrants often perform jobs that a country's own citizens
consider beneath them. With the aging population, there will
soon be innumerable jobs that the population of the Land of
Plenty will have a hard time finding enough people to fill. So
why turn our productive entrepreneurs, engineers, scientists,
and scholars into carers, cleaners, and tomato harvesters
when we can call in the help of foreign workers? Any
displacement, should it occur, will be only temporary and
local. Moreover, immigrants mostly assume jobs previously
filled by other immigrants.

45 George Borjas, "Immigration and the American Worker. A Review of the Academic Literature," Center for Immigration Studies (April 2013). http://cis.org/sites/cis.org/files/borjas-economics.pdf.

46 Heidi Shierholz, "Immigration and Wages: Methodological advancements confirm modest gains for native workers," Economic Policy Institute (February 4, 2010). http://epi.3cdn.net/7de74ee0cd834d87d4_a3m6ba9jo.pdf. Also see: Gianmarco I. P. Ottaviano and Giovanni Peri, "Rethinking the Effect of Immigration on Wages." http://www.nber.org/papers/w12497.

47 Frederic Docquiera, Caglar Ozden, and Giovanni Peri, "The Wage Effects of Immigration and Emigration," OECD (December 20, 2010). http://www.oecd.org/els/47326474.pdf.

48 Tyler Cowen, *Average Is Over. Powering America Beyond the Age of the Great Stagnation* (2013), p. 169.

49 Corrado Giulietti, Martin Guzi, Martin Kahanec, and Klaus F. Zimmermann, "Unemployment Benefits and Immigration: Evidence from the EU," Institute for the Study of Labor (October 2011). http://ftp.iza.org/dp6075.pdf.
    On the U.S., see: Leighton Ku and Brian Bruen, "The Use of Public Assistance Benefits by Citizens and Non-Citizen Immigrants in the United States," Cato Institute (February 19, 2013). http://object.cato.org/sites/cato.org/files/pubs/pdf/workingpaper-13_1.pdf.

50 OECD, "International Migration Outlook," p. 147. http://www.globalmigrationgroup.org/sites/default/files/Liebig_and_Mo_2013.pdf.

51 Mathias Czaika and Hein de Haas, "The Effect of Visa Policies on International Migration Dynamics," DEMIG project paper (April 2014). http://www.imi.ox.ac.uk/publications/wp-89-14.

52 Doug Massey, "Understanding America's Immigration 'Crisis,'" *Proceedings of the American Philosophical Society* (September 2007). https://www.amphilsoc.org/sites/default/files/proceedings/1510304.pdf.

53 Gallup, "700 Million Worldwide Desire to Migrate Permanently." http://www.gallup.com/poll/124028/700-million-worldwide-desiremigrate-permanently.aspx.

54 Dick Wittenberg, "De terugkeer van de Muur," *De Correspondent.*

https://decorrespondent.nl/40/de-terugkeer-van-de-muur/1537800098648e4.

55 Dylan Matthews, "Americans already think a third of the budget goes to foreign aid. What if it did?" *Washington Post* (November 8, 2013). https://www.washingtonpost.com/news/wonk/wp/2013/11/08/americans-already-think-a-third-of-the-budget-goes-to-foreign-aid-what-if-it-did/.

56 Terrie L. Walmsley, L. Alan Winters, S. Amer Ahmed, and Christopher R. Parsons, "Measuring the Impact of the Movement of Labour Using a Model of Bilateral Migration Flows," World Bank. https://www.gtap.agecon.purdue.edu/resources/download/2398.pdf.

57 Joseph Carens, "Aliens and Citizens: The Case for Open Borders," *Review of Politics* (Spring 1987). http://philosophyfaculty.ucsd.edu/faculty/rarneson/phil267fa12/aliens and citizens.pdf.

CHAPTER 10 HOW IDEAS CHANGE THE WORLD

1 Joe Keohane, "How facts backfire," *Boston Globe* (July 11, 2010). http://archive.boston.com/bostonglobe/ideas/articles/2010/07/11/how_facts_backfire/.

   See also: Leon Festinger, Henry Riecken, and Stanley Schachter, *When Prophecy Fails: A Social and Psychological Study of a Modern Group That Predicted the Destruction of the World* (1956).

2 The research group's website is: http://www.culturalcognition.net.

3 Ezra Klein, "How politics makes us stupid," *Vox* (April 6, 2014). http://www.vox.com/2014/4/6/5556462/brain-dead-how-politics-makes-us-stupid.

4 Nicholas Bakalar, "Shorter Workweek May Not Increase Well-Being," *New York Times* (August 28, 2013). http://well.blogs.nytimes.com/2013/08/28/shorter-workweek-may-not-increase-well-being/.

5 Katie Grant, "Working Shorter Hours May Be 'Bad For Health,'" *Telegraph* (August 22, 2013).

6 Of course, since then I have looked at the study. To quote from the abstract: "While satisfaction with working hours increased, reductions had no impact on job and life satisfaction . . .

Moreover, positive SWB effects might be offset by rising work intensity." In other words, the South Koreans had switched to working shorter weeks, but they were also working harder.

7   James H. Kuklinski et al., "Misinformation and the Currency of Democratic Citizenship," *Journal of Politics* (August 2010), p. 810. http://richarddagan.com/framing/kuklinski2000.pdf. That shocks can work wonders was proved on that December night in 1954. When no flying saucers arrived, one sect member decided he'd had enough. He stopped believing after the massive "disconfirmation" at midnight, Festinger recorded. (Not surprisingly, he had also invested the least in his conviction, only having had to cancel a Christmas trip to Arizona to be there that night.)

8   Solomon Asch, "Opinions and Social Pressure," *Scientific American* (November 1955). http://kosmicki.com/102/Asch 1955.pdf.

9   Alan Greenspan, "Speech at the American Bankers Association Annual Convention, New York" (October 5, 2004). http://www .federalreserve.gov/boarddocs/Speeches/2004/20041005/ default.htm.

10 Quoted in: Edmund L. Andrews, "Greenspan Concedes Error on Regulation," *New York Times* (October 23, 2008). http://www .nytimes.com/2008/10/24/business/economy/24panel.html.

11 He said this on ABC News: http://abcnews.go.com/ThisWeek/ video/ interview-alan-greenspan-10281612.

12 Edward Krudy, "Wall Street cash bonuses highest since 2008 crash: report," *Reuters* (March 12, 2014). http://www.reuters. com/article/us-usa-bonuses-idUSBREA2B0WA20140312.

13 Jurgen Tiekstra, "Joris Luyendijk: 'Dit gaat helemaal fout,'" *Volzin* (September 2013). http://www.duurzaamnieuws.nl/ joris-luyendijk-dit-gaat-helemaal-fout/.

14 See for example: Milton Friedman, "Neo-Liberalism and its Prospects," *Farmand* (February 17, 1951). http://0055d26 .netsolhost.com/friedman/pdfs/other_commentary/Farmand .02.17.1951.pdf.

15 F. A. Hayek, "The Intellectuals and Socialism," *University of Chicago Law Review* (Spring 1949). https://mises.org/etexts/ hayekintellectuals.pdf.

16   Quoted in: Angus Burgin, *The Great Persuasion. Reinventing Free Markets Since the Depression* (2012), p. 13.

17   Quoted in: ibid., p. 169.

18   Ibid., p. 11.

19   Ibid., p. 221.

20   Francis Fukuyama, *The End of History and the Last Man* (1992).

21   At the end of his life, Friedman said there was only one philosopher he had ever really studied in depth: the Austrian Karl Popper. Popper argued that good science revolves around "falsifiability," requiring a continual search for things that don't fit your theory instead of only seeking confirmation. However, as we've seen, most people approach theories the other way around. This also seems to be precisely where neoliberalism – and Friedman himself – went wrong.

22   Stephanie Mudge, "The Social Bases of Austerity. European Tunnel Vision & the Curious Case of the Missing Left," SPERI Paper No. 9 (February 2014). http://speri.dept.shef.ac.uk/wp-content/uploads/2013/01/SPERI-Paper-No.9-The-Social-Bases-of-Austerity-PDF-579KB.pdf.

23   John Maynard Keynes, *The General Theory of Employment, Interest and Money* (1936), last paragraph.

24   Oscar Wilde, 'The Soul of Man under Socialism' (1891).

25   Quoted in: Burgin, *The Great Persuasion*, p. 217.

26   Keynes, *General Theory*, last paragraph.

EPILOGUE

1   And now that we're on the subject, who better to get us started than history's biggest venture capitalist: government. Almost every groundbreaking innovation is financed by taxpayers, after all. Every sliver of fundamental technology in your iPhone, for example – capacitive sensors, solid-state memory, GPS, Internet, cellular communications, Siri, microchips, and the touchscreen – was invented by researchers on the government payroll. See: Mariana Mazzucato, *The Entrepreneurial State: Debunking Public vs. Private Sector Myths* (2013).

2   Bronnie Ware, *The Top Five Regrets of the Dying. A Life Transformed by the Dearly Departing* (2012).

INDEX

ACKNOWLEDGEMENTS

No book is ever written alone, but never before have I had such a wealth of support. My thanks firstly to the members of *The Correspondent*, my home as a writer, who provided input and tips on articles and books, as well as pointing out various errors. Also to my coworkers, especially those who read all or parts of the manuscript — Jesse Frederik, Andreas Jonkers, Erica Moore, Travis Mushett, and Rob Wijnberg — I owe a huge debt of gratitude.

A big thank-you to the Momkai design team — Martijn van Dam, Harald Dunnink, Shannon Lea, Cynthia Mergel, Leon Postma, and Frazer Sparham — for the great infographics (and for their endless patience all those times I made yet another small change).

I had the great honor to have Wil Hansen as my editor for the original Dutch version of this book, who once again saved me from faulty logic and awkward turns of phrase. I am equally grateful to Elizabeth Manton, the book's translator, for her feel for language and her invaluable input. When people asked how the English translation was coming along, I was soon confessing concern that it might turn out to be much better than the original.

This book could never have been a success without my amazing Dutch publisher, Milou Klein Lankhorst. She also put me in touch with my agent-to-be, Rebecca Carter, who was convinced my book had potential and in short order introduced me to my editors Ben George at Little, Brown and Alexis Kirschbaum at Bloomsbury, whose insights have further improved this book.

Last but not least, I have been blessed to have the support of my family, friends, and, above all, Maartje. She provided criticism that was sometimes tough to take but that I couldn't have done without, for the simple reason that she was usually right.

For any faulty logic, awkward phrases, and unachievable illusions that remain, I take full responsibility.

Rutger Bregman, a member of the *Forbes* 30 Under 30 Europe Class of 2017 and one of the continent's most prominent young thinkers, has published four books on history, philosophy, and economics. His *History of Progress* won the Belgian Liberales prize for best nonfiction book in 2013, and he has twice been nominated for the prestigious European Press Prize for his journalism work at *The Correspondent*. The Dutch edition of *Utopia for Realists* sparked a basic income movement that made international headlines. His work has been featured in the *Washington Post*, the *Guardian*, and on the BBC.

A NOTE ON THE TRANSLATOR

Elizabeth Manton is an American-born translator currently living in the Netherlands. She has an MA in art history from the Courtauld Institute of Art in London and an MA in translation from VU Amsterdam. Her previous translations into English include *Financing Cathedral Building in the Middle Ages* and *Revolution Justified*.